OYSTERS TO ANGUS

Copyright © 2014 Elizabeth Terry Historical Research

Cover design: Paula L. Warner

Photos on the cover:

Tony Faust. From the Collections of the St. Louis Mercantile Library at the University of Missouri-St. Louis

Tony Faust's Restaurant, with the garden terrace, before 1889. Courtesy of Missouri History Museum, St. Louis

Printed in the United States of America

Bluebird Publishing Co.
St. Louis, Missouri

ACKNOWLEDGMENTS

This book project began with my family attending a weekend event at Faust Park on a lovely spring day. I asked a guy in a St. Louis County Parks polo shirt, "Do you need help?" The next thing I knew, I sat with Jesse Francis, Curator, and he suggested I delve into the history of the Faust family. Challenge accepted. Soon, though, the project took on a life of its own. Jesse looked me in the eye and said, "You need to turn this into a book." *What?* His faith in me from the beginning was soon followed by the kindness and encouragement of his fellow Faust Park forces: Lori Ritchey, John Honewinkel, Janet Wilzback, and Director Jim Foley fueled my research and writing journey. Thank you, Jesse.

I'm indebted to those who burrow deep in the libraries and archives of St. Louis. Those keepers of The Lou's documented history made this book happen. Among others, much appreciation goes to the Special Collections staff at the St. Louis County Library Headquarters, specifically for providing the digitized historic *Post-Dispatch*, whose accounts make up much of this book. Great archivists of those hallowed repositories, like Dennis Northcott of the Missouri History Museum Library and Research Center, and Sonya Rooney and Miranda Rechtenwald of Washington University Archives, facilitated my research as much with their professional prowess as with their conversation and rapport.

Book writing is a long and lonely road, though. Little tidbits, quiet discoveries, and *Eureka!* moments that mean the world to an author and nothing to the population at large demand more than a lone celebration. Near daily phone calls with my beloved mother who asked, "What did you learn about Tony/Edward/Leicester today?" balanced my soul and my sanity. Thank you, Mom.

Along the way, I was blessed with encouragement (a.k.a. life support) from good friends: Autumn Kowalski, Karina Crouch, Jenn Lupo, Karen Spencer, Victoria Portell, Katie Hotard, Kristina Thomas, Mindy Davis, Kristin Schinzing, Angela Shah, Amanda Lester, Kayla Dye, and Susan Terry. I'm grateful for the incredibly helpful advice from my friend Dr. Catherine Seltzer. And words cannot describe my appreciation for the props given to me by my very dear friend and fellow public historian, Jamie Kuhns.

Getting to know Jane Keough, granddaughter of Leicester and Mary Faust, has been a delightful bonus in this bookmaking project. I first made her acquaintance as we visited what once was the Big House: she, who captivated me with her stories of her Cici and Booba; and me, privileged to feel the presence of her ancestors with every turn. It has been my honor to delve into the history of this family, and I value my friendship with Jane.

As the words on paper evolved into book form, it was Karina Crouch who first read the manuscript, setting the editing process in motion. Thank you, Karina. I also thank Esley Hamilton, Historian for St. Louis County Parks, who read my manuscript and has been a great resource for me. Thanks to Carmen Freeman for her German translations. I'd like to thank the ever-kind Rebecca Dellegrazio for her numerous facets of support from within the former Big House. Many thanks to Dan Thompson at Bluebird Publishing and Fran Levy, my editor. It's been fun!

Nothing, of course, is possible without my family. I like to think I share pioneer strength with my sister, Autumn Kowalski, my brother, Russ Warner, and my parents, Paula and Randall Warner. It's my dad who fostered my love of history since my childhood on the northern plains. And Dave, my husband: you built me a beautiful writing table for future projects, and together we built the best project of all.

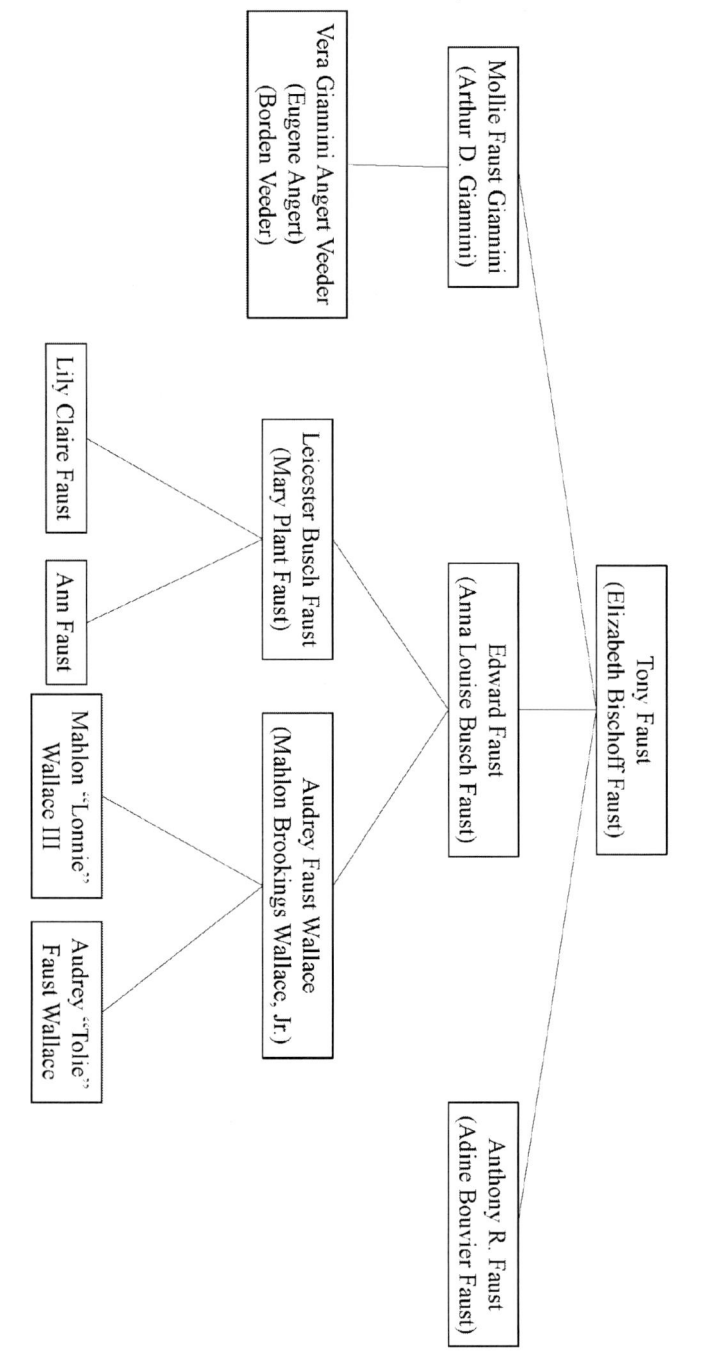

TABLE OF CONTENTS

INTRODUCTION viii

BOOK ONE
- Chapter 1 - The Industrious German 2
- Chapter 2 - The Perils of Beer 25
- Chapter 3 - Enterprising and Active 36
- Chapter 4 - The 1904 World's Fair 48
- Chapter 5 - Tony's Family 55

BOOK TWO
- Chapter 1 - Life and Death 73
- Chapter 2 - A Member of the Posse 84
- Chapter 3 - The American German-American 105
- Chapter 4 - The Art of Making Money 119

BOOK THREE
- Chapter 1 - The Joys of Youth 136
- Chapter 2 - Golf, Tulips, Angus, and Finally, Beer 149
- Chapter 3 - The Great Depression 163
- Chapter 4 - Life on the Farm 174
- Chapter 5 - Times are Changin' 186
- Chapter 6 - Sunset on the Farm, Sunrise on Faust Park 195

EPILOGUE 205

NOTES 207

INTRODUCTION

St. Louis was full of promise and full of potential in the mid-1850s. Tony Faust settled there like so many others who fled Germany after the failed Revolution of 1848. As an emerging industrial city, his new hometown epitomized mid-America, teeming with immigrants while the Civil War loomed on the horizon. Likewise, Tony embodied the new citizen, full of hope in a city resentful of the flood of German humanity. He clawed his way to social and financial standing by way of good investments, good humor, and good luck.

Three generations of Faust men made St. Louis their home: Tony, his son Edward, and his grandson Leicester. But, *where* in St. Louis each made his home is significant. Tony resided in a lavish apartment in the city center, adjacent to the restaurant which funded the lives of leisure enjoyed by him and subsequent generations of his family. While Tony remained firmly entrenched in the German community, Edward desired a home in the exclusive West End. This gained him admittance into the most exclusive club in town – he joined the coterie of wealthy capitalists unaffectionately known as the Big Cinch. Leicester set his sights even farther west, and he used his wealth in an entirely different manner. He settled into his quiet, steady life in farm country located on the perimeter of metro St. Louis. His vision of a picture-perfect, self-sustaining farm became a reality, built jointly from his head for agribusiness and the hard-working hands of his dedicated employees.

Despite their wealth, the Faust men were not exempt from the struggles that beset other St. Louisans. Their personal stories are set into the context of local, national and world events. Tony, who found himself a target of the Temperance Movement, battled to serve alcohol on Sundays while barroom brawls raged in his saloon deep into the night. Edward fought the stigma of being the son of a German immigrant during the volatile days of World War I. Leicester, through the fertile soil of his farm, fed his employees' families during the dark days of the Great Depression.

Due to the external factors of the world in which they lived, the Faust men's lives were full of contradictions. Tony paid trappers to venture into the frontier that bordered St. Louis to the north and the west, and he sold the wild game in his market. However, he also sold oysters procured from the Chesapeake Bay as well as cheeses shipped from Europe, a nod to St. Louis' prominent location along rail lines and its vital port on the Mississippi River. Tony's thriving business simultaneously characterized St. Louis' economic past and future. Ever obsessed with his reputation, Edward labored to shed his second-generation German immigrant status in the eyes of those in his "American" social network. Yet, he continued to serve as an officer in the Liederkranz Club, the most exclusive German club in St. Louis. And Leicester, true to his nature, cherished his friendships with his hired men just as much as his associations with fellow members of the Merchant's Exchange, eschewing the powerful pull of status that entrapped his father.

The Faust family's tapestry cannot be woven without the threads of the Busch family – a name synonymous with St. Louis. The story begins with Tony's close friendship with the Busch patriarch, continues as Edward's relationship with the Busch family slowly begins to unravel, and terminates with Leicester angrily severing the ties. Neither family's story can be fully told without the other. The Busch family played a profound role in the lives of the Fausts.

Each generation of the Faust men used their wealth differently, and each within the context of his time and character. Their residential choices, their associations to the Busch family, their connection to their German heritage and their varying degrees of concern for their social status set them apart from one another. Even so, affection for St. Louis ran deep in Faust blood. All three Faust men built their own legacies through their unique philanthropic contributions to their beloved city, and still today St. Louis is the better for it.

BOOK ONE

Tony Faust.
Courtesy of Missouri History Museum, St. Louis

Chapter 1
THE INDUSTRIOUS GERMAN

St. Louis boasts a deep French history. Pierre Laclede, in 1764, began his fur trading post on a bluff south of the confluence of the Mississippi and the Missouri rivers. French inhabitants sailed up the Mississippi from the port of New Orleans and down the Illinois River from French Canada. By the time Napoleon sold Louisiana to the United States in 1803, St. Louis was a thriving French village.[1] It was still a little community by 1818, with only 2,000 inhabitants, two-thirds of them French. Near Carondelet Road lived legendary St. Louis families such as the Chouteaus, Soulards, and Pages. In a tightly knit French community, many became wealthy and kept to themselves. They had disdain for the Americans, viewing them as rough and crude and extended those opinions toward the Germans as they began to immigrate.[2]

Irish and Germans poured into St. Louis after Ireland's potato famine had begun in 1845 and following the defeat of German Liberalism in the Revolution of 1848. The Germans, called the "Damned Dutch" by the St. Louis natives, invaded Frenchtown, bringing their beer-brewing skills and their oompah bands. "After 1850, the German atmosphere was such that a person wandering through some of the streets could believe that he had been transported to Germany, since he heard only German spoken."[3] Between 1847 and 1850, the population of St. Louis increased by 30,000 people. By 1860, it had grown by 373 percent to 77,860 people. Many in this fresh wave of German immigrants were impoverished and unskilled. They lived anywhere they could in Frenchtown, crowding tenement houses and living in squalor. Others, however, opened successful shops along Carondelet and Lafayette Avenues. Through the 1850s, the Germans engaged in violent riots, defending themselves against St. Louis natives and even the Irish. To make matters worse for longtime St. Louisans, Germans quickly became naturalized and voted Democrats into office.[4]

Seventeen-year-old Tony Faust arrived in New York from Germany in 1853. He came to St. Louis after a brief stay in Dubuque, Iowa. Like many of his German counterparts, he settled in Frenchtown. While the clannish French sorrowfully watched their culture fade from dominance in St. Louis, Tony established himself in his trade as an ornamental plasterer. The Civil War loomed on the horizon.

In 1861, secessionist Missouri Governor Claiborne Fox Jackson knew that the St. Louis Arsenal, located in South St. Louis and billed as the largest weapon storage in the South, was vital for Confederate control of Missouri. However, Unionist Senator Frank P. Blair designated Captain Nathaniel Lyon commander of the arsenal. Lyon proceeded to send the majority of the weapons to Illinois. Knowing that Confederates would ship weapons up the Mississippi to St. Louis, Lyon encircled the arsenal with Union agents. In turn, southern sympathizer Brig. Gen. Daniel Frost set up Camp Jackson at the end of Olive Street on the western part of St. Louis. He called it a "training camp," ultimately planning to take over St. Louis. When a shipment of weapons stolen by Confederates from an arsenal in Baton Rouge arrived at Camp Jackson, Lyon marched two companies of US Regulars and 7,000 volunteers, mostly German, to Camp Jackson. He surrounded the camp and forced the Confederates to surrender. After the prisoners lined up for their march away from Camp Jackson, Lyon was knocked out by a horse's kick. The prisoners jeered and taunted the German volunteers by shouting "Damn the Dutch." A skirmish broke out and 28 people were killed. The prisoners were at last marched away and held for a time at the St. Louis Arsenal. The flawed capture of Camp Jackson prompted bitterness, and Germans bore the brunt of the blame.[5]

Tony Faust was painting that day in 1861 when the German volunteers marched to take Camp Jackson. He stood along the street with others, watching the parade, when a soldier's gun accidentally discharged and shot him in the leg. No longer physically capable of working as an ornamental plasterer, he opened his first café at 295 Carondelet Road in Frenchtown.[6] Perhaps, though, he was inspired by the many German volunteers who marched past him that day; perhaps he was tired of the violence and ethnic discrimination against Germans; perhaps he felt strongly for the Union cause. In any case, on September 13, 1862, Tony volunteered for the Enrolled Missouri Militia, 3rd Regiment, Company A. His regiment was organized in St. Louis with 921 soldiers under the command of Colonel N. Schittner. His regiment never saw active duty, and Tony Faust returned to his café in Frenchtown.[7]

In 1870, Tony Faust opened a new restaurant 20 blocks north on the corner of Broadway and Elm. Tony's early success was built on his oysters, a product of the bourgeoning river commerce. Steamboats began powering up the Mississippi from New Orleans in the 1830s. By the 1850s, St. Louis's wharf was a spectacle of steamboats, docked several deep, while others waited a mile up and down river. In fact, by 1857, St. Louis boasted steamboats carrying an average of 250 tons of goods, with three to ten departures per day, likely exporting furs.[8]

Though the Transcontinental Railroad bypassed St. Louis in favor of Chicago and Omaha, many railroads came as far as East St. Louis by 1870. By then, the Wiggins Ferry Company had established a rail-car ferry system. It hauled railroad cars one by one across the Mississippi River to the St. Louis side. That changed in 1874 when James B. Eads built his phenomenal bridge across the river that accommodated horse-drawn and rail traffic. The Eads Bridge connected East St. Louis with St. Louis, Illinois with Missouri, and East with West. This enabled Tony Faust, by then known as the Oyster King, to ship his oysters with ease.[9]

Tony Faust's restaurant on Broadway and Elm was a landmark in its own right, but its location adjacent to the Southern Hotel can't have hurt business. Built in 1863 and proclaimed by the *New York Times* to be "unsurpassed in any building of the kind in the land," the hotel was state-of-the-art and the largest in St. Louis.[10] "Tony Faust Oyster House & Saloon" stood on the southwest corner of the block. Tony leased the property from the hotel's owner, St. Louis business magnate Robert Campbell. Business in that thriving section of the city was brisk.[11]

That successful commerce was tragically interrupted on the night of April 10, 1877; a fire broke out in the Southern Hotel. The fire started in the basement of the building, traveled briskly up the elevator shaft, and quickly consumed the hotel. Horrible stories of death and injury sprang from the catastrophe. Fatalities included actresses who performed at the Olympic Theater across the street, young couples who boarded at the hotel, and servant girls and other employees who lived and worked there. The destruction was such that even the *New York Times* followed the story for days, reporting on the suffering, the investigation, and the ensuing inquest. It was resolved that the hotel management was negligent in several areas, making the tragedy worse than it otherwise might have been.[12]

Tony Faust's restaurant's roof was used by firemen to prop ladders up against the hotel during the fire. His establishment was heavily damaged, but salvageable. In fact, the *St. Louis Post-Dispatch* congratulated him the day following the fire:

> Tony Faust re-opens his saloon this afternoon on the ashes of his former place of business in the Southern Hotel block. The example of Faust is a good one, and shows genuine enterprise and determination, which will overcome all obstacles and assure success. Long live Faust and longer still his example.[13]

Plans to rebuild the hotel began immediately for a structure just as magnificent, only fireproof. Not to be outdone, Tony Faust set to work himself.

Firemen on the roof of Tony Faust's Restaurant when the Southern Hotel burned, 1877.
Courtesy of St. Louis County Parks

German immigrants brought to America the concept of beer gardens, a beloved institution in their homeland. St. Louis boasted numerous beer gardens in the last half of the nineteenth century. The gardens were favored as gathering places for working men and women, couples, and families as a place to relax and enjoy fresh air and camaraderie. Keen on this concept, in 1879 Tony Faust created a "garden terrace" on the roof of his restaurant building. "Tony's Terrace" was "above and removed" from the bustle of the city. Opened every spring when the weather turned warm, the rooftop was beautifully landscaped with rocks and grottoes, shrubs, tropical flowers, and even a fountain created by a horticulturist. Extremely popular, the terrace provided a garden-like setting with the comforts of a restaurant, often illuminated with lights, featuring orchestral music.[14]

Tony Faust's Restaurant with garden terrace, before 1889.
Courtesy of Missouri History Museum, St. Louis

The *St. Louis Post-Dispatch* ran an article in 1888 about the financial costs of running a saloon. One of the city's longtime saloon keepers estimated Tony Faust's daily expenses to be approximately $175 per day, with yearly rent around $10,000 and profits between $15,000 and $20,000. The interviewee explained that such rent was an excellent deal considering the vast square footage of Tony Faust's enterprise. The building had the benefit of various entrances including Fulton's Market, the ladies' restaurant, and "The Cabin" (the gentlemen's dining area) in the rear of the premises. It also had the distinct advantage of being located in the theater district, across from the Olympic Theater.[15] Visiting troupes stayed at the Southern Hotel and dined at Tony Faust's restaurant. Tony hosted grand after-show dinners and toasted the actors and actresses on their performances. The Olympic thrived in the early days on vaudeville acts and minstrel shows, then produced drama after 1869. Tony's continued success was assured when the Olympic built a new theater in 1882, still across the street from Tony Faust's restaurant and terrace.[16]

Having the means to be a world traveler, Tony attended the Paris Exposition during the summer of 1878. Also called the Paris World's Fair, it was the grandest such event up to that time. Surely he was mesmerized by the art and architecture displayed on the 66 acres. He was perhaps enthralled by the completed head of the Statue of Liberty of the United States exhibition, displayed in the garden of the Trocadero Palace. Obviously, though, Tony Faust was enamored by the illumination of the Avenue de l'Opera.

The avenues were aglow with electric lighting invented by

Russian engineer Pavel Yablochkov. Tony returned to St. Louis from Paris with a Yablochkov electric arc lamp and the Gramme dynamo, the apparatus powering the lamp. The introduction of electric lights in St. Louis elevated Tony Faust's celebrity.[17]

If Tony's goal was the successful use of electric lighting in his restaurant for the long term, the experiment was a complete and utter failure. After two or three nights of glorious illumination, the electric dynamo burned itself out. Charles Heisler, proprietor of an electric bells and instruments factory, served as Tony's technician for the new lights. Undaunted, Mr. Heisler took the machine to St. Louis's Polytechnic Building to study and perfect the design. Within two years Mr. Heisler demonstrated and sold his improved electric lights. This was the first known commercial sale of electric service in St. Louis. By 1885, he was president of Heisler Electric Lights.[18]

Regardless of the brevity of the early illumination in his restaurant, Tony Faust achieved "pioneer" status. When describing Tony Faust's electric light experiment, the *St. Louis Globe-Democrat* prophesized in 1878, "The time is not far distant when gasworks will be abolished, and the streets and buildings of our cities will be lighted by electricity."[19] Sure enough, the Brush Electric Association was established in 1881 as the first commercial electric-generating enterprise in the city. By 1891, electric workers established the International Brotherhood of Electrical Workers. By 1903, the creation of Union Electric merged more than 30 St. Louis companies that provided electric service. By the time visitors from around the globe dined at Tony Faust's restaurant at the 1904 World's Fair, the entire exposition was electrically lit for the world to see.[20]

Electric success was not without bumps in the road. The *St. Louis Post-Dispatch* reported in 1885:

> About 6 o'clock Saturday evening the electric light attachment to the gas fixtures in Tony Faust's came in contact with the gas and in an instant the ceiling of the dining-room was covered with flames.[21]

Tony Faust's Restaurant, 1889.
Courtesy of Missouri History Museum, St. Louis

Ten years after the Southern Hotel burned, Tony tore down his restaurant and built anew. He had traveled around Europe studying architecture, kitchens, equipment, and foods. Upon his return to St. Louis, he hired architect Isaac S. Taylor. When Tony held the grand opening to his new establishment in 1889, few could believe the size and luxury. Even the 72-foot by107-foot basement with high ceilings, wine cellar, laundry, and cooling rooms was state-of-the-art. The "magnificent, spacious bar" and gentlemen's restaurant were located on the ground floor with the kitchen in the rear. The ladies' parlor was located on the second floor with its own entrance, decorated with oil paintings and mosaic flooring.[22] Estimated to cost $98,000, the restaurant could accommodate 1,500 people. One table was known as the "millionaire's table," a nod toward the pre-income-tax Gilded Age.[23] Tony sacrificed his patrons' beloved garden terrace to enclose the second floor, but it's likely that few complained as they dined in the lap of luxury.

Tony Faust's restaurant was commonly referred to as "Delmonico's of the West." Opened in 1837 in New York by the Delmonico brothers, that restaurant was known for its private dining rooms and for its house special, the Delmonico steak. The Delmonico brothers adopted the Parisian style menu of bill of fare, which offered choices of foods with individual prices rather than set meals with set prices. This was an entirely new menu format for the United States's dining public, and proved to be very popular. The period from 1876 until 1896 was Delmonico's golden age. Delmonico's moved north to Madison Square, following the shift in New York's population. There the brothers built a luxurious restaurant complete with ballrooms, silver chandeliers, frescoed ceilings, a fountain, and mahogany furniture. Delmonico's raised culinary standards. That Tony Faust's was compared to such an enterprise was an accomplishment indeed.[24]

Dedicated to his business, Tony lived next door to his restaurant. Plans indicated that "East of this will be Mr. Faust's residence quarters for himself and family, where all the comforts and conveniences of a modern residence will be enjoyed."[25]

Menu for Tony Faust's Restaurant, September 1889.
Courtesy of Missouri History Museum, St. Louis

Tony Faust took customer service seriously. He worked in tandem with his staff to cater to his customers. He employed as many as 100 people at a given time, the majority German. In fact, part of his large enterprise served as living quarters for waiters and other employees. Tony was known to be liberal with his money, and his employees were likely paid well. Until 1895, every employee was allowed as much beer as he desired throughout the workday.

In 1881, Frank Hanni, the headwaiter at Tony Faust's, attended the first meeting of waiters in St. Louis. The group of waiters from St. Louis restaurants and hotels met with the purpose of establishing a Waiters Association. It was to protect themselves *and their employers* against irresponsible and disreputable restaurant employees. A committee was formed to develop a system of rules and bylaws based on good character. The new society's chair proposed that the organization have a blacklist, "with a committee of grievances, before whom the aggrieved waiter might state his side of the case." So dedicated to his employer, Frank Hanni was appointed to and served on the committee.[26]

People loved Tony Faust. He moved about his restaurant, visiting and joking with his customers. Known to be jovial, Tony Faust delighted in whimsy. To the amusement of his customers, he blatantly disregarded a city ordinance against obstructing sidewalks. He placed a replica of a loggerhead turtle, three feet in diameter, in front of his restaurant.[27] The *St. Louis Globe-Democrat*, the newspaper of his political choosing, printed in 1878, "We acknowledge the receipt of a small bottle of wine converted into a pencil, a novelty presented by Tony Faust."[28] In 1880, Tony Faust happily hosted Albert Michaelis, Superintendent of the Louisiana Ice Manufacturing Company of New Orleans, who set up his headquarters at Tony Faust's while making sales calls in St. Louis. People flocked to the restaurant to see the mammoth blocks of ice containing curiosities like flowers, bottles of wine, fish, and a chromo of Tony Faust.[29]

Tony hosted thrilling eating competitions as well as popular oyster-opening contests. Sadly, in 1878, his expert oyster opener lost the prized silver cup to fellow restaurant Sprague & Butler's oyster opener. The winner "accomplished the unprecedented feat of opening fifty oysters in two minutes and ten seconds – best on record." Sprague & Butler, having earned bragging rights, placed an ad in the newspaper proclaiming victory and inviting all to come to their restaurant. Both the silver cup *and* their star oyster opener were on exhibit.[30]

Tony Faust was known especially for his New Year's Eve parties. Seats in his restaurant were often reserved a year in advance. In 1887, guests each received a card with a caricature of Tony getting out of bed on New Year's Day with cherubs blowing trumpets with salutatory messages in both French and German.[31] Tony hired away a new headwaiter from a restaurant in New York for his 1900 New Year's Eve party, which included a standing-room-only crowd and a band.[32] The 1901 New Year's Eve celebration was an even bigger event, with large parties sitting in long-reserved seats. The most sought-after seats were located at the Faust-Busch table. That year 16 people claimed these spots. As midnight neared, the orchestra played and curtains drew back. Tony emerged playing "Mephisto" from *Faust,* donning the red hat with the signature rooster's feather and bidding farewell to the previous century. At midnight, the room was illuminated with an electric sign that read "Twentieth Century." The crowed joined together and sang "Auld Lang Syne" and the American national anthem.[33]

*Interior of Tony Faust's Restaurant.
Courtesy of Missouri History Museum, St. Louis*

In spite of his popularity, other business owners in town were aware that prominent men such as Tony Faust had unfair advantages. Tony "rented" the space along the city street in front of his restaurant to the Hansom Cab Company. In this manner, the Hansom Cab Company and a couple of livery stables secured the choicest cab stands in the city. Finally, in 1887, Judge Noonan, a well-known judge in the St. Louis courts, ruled this illegal in that "wherever a stand was created all cab-drivers and owners had equal rights to occupy it." This ruling dealt a blow to Tony, who had enjoyed a tidy profit from this arrangement.[34]

When the government proposed in 1883 that each saloon pay $500 per year for a liquor license, small-saloonkeepers asked, how is that fair? Said one spitefully,

> Those fellows who run whisky shops on Elm street (Tony's location) and Sixth street and Christy

avenue... are the very chaps who have money and will be able to pay a high license.... As it is now, Tony Faust, who does an immense business, pays no more to the city than does the poor saloon-keeper out on the Bellefontaine road. Such a condition of affairs is not right.[35]

The tables were turned six years later when Jefferson City announced a bill that would raise annual liquor licenses to $4,000. Saying war was being made against them, Tony Faust, P.J. Carmody, and other large-saloon owners claimed that this was the government's way to shut them down. They blamed the small-saloon owners: "A drunk in one of those places sometimes costs a man very dear, and such outrages...are frequently reported." So, why should the *reputable* establishments, where *of course* men do not become drunks and squander away their livelihoods, have to suffer? Tony Faust called it "prohibition," and when asked what he thought was the real object of the bill, P.J. Carmody replied, "Spite."[36]

However, saloon keepers across the spectrum found themselves in alliance with each other when it came to certain issues. When threatened with the Moffett Bell Punch law in 1878 and 1879, they were outspoken as a group. The law suggested that a machine be placed on every bar; when a glass of beer was sold, an employee marked the glass and rang the bell on the machine. The bell indicated that the patron paid a 2 ½ cent tax on that beer. How, the saloon-keepers questioned, was this supposed to work? Who wants that bell ringing all day? How can we spare an employee to stand at that machine full-time? Our bar will be clogged – are the patrons and waiters supposed to line up and wait for each glass to be marked? They fumed, we are being labeled as criminals! Why aren't we trusted to report the taxed beers without a machine? And of course: it is only the *honest* establishments, like ours, that will end up paying the taxes.[37]

During the era of trusts, a more serious concern bonded not just the saloon keepers but nearly everyone involved in food service businesses. All were at the mercy of the meat trust, which comprised Philip D. Armour, Nelson Morris and Gustavus F. Swift. These gentlemen were tagged the "Big Three." Based in Chicago, they purportedly met weekly to set prices for meat. The "soulless combine," as they were also known, controlled the price of meat from the steer to the table and wreaked havoc on the market system. Realizing that they could profit more from selling meat than heads of cattle, they shipped the beef out of Chicago in their own fleet of refrigerator cars. The men and their companies gave rebates to butchers who purchased beef from their controlled packers. They set up shop next to butchers who boycotted them and undercut their prices, forcing them out of business. Tony Faust's saving grace was his specialty in oysters, seafood, and other delicacies, not beef. But he, like other restaurateurs, was forced to maintain the Big Three prices on his steaks and take a loss. Armour, Morris, and Swift formed the National Packing Company in 1902. They began buying smaller meat companies, stockyards, and slaughtering plants. The "Big Three" were first investigated by a federal grand jury in 1896. The National Packing Company finally dissolved in 1912 under governmental pressure. But the "Big Three" had grown to the "Big Five" by 1920, when they sold their holdings under the Sherman Anti-Trust Act. It had been a difficult era for Tony and other restaurant owners who came after him.[38]

As early as 1876, Tony began selling oysters retail and wholesale. This side business was a great addition to his restaurant, and he prospered. The Oyster King called his side business "Faust's Fulton Market: Oyster Depot and Packing House." He stocked his market with saddle rock oysters, tub oysters, bulk oysters, and shell oysters in addition to fresh sea fish, lobsters, crab, and clams. Tony hired his oyster opener directly from the Fulton Market in New York so that his customers might be "served in the most skillful and efficient manner."[39] Using endless self-promotion, Tony guaranteed freshness and top-quality products to his customers. The newspapers also promoted his market. The *St. Louis Globe-Democrat* touted, "…that his patronage has been liberal has been due not alone to the popularity of the dealer, but as well to the high quality of goods that he has dealt in."[40] By 1879, Fulton Market sold imported cheeses from England, Switzerland, France, and Germany, as well as game in season.

And, Tony offered, the goods will be "delivered to any part of the city."[41] For this purpose, Tony managed a fleet of delivery wagons, which rumbled over the poorly maintained St. Louis streets. Of course, collisions occurred from time to time. In 1878, a collision between one of his delivery wagons and a man driving a spring wagon injured the man's face and caused $25 worth of damage on the man's wagon.[42]

Heavy traffic on the unpaved city streets inspired the *St. Louis Post-Dispatch* to declare a war on dust in 1880. The newspaper pressured men of means to voluntarily pay a monthly subscription of $1 to have the streets sprinkled. The newspaper reminded wealthy readers that instead of only one dollar, "…gentlemen may assure themselves that there will not be the slightest jealously or ill-feeling if they see fit to subscribe more than that amount." The newspaper went so far as to suggest, "Ten dollars a month is not too much too [sic] pay for a pleasant drive by those who can afford it, and each subscriber should grade his subscription by the amount of enjoyment he proposes to have on the sprinkled avenues."[43] The *Post-Dispatch* then printed the lists of subscribers and their monthly donations. Tony Faust paid $5.[44]

Many of the city streets had been paved by 1891, which helped solve the dust problem. The Team Owner's Association and the Liverymen's Association then proposed that the cost of a vehicle license be reduced. At the time, every delivery vehicle owner paid taxes twice to the city: once for the vehicle merchant's license, then again for the vehicle license. The Associations' representatives argued that since many of the city's streets had been paved and wagons no longer damaged the streets, the vehicle license tax should be reduced. Additionally, as a result of the paving, the horses needed to be shod more often, and wagon wheels needed more repairs. They sent out a petition and gathered several hundred signatures, including those businessmen who had a large volume of deliveries around St. Louis. Signatories included brewers W.J. Lemp and Adolphus Busch, the owner of the messenger-service American Express Co., and oyster retailer Tony Faust.[45]

The Fulton Market wholesale oyster business was booming. When the Southern Hotel opened its brand new fireproof doors in 1880, the Fulton Market secured its own space on the hotel's first floor, conveniently located next door to Tony Faust's restaurant. "No Western city has anything like it" proclaimed the *Post-Dispatch*,
> From the outside, looking through large crystal plate glass, the passerby sees, appetizingly arrayed in a glass refrigerator, the delicacies of the season. Fish from the St. Lawrence and the Gulf of Mexico, from

the straits of the great chain of lakes and the briny Atlantic itself.[46]

The Fulton Market offered an impressive variety of fish, including shad, pompano, salmon, cod, striped bass, Spanish mackerel, brook trout, red snapper, halibut, haddock, and cod, as well as vegetables, cheeses, wild game, canned goods, and even condiments. And, true to form, Tony Faust spared no expense in the décor, "...a lofty ceiling that cost $1,800 in its ornamentation, a marble tiled floor, pure marble counters...polished walnut cases against the walls..." The market had an "upstairs office of French plate and ornamented glass in polished walnut... that cost at least $2,000." Equipped with modern appliances and a large staff, the Fulton Market was a St. Louis treasure.[47]

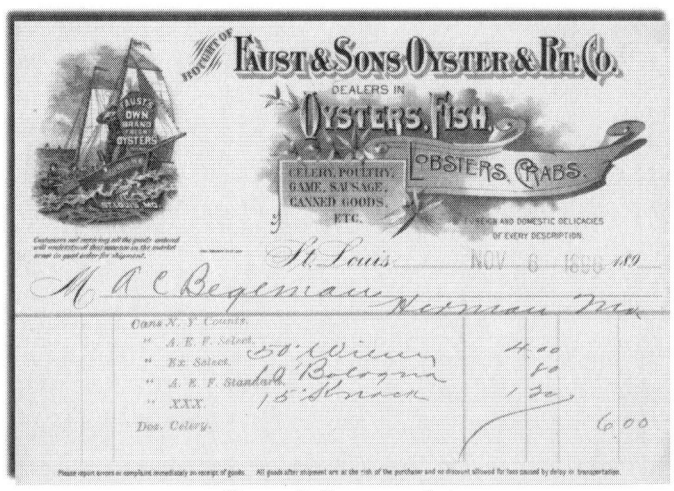

Faust & Sons receipt.
Courtesy of Missouri History Museum, St. Louis

Tony Faust soon added a summer garden at the rear of the Fulton Market. Complete with elegant awnings and stylish furniture, the garden also served as a café and a shady spot for a cocktail. In the evenings, the garden was illuminated with electric lights. The garden was often reserved for private parties and banquets, and was especially popular with the after-theater crowd.[48]

Tony awed his customers by offering elaborate Christmas dinners of Minnesota venison, Wisconsin fat geese or turkey with oyster dressing, and fresh Florida strawberries. Game included prairie chicken, grouse, woodcock, and ducks. Care to go international? The Fulton Market sold Westphalia ham, Braunschweig, Cervelat and Salami sausage; Brie Neufchâtel and Brie Québec, Roquefort, D'lsigny, and Swiss cheeses. Of course oysters were sold along with anchovies, *sprotts*, sardines, clams, crab, and lobster. Also for sale: frogs, terrapin, and turtle. Condiments, salads, fruits, wine, and champagnes were available. Customers chose the preparation: raw, canned, or cooked, and the meal was delivered right to their tables.[49]

So dedicated was Tony Faust to his oyster empire that he had a schooner built in the Chesapeake Bay. Tony commissioned 27-year-old boat maker Charles W. Crocket of Pocomoke City, Maryland, to fabricate his vessel, the third boat ever built by Crocket. Completed in June 1884, the boat was impressive: overall 58 feet on keel, 22-foot beam, and 6-foot depth of hold. It was lauded as a beauty by the *Baltimore Sun*. The boat was built with a carrying capacity of 2,000 bushels of oysters and was used by H.J. McGrath, the oyster packer hired by Tony. Sparing no expense, the vessel was ornamented with its name "Tony Faust," and at the bow stood a bust of the man himself.[50]

Soon Tony began to import more oysters then he could sell in St. Louis. He stepped into the lucrative position of middle man. Goods were shipped to St. Louis by rail from the East.

Tony also received shipments of oysters on the Mississippi River from points north and south. He then transported the products by rail to clients in the West. American railroading was in an ugly state of affairs at this time. Railroad companies formed trusts and fixed rates, and they granted rebates only to mammoth business owners like John D. Rockefeller of Standard Oil to secure their patronage. The railroads charged more for short hauls than long hauls, which enraged farmers and small business owners. Tony Faust, though, shipped his oysters great distances, enjoying the lower rates of long hauls.

Railroad magnates treated their employees horribly. Fed up, railroad workers around the country went on strike in 1877. The country was in a depression, yet railroad workers' already low wages were cut. This further angered the workers, whose jobs were difficult and dangerous. Industry in St. Louis and East St. Louis shut down as the railroad strike morphed into a general strike of the working man, represented by the Workingmen's party. A rally of 10,000 people disrupted commerce in St. Louis. Though it was a strong showing, the strike lost momentum and was put down by the police and the military. A decade later, in 1887, the government created the Interstate Commerce Act. It moved the country toward federal regulation, which required railroads to publish their rates and prohibited discriminatory fares and rebates.[51]

Tony Faust's business persevered. In 1881, he joined the Spanish-American Commercial Club. The club was begun with the "object of advancing the commercial interests of St. Louis in its trade with Mexico." Clearly hoping to ship his oysters beyond the boundaries of the United States, Tony was a loyal member of the group, which offered Spanish lessons three times per week.[52]

By 1895, Tony was shipping goods to the entire western United States, from the Ohio River to the Pacific coast, from the Canadian border to the Gulf of Mexico. That same year the Fulton Market outgrew its space in the Southern Hotel. Tony built a three-story building across the street. An underground tunnel connected the new Fulton Market to Tony Faust's restaurant.[53] By 1897, Tony had expanded again; he opened his "west branch" of the Fulton Market on Olive Street. In 1903, he had added yet another branch on Fourth Street.[54]

In spite of his thriving trade, Tony could not compete with Mother Nature. In September 1878, a storm swept over the East Coast that damaged railroad tracks, resulting in an "oyster famine" in the West. A local newspaper reported that Tony Faust had more than 100 orders from his clients whose shipments would be delayed.[55] A few years later, a vicious March snowstorm left Tony's Fulton Market without much inventory. The *St. Louis Globe-Democrat* reported that game supplier W.W. Judy, hunting in Indian Territory, was able to supply Tony Faust with some wild pigeons and duck. Game such as grouse, pheasants, quail, woodcock, venison, antelope, elk, buffalo, bear, and opossum were unattainable, but rabbits, jackrabbits, and squirrels remained in stock. Squirrels sold for $1 per dozen.[56]

Tony Faust was truly a leader of commerce and an example of the rapidly changing economic atmosphere of St. Louis. Alongside his hard-won squirrels, Tony sold international cheeses, vegetables, and meats in his market. St. Louis became a port of entry in 1871. Tony and other merchants could then receive their European goods directly. This was a great improvement compared to the years their goods arrived by rail, having been shipped first to New York. By

1883, 400 St. Louis merchants directly imported their goods from Europe. Tony frequently traveled by ship to Europe as a buyer to secure future imports. Many of the foods on his menus were German to accommodate St. Louis's large German population and their appetites. For example, between October 1886 and December 1887, Tony Faust received six shipments from Germany alone:[57]

    A.E. Faust, 13 cases vegetables, per steamer *Elbe,* from Bremen.

    October 1886

    A.E. Faust, 15 cases vegetables, per steamer *Saale,* from Bremen.

    February 1887

    A.E. Faust, 15 cases sausage and 1 case hams, per steamer *Werra,* from Bremen.

    April 1887

    A.E. Faust, 32 cases canned goods, per steamer *Lessing,* from Hamburg.

    September 1887

    A.E. Faust, 4 cases canned goods, per steamer *Werra,* from Bremen.

    October 1887

    A.E. Faust, 15 cases meat, per steamer *Alter,* from Bremen.

    December 1887

Chapter 2
THE PERILS OF BEER

Despite glowing reports about the architecture of the building, the imported food, and the décor, Tony Faust's restaurant had a counter-image. As many times as it was called a "restaurant" it was synonymously called a "saloon." Though the restaurant was lauded as a place for ladies and gentlemen to dine on imported delicacies, the saloon made the papers for raucous behavior. Just as the newspapers mentioned the orchestral music on the terrace, they also reported brawls in the saloon late at night. Tony was not just a jovial host for his guests in their finery. He rolled out the red carpet for *all* patrons, even those who used their fists to resolve disputes that erupted over their steins.

It wasn't unusual for the bar fights to include the wait staff. An article about one such brawl in 1882, reported in the *St. Louis Post-Dispatch*, read simply: "A lively fight occurred in Tony Faust's saloon last night, in the course of which four unknown men beat a number of waiters rather severely."[1] In 1883, three railroad men caused trouble with two waiters. One of the railroad workers pulled a knife but "before he could use it he received a severe blow to the back of the head." The men left quickly.[2]

A brawl in 1893 proved the mettle of Tony's waiters. Around midnight one evening in June, Sam Yungling, a former bartender of another saloon in St. Louis who was known for shooting a patron, grew angry over his bill at Tony Faust's. The waiters threw him out. On the sidewalk a group of his friends joined him and threatened to "do up" the waiters. The waiters outnumbered the group and the fight took place "in which glasses, sticks and umbrellas were freely used." Even people in the crowd tussled a bit. A city alderman received a blow. A prize fighter jumped into the fray before police broke up the brawl.[3]

The newspaper printed vivid accounts of bar fights. One such article in 1896 detailed a man willing to "lick" anyone of "doubtful birth" one night at Tony Faust's. A man standing nearby took exception to this remark, so the troublemaker "immediately put him to sleep."[4] The *St. Louis Post-Dispatch* recounted horrible beatings. One late night in 1895 at Tony Faust's, a bookmaker ("bookie") "was nearly murdered" by a man who was a paid racetrack informant and owed the bookie money.[5] Sometimes patrons used weapons, as in October 1896, when one man drew a pocketknife on another as they supped at Tony Faust's around 7:00 in the evening. "A scattering of chairs" and tough talk preceded the assault. The man with the knife cut the other's face.[6]

A hilarious account in the local newspaper described how two actors with a theater group entertained diners one night in 1889 at Tony Faust's. One actor accused the other of indulging in "what the variety profession has called 'guying.'" Seeing him incensed, the accuser's first impulse was "to wipe up the floor" with him, "but he compromised by slapping his face" with an "absolute lack of ceremony." The article continues:

> The salient features of the performance were loud talk, flying beer steins, fried oysters, bread and butter, prepared mustard, condiment bottles and other things of that description filled the air while the rapid and uncomplimentary exchanges of words between the men worked up the proper orchestral effect. A waiter who undertook to interfere was

covered with oyster soup and French dressing for his pains. Finally the men were separated and departed in peace.[7]

Then there was the time in June 1882. The *St. Louis Post-Dispatch* went into great detail describing two women of "unsavory notoriety." The women, one wearing a red silk dress, arrived drunk at midnight on the veranda at Tony Faust's. Angry that the waiters declined to serve them based on their "boisterous and unseemly" behavior, one "made a display of her person that caused the genteel waiters to turn their heads and blush." A watchman, a security guard of sorts, forcibly removed them. They kicked and screamed until he threw them onto the street. Alerted by the hubbub, the police took them away. The newspaper concluded that the "sufferers are the private watchman and Tony Faust."[8]

Like all bars, Tony Faust's saloon served as a venue for emotions that sometimes ran high. The manager of the St. Louis Browns chased a sportswriter out of the establishment one night in 1896. Henry "Harry" Diddlebock, the Browns manager, was angry at the sportswriter for malicious comments in his column. The sportswriter was irate at not being named the official scorer for the Browns.[9] On a more violent night in 1897, the unappreciated lightweight boxing champion, Jack McAuliffe, tried to beat a man "to death" in Tony Faust's saloon when the bar patron refused his terms in his challenge for a fight.[10]

Even a physician, Dr. Engelbert Voerster, started brawls at Tony Faust's restaurant. In September 1886, the doctor suffered a blow to his jaw with a rock in retaliation for punching a man. After the physician and his opponent were removed by the police, the doctor's friend continued the fight and pulled a revolver. Dr. Voerster, known for raising his fists around St. Louis, returned to Tony Faust's a few months later. According to a waiter, he was found at 2:20 in the morning in the rear of the restaurant "pounding the face of a small-sized man." The waiter managed to pull the doctor off, but not "until the doctor had succeeded in pulling off with his nails a piece of the gentleman's ear."[11]

Could this negative publicity, reported in an English-speaking newspaper, have contributed to the rapidly-growing temperance movement? Tony Faust's saloon was certainly no different than any other beer-drinking establishment in St. Louis. Temperance proponents viewed drinking as a contributor to the ills of urban society; domestic conflict plagued overcrowded cities full of immigrants in the nineteenth century. One example of many appeared in the *St. Louis Globe-Democrat* in 1879: a woman wished to divorce her husband who was known for spending his time in saloons, even claiming to be the champion *leber wurst* eater at Tony Faust's old place on Carondelet Avenue. He squandered his salary, leaving the woman and her child with a pittance while he bellied up to the bar.[12] Many in the temperance movement blamed society's problems on alcohol. Drinking was viewed as an ethnic and inferior practice. Though many German men in St. Louis achieved professional and financial success, most immigrant men toiled for little pay at backbreaking jobs. They sought comfort and camaraderie in their places of refuge: saloons.[13]

The role of the government was questioned by those for and against temperance. Temperates argued for government regulation. They advocated laws that would "moralize" members of society. Beer-drinking immigrants, however, whose European backgrounds made them familiar with hierarchy of authority rather than independent political participation, placed personal loyalties over abstract regulation. Immigrants therefore directly contributed to tarnished political systems by voting for ward bosses and city officials who not only understood the immigrants' issues but assured them of their loyalty.[14]

The conflict played itself out in the allegiance to political parties. Many immigrants aligned themselves with Democrats, who preferred *laissez faire* and opposed governmental interference. Republicans offered a place for reformers to advance creative, all-encompassing uses of governmental authority.[15] Tony Faust, whose business interests were directly affected by his political adherence, was proudly aligned with the Democratic Party. He served on fund-raising committees in 1888 and 1889 for the Democratic National Convention.[16] And on November 4, 1888, Tony, his close friend Adolphus Busch, and other prominent Germans presided over a rally of about 2,000 German Democrats. Speaking in German, the leaders of the rally called the Republican party "tyrannical" while the Democratic party leaders promised personal liberties and consideration for American citizens of foreign birth.[17] Inevitably, such political fervor played out at fever pitch in drinking establishments.

The *St. Louis Post-Dispatch* wrote of an incident in 1888 in which a former member of the House of Delegates pulled a knife in anger at Tony Faust's restaurant. At another table a judge and an attorney spoke disparagingly against the mayor, who was running for governor. The former delegate vehemently defended the candidate and drew his weapon after, in the worst of all insults, he was called a "Republican."[18]

Not all blows came at night. Judge Noonan of the Court of Criminal Correction in St. Louis sat having lunch at Tony Faust's restaurant at 10:00 a.m. one day in 1887. As Frank O'Neill, managing editor of the *Republican* passed by, the judge began a tirade against him. The editor, who bitterly opposed the judge during his previous campaign, took the verbal abuse silently. The judge called over the clerk of the Supreme Court from Jefferson City, who was lunching at a nearby table, for support in his rant. Finally, still saying nothing, the editor punched the judge in the face. Then each went his separate way.[19]

As early as 1882, brewers and saloon keepers heard rumors that Republicans planned to pass a bill that would shut their businesses down, if not completely, then at least on Sundays. A group of 50 St. Louis brewers filed for their naturalization papers that year in July so they could vote for the Democrats in the next election. Of the rumors, brewer William J. Lemp said, "We must fight this fanatical desire to wipe out everything connected with the liquor traffic, for there are some people who want to drink beer… Every man has some rights which others must respect, and I consider this desire one of those rights." Another said, "I have a great respect for a sincere, high moral churchman, but he has no right to force his opinions on me, nor has he the right to legislate against my business, which is a lawful one." Tony Faust agreed, "I feel that my business is a legitimate one, and I do not propose to be regarded as a criminal…"[20]

A year later, things became more heated, and the proposed saloon closings divided the ranks of city and state officials. The governor of Missouri declared that when the law came into effect to close saloons on Sundays, he expected the law to be enforced without question. He hinted that, if it was not enforced, resignations of police officials under his appointment might be forthcoming. Meanwhile, the president of the Saloon Keepers Protective Association declared that Sunday was the working man's holiday. Beer gardens were simply too popular an institution to close. Missouri's state senator agreed. He believed that the city of St. Louis had too diverse a population to enforce such an unreasonable law.[21]

With the proposed law in mind, the *St. Louis Post-Dispatch* surveyed the crowds one Sunday in July 1883, to ascertain just how many of the citizens spent their time in beer gardens on the Sabbath. The newspaper reported that nearly 100,000 people patronized beer gardens all over the city. It reported that 10,000 people, largely of "foreign extraction," visited Tony Faust's throughout the day.[22]

The law was put into effect at the end of July, 1883. The city of St. Louis was abuzz. City officials were left with the burden of interpreting the so-called Sunday law, which was called a "farce" and an "absurdity." It required non-essential revenue-producing businesses to close their doors. Though the Saloon Keepers Protective Association vowed open defiance, Tony Faust agreed to close his bar, but keep his restaurant open.[23] Public services such as railroad offices were also forced to close on Sundays. The *Post-Dispatch* complained that the Sunday law "classed railroad offices with saloons and other places tending to disturb the peace and quiet of the Sabbath day."

For a place of the size and importance of St. Louis, where numerous railroads center it is thought that this is too much of a back-country, one-horse policy to follow, and it frequently subjects travele[r]s to great inconvenience.[24]

31

The deeply contested law was short-lived. Judge Noonan, friend of the drinking public, delivered a victory to the alcohol industry. During the trial of brewer and saloon keeper William J. Lemp, who had violated the Sunday law, Judge Noonan declared that the Act of 1857, which stated that alcohol may be served seven days a week, overrode the Downing Law, the part of the Sunday law which specified that liquor-selling businesses must close on Sundays.[25] Tony Faust and his brethren could again sell beer seven days a week and did so for the next four years.

Once again, though, in 1887, Missouri state lawmakers voted for the Sunday law, officially repealing the Act of 1857.[26] Members of the St. Louis police board were again burdened with deciphering which businesses could or could not remain open on Sundays. The St. Louis Browns were not even allowed to play visiting baseball teams at Sportsmans Park on a Sunday.[27]

Tony Faust, now on the Board of Trustees of the "Liberal Brotherhood of America," (formerly the Saloon Keepers Protective Association and soon to become the Retail Liquor Merchants Protective Association) once again agreed to be law abiding, in spite of rumors of his defiance. How effective was this law, anyway? The vast majority of those saloon keepers tried were acquitted. In one case the jury deliberated for as long as two minutes. No wonder, as the juries were handpicked by the court deputy and were called "decidedly German" by a member of the temperance movement. Judge Noonan said, "A Judge is human....and need not be expected to turn away from his friends."[28]

And so it went. For the next eight years, Tony Faust kept the doors of his establishment closed on the Sabbath. However, he was arrested in 1895 for violating the Sunday law. Charged with another prominent saloon keeper, Pat Carmody, Tony offered the Sabbath Association a compromise, "Now, in the old country the beer gardens and saloons close up during church hours... I would gladly do this if an agreement of this sort were reached." Even more eloquent, Pat Carmody said,

> I am thoroughly in sympathy with all truly religious people and will aid them in any way that I can to uphold the law, but I have no use for hypocrites who use religion as a cloak. ...the saloons can never be closed on Sunday. The great masses should have their right to drink as well as the rich man, who has his stock of liquors in his cellar. The Liquor Dealers' Association is willing to meet the Sabbatarians half way. They should have their part of the day and we ours." [29]

Perhaps it was the arrest of these two prominent citizens of the German community that persuaded the law enforcement officials of St. Louis to declare war. The prosecuting attorney's office planned to arrest absolutely every business owner who operated on Sunday, pronouncing them all non-essential. Streetcars, theaters, and ice cream shops were fair game. Expecting to debilitate the city and clog the courts, the city attorney hoped to show the absurdity of the law. The St. Louis prosecuting attorney asked, "Why should the standard theater or any of the other places of amusement be allowed to remain open, and Tony Faust's be forced to close...?"[30] In response, Rev. Werlein, president of the Sabbath Association, spoke with venom,

> ...I believe the intelligent element of our city is strong enough to render such an effort unsuccessful. It is the aim ...of violators of law to endeavor to debauch the minds ...of the people down to their level. We are engaged in a warfare against the

oppressor in the interests of the oppressed. ...we must do something practical for poor, suffering humanity.[31]

Of course, each side claimed allegiance with the working class: one wished to free them from the debauchery of the saloon on Sundays, while the other wished to provide them with a place to relax with a beer.

After the laws took another turn, Tony Faust proudly posted this advertisement in 1905, "**On and after Sept. 3 Tony Faust's world-famous restaurant will be open Sundays.**"[32]

Temperance during this era incited passion. Out of this came a multitude of groups, including the American Society for the Promotion of Temperance, the Anti-Saloon League, the Women's Christian Temperance Union, the American Temperance Society, and the Sons of Temperance.[33] Tony Faust was only one of the great many American saloon keepers who struggled to defend his business and his culture against well-intentioned reformers. In the summer of 1889, 40 Kansas City saloon keepers were arrested in one Sunday under the Downing law. Those who had admitted customers through side alleys were also found to have broken the law and were taken into custody by police disguised in street clothes.[34]

Ambiguous boundaries separated each side of the temperance conflict in the late nineteenth century: natives vs. immigrants; established immigrants from western Europe vs. the influx of new immigrants from southeastern Europe; and middle/upper class vs. working class. Nothing regarding temperance was straightforward in this era. There were endless dichotomies: reformers citing religious reasons for temperance, and immigrants serving alcohol during weddings and wakes; dogmatic women venturing out of their place in the home in the name of reform to invade the homes of working-class women with their messages of temperance; and male "dries" allowing women to further their political cause without giving women franchise rights in return.[35] The never-ending paradox begged the question: where was the balance between needed reform and reform overdone?

Voters found their ballots more important than ever. The establishment of the Progressive Party in the early twentieth century serves as an example of Americans' better-defined goals. Politics raced onward toward the inevitable: Prohibition.[36]

Chapter 3
ENTERPRISING AND ACTIVE

Hunters and sportsmen provided quail and other game for Fulton's Market and Tony Faust's restaurant. In fact, in 1881 the St. Louis City Comptroller sent a package of Tony Faust's pheasants, quail, and guinea hens to President Garfield, who, according to a grateful letter from his private secretary, loved it.[1] Two years later, quail- eating contests were all the rage. St. Louisans took up the event after a highly publicized match in New York. At one St. Louis restaurant a man set out to prove that he could consume two quails each day for 30 days. Meanwhile, Thomas Wood bet Henry Dahmer (both employees of the *St. Louis Post-Dispatch*) $1,000 that he could not eat 35 quails in 35 days. Under the terms of the wager, Mr. Dahmer was to order his quail at Tony Faust's restaurant between 11:00 a.m. and 1:00 p.m. every day.

Beginning his "gastronomic feat" on January 27, 1883, Mr. Dahmer experimented with his quail and decided he preferred it broiled. Tony served it up with bread and butter, potatoes, pickles, and beer. The proprietor was well stocked with quail to feed his competitor through the duration of the competition. He was not concerned that the Missouri game law prohibited the sale of out-of-season quail between February 1 and October 15. On February 10, Mr. Dahmer ate his fifteenth quail just as the president and secretary of the Game and Fish Protective Association showed up at Tony Faust's. They felt obliged to tell Tony that from that day forward the law would be enforced. Tony stated he would follow the letter of the law by no longer serving quail. The fun was over and each participant claimed victory.[2]

The next 14 years brought similar disregard for gaming laws. Like the hundreds of other merchants who sold out-of-season game in open markets, cafés, and restaurants across the city, Tony thought nothing of meeting the demand for game, since the laws were never enforced. To get around the law, restaurateurs listed quail as "snow birds," prairie chickens as "young owls," and venison as "antelope." When patrons ordered their food, waiters would carefully call the items by their names on the menu. In 1897, unsuspecting waiters readily divulged the true menu item when asked by undercover deputies of the State Game and Fish Warden's department.

The *St. Louis Post-Dispatch* reported, "The opening gun in what promises to prove a bitter war between the State Game and Fish Warden and the game and commission dealers of the city was fired Saturday" with the arrest of Tony Faust and nine other sellers of out-of-season game. The day prior to the arrest, an angry city judge promised that 10 violators would be selected of the 740 game dealers in the city "as a test" to determine whether the courts would uphold the law and prosecute them. He railed, "I do not know who the ten will be, but Tony Faust... will be among the number." And sure enough, he was.[3]

Tony Faust's case probably ended there. At that time, most game law violators were fined, or their cases were quashed in St. Louis courts.[4] In December of that year – when game was again in season – the *St. Louis Post-Dispatch* reported:
> The express companies have been kept busy shipping boxes of game to the East, being Christmas presents from St. Louis. Wild turkeys...[are] the most popular game, though prairie chickens, quail,

grouse, wild geese and venison is being shipped largely. Faust's Fulton Markets, 610 Olive street and Broadway and Elm, are the markets that are supplying the demand, and their patrons are keeping them busy with orders for game for the East.[5]

It would be reasonable to speculate that Tony's brisk sale of quail was *not* the item on Tony Faust's menu that piqued the ire of the authorities... it was the alcohol.

Tony often used his restaurant business as his philanthropic tool. The *St. Louis Globe-Democrat* directed in 1878, "Go to Tony Faust's to-day. His *gross receipts* during the day will be given to the Southern sufferers."[6] In 1880, Tony sat on the committee of liquor retailers of the Merchant's Exchange and sought subscriptions for a new handbook to be distributed to future immigrants from around the world. The Missouri Immigration Society hoped to entice new settlers to the state. Tony's employees joined him in giving generously for flood relief in 1892 and tornado relief in 1896.[7]

Tony Faust was a wealthy, philanthropic business owner in the Gilded Age. His bankbook, though, was nowhere near the likes of those who made their fortunes in growing industries during this pre-income tax era. Such men included J. Pierpont Morgan, John D. Rockefeller, Andrew Carnegie, and even Adolphus Busch. Most had a reputation for unscrupulous business practices. The term "Robber Baron" was bitterly applied. Some believed those business titans donated money only to restore their reputations. Nevertheless, the great institutions created by men of their financial stature often succeeded in establishing their own prestige. Libraries, hospitals, and colleges built by those men benefitted everyone. One cannot argue that, said one author, "moral responsibility, like the ambition to succeed, knew no class lines."[8]

During the latter part of the nineteenth century, Social Darwinism was drawn from Charles Darwin's theory of evolution. It was the attitude that those who were rich were superior to those who were poor. By that theory, being poor was a sign of personal failure. Some even suggested that assisting the poor, whether through philanthropy or governmental intervention, was only prolonging their state.[9] When Supreme Court Justice David J. Brewer addressed the New York State Bar Association in 1893, he suggested that only few had what it took – stamina and strength – to become wealthy:

> The great majority of men are unwilling to endure that long self-denial and saving which makes accumulations possible…and hence it always has been, and until human nature is remodeled always will be true, that the wealth of a nation is in the hands of a few, while the many subsist upon the proceeds of their daily toil.[10]

This notion of superiority was plainly exhibited in an 1898 article in the *St. Louis Post-Dispatch.* The reporter played the role of Rex M'Donald, a horse at an equine event at the St. Louis Coliseum. He wrote the article through the eyes of the horse as he surveyed the crowd. When his eyes moved to Tony Faust's wife and daughter sitting with the Busch group, he commented, "Adolphus Busch looks the part of a rich man and good citizen. All men like him ought to have money, and everybody with money ought to spend it as liberally and judiciously as he."[11]

Superior or not, it was a coup to be recognized for helping

others. Newspapers awarded accolades to those who gave. Tony served as chairman of the dinner committee of the 1904 Christmas Festival at the St. Louis Coliseum, in which "prominent men and women aid the cause." Ten thousand poor children and their families attended the event; Christmas trees were decorated and gifts were distributed. The *St. Louis Post-Dispatch* heralded Tony: "Through the great kindness of A. E. Faust, the chef of his restaurant, Carl H. Dietz, will have charge of the menu in its framing, preparation, and service."[12]

Tony was wise. Such benevolence was not only good for business, but perhaps he had an ulterior motive? Saloon keepers were often viewed as contributors to the domestic ailments of the poor. Yet, his generosity enabled him to join hands with those with whom he battled. It indisputably proved that one did not have to be in the temperance movement to provide for the less fortunate. Whether this bought him and other saloon keepers favor in the eyes of the temperate, however, is less likely.

Tony Faust took his restaurant fare on the road. Among his many catering jobs, he provided the first meal under the new roof of the rebuilt Southern Hotel in 1881. There he served the construction workers and a variety of dignitaries.[13] Tony's "kitchen corps" also had the honor of preparing the Twenty-fifth Anniversary meal for his dear friends Adolphus and Lilly Busch. Though he was undoubtedly considered a guest rather than kitchen help, Tony oversaw the lavish dinner at the Busch residence, which seated the 175 guests around one table.[14]

Tony was awarded catering privileges at the newly built Delmar Gardens theater in St. Louis in 1900. Until then, his largest catering job had been at the Exposition Hall.[15] The St. Louis Exposition and Music Hall was a magnificent building. Business-savvy Tony paid $250 in stock subscriptions toward the construction of the hall, which was built in 1883. He then leased the immense restaurant space in the building.[16] Fall festivals at the Exposition Hall were extremely popular and well attended. During the first year the Hall was open, 500,000 people attended during one week in October. There was something for everyone: "Leiderkranz Night," "Classical Night," "Veiled Prophet Week," and "Merchant's & Manufacturer's Day" as well as sold-out orchestral concerts and appearances by the great John Phillip Sousa's marching bands.[17]

Tony didn't limit his business interests to food service. He and his pal Adolphus Busch traveled the country together seeking real estate and business opportunities. In 1887, they and several other St. Louis businessmen made a trip to Arkansas. The region was booming in the post-Reconstruction era. Both logging and agricultural products like strawberries had become a big industry. Both required a route to larger markets. There the businessmen scouted the site of the proposed railroad line in the Beebe, Arkansas, area, and considered purchasing property near Little Rock. Tony and Adolphus had joined the ranks of carpetbaggers: wealthy northern businessmen who headed south during and after Reconstruction to get a piece of the financial-growth pie while the South recovered and industrialized.[18]

Tony also joined his brewer friend on many trips to Texas, including one trip in 1889 to Denison, Texas, 75 miles north of Dallas. There they invested in property "adjacent to the Busch Beer Depot." But Adolphus Busch made it known that the most important reason for their trip was to "perfect arrangements for the protection of the St. Louis trade against any encroachments...for the Texas beer supply." For Adolphus Busch, his interest was to remain the primary beer supplier for the state. Anheuser-Busch not only shipped beer from St. Louis but built breweries in San Antonio, Houston, Galveston, and Fort Worth.[19]

Tony Faust was known for spending his money on public entertainments. He mesmerized St. Louis crowds in 1881 with a fireworks display fired from his restaurant's rooftop during a parade. He purchased his pyrotechnics from a manufacturer in New York and had them shipped to St. Louis at a whopping cost of $700.[20] Tony also generously donated money and raised funds for a show of lights during St. Louis fairs and the city's annual Illumination.[21] In 1889, he invested in an enormous fish tank (supposedly the largest in the country), built by the Missouri Fish Commission for display at the Exposition.[22]

Tony gave back to his community in other ways, too. In 1875, he served on a fund-raising delegation for the Philadelphia World's Fair. He was a member of the Knights of St. Patrick and the Order of the Elks. In 1886, Tony served on the planning committee for the twenty-fifth anniversary celebration of taking Camp Jackson, and in 1894 he became a member of the St. Louis Historical Society.[23]

Tony was also a member of two German societies: the Germania Club and the Turner Society. The purpose of the Germania Club, founded in 1866, was to provide entertainment for its members, including lectures, concerts, and dances. The Turner Society was founded in St. Louis in 1849, just as German immigrants began to inhabit St. Louis in droves. The principal object of the group was to provide gymnasiums for exercise and to "develop children into healthy, able-bodied men and women" – a philosophy brought from the Fatherland. And for years, Tony and the others celebrated the Turners' company of sharpshooters, which had comprised a large portion of the volunteers who marched on Camp Jackson.[24]

And he sang, too. When a St. Louis singing group performed at a German festival in Chicago, singer Tony Faust saved the day. "The St. Louisans could not stand the Chicago beer, and had it not been for Tony Faust, who brought up a lot of St. Louis brewed fluid, the tuneful boys would have had to go thirsty."[25]

Tony Faust was a fan of rowing. In 1878, he was one of the founding members of Modoc, a rowing club made up of businessmen like him. He, the newly elected vice president of the club, sent a letter to the new president,

> Dear Sir-
> Allow me to present to the oarsmen of St. Louis the cup sent herewith, to be offered as a prize for annual competition of the eight-oared barges. Trusting it will be the means of advancing the boating interests of this city, I remain yours respectfully, A.E. Faust.[26]

This was the first race for the Faust Cup, a silver trophy 14 inches tall with gold lining, ornamented with oars, cables, and anchors, and inscribed "Faust Prize Cup, Presented by A.E. Faust." The race was held on the Mississippi River. The newly formed Modoc rowing team competed against teams from two other St. Louis rowing clubs.[27]

In 1879, the University Club merged with Modoc. The

merger gave Modoc a new batch of young, strong rowers. Still vice president a year later, Tony commissioned a new racing barge for Modoc, called none other than the "Tony Faust." It was "considered the finest six-oared barge ever built." It was 42 feet long and 46 inches wide with swivel rowlocks and a new style of sliding seat. The vessel was exhibited for the public to admire at the club's boathouse on the Mississippi River before it was put to the test by the rowers.[28]

Modoc's first boathouse stood at the docks on the Mississippi River at the end of Spruce Street. A terrible accident occurred in 1881 at this busy location on the river. A steamer ran down a Modoc racing boat and killed three oarsmen. The club moved its boathouse to a quieter area of the river, south of the busy waters and the ferries, near Anna Street. That same year, Tony donated $200 toward a new boathouse at Creve Coeur Lake, a lovely spot with calm waters 20 miles west of St. Louis. A rowman proclaimed that, "if there is a better three-mile course in the world he has yet to see it."[29]

By 1885, the Modoc Rowing Club was one of four rowing clubs in St. Louis. It boasted the largest fleet of racing barges: 40 in all, and the "Tony Faust" was still one of the primary vessels. Called one of the principal backers of the club, along with his good friend Adolphus Busch, Tony cheered the Modoc rowers in their tan jerseys and blue knee trunks. In 1886, Tony held a banquet in the club's president's honor at the Cabin in his restaurant. "About twenty-five as genial gentlemen as ever sat down to a champagne supper drank toasts with friends." The Cabin was decorated with a single scull ornamented with flowers and suspended from the ceiling. After a feast and many toasts, the men jovially sang aquatic selections such as "The

Skipper."[30]

On April 8, 1875, Tony Faust became a member of the Free and Accepted Masons, Naphtali Lodge No. 25. His membership certificate, written in both English and German, reads,
> Anthony E. Faust has been regularly initiated as an Entered Apprentice, Passed to the degree of Fellow Craft, and Raised to the Sublime Degree of Master Mason, and is distinguished for his Zeal and Fidelity to the Craft. We do therefore recommend, that he be received and acknowledged as such by all true and accepted Freemasons, wheresoever dispersed.[31]

The Masonic fraternity is believed to have its beginnings in stonemasons' guilds during the middle ages. Its documented history begins in 1717 with the formation of Masonic lodges in England. Freemasonry became popular in colonial America, with many Founding Fathers as members. The first Missouri Masonic Lodge was constituted in 1807, with Meriwether Lewis as its master. The Masons continued their tradition of emphasizing self-improvement and personal study as well as philanthropy well into the nineteenth century, founding orphanages and homes for widows and the elderly.[32]

The Naphtali Lodge was described as one of the wealthiest of the St. Louis lodges. Tony was an involved member in the Masons' philanthropic activities. For example, in 1878 he served on the reception committee for a charity ball held at the Masonic Hall.[33]

In 1887, the Grand Lodge of Missouri noted that the Naphtali Lodge's membership included those who were connected with the manufacture, sale, and handling of intoxicating liquor – strictly prohibited by the Masonic Lodge. So the Naphtali Lodge dutifully charged, quietly tried, and quickly acquitted Tony Faust and two of its other saloon-keeper members. Angered by this act of defiance, the Grand Lodge of Missouri arrested the Naphtali Lodge of St. Louis, rendering the lodge nonexistent. Tony demitted, or relinquished, his membership.

Tony's occupation was "saloon keeper" when he was received as a member of the Masonic Lodge in 1875. So why had his membership been accepted? And why did the lodge wait 12 years to act? Tony Faust had only one answer: "Prohibition."[34]

Besides the Naphtali Lodge, there were 25 Masonic lodges in St. Louis. A half-dozen of them had saloon-keeping members. Yet only the three from the Naphtali Lodge faced the Grand Lodge's justice system. It was deeply embarrassing. The *St. Louis Post-Dispatch* called the situation a "spectacle" in an article titled "A Masonic Muddle." Speaking to a *Post-Dispatch* reporter about the three saloon keepers, the District Deputy Grand Master of the Grand Lodge of Missouri explained that "a saloon-keeper is not such a member as a fraternity like the Masons ought to have" and that "saloon-keepers are not desirable members."[35]

It didn't stop there. Many of the Masonic Lodges offered a life insurance policy to their members. While a member, Tony paid dues toward his policy. The District Deputy Grand Master rationalized that saloon keepers had a shorter life expectancy (owing to the drink). Yet, he suggested, the insurance money allowed them to go into the afterlife in style,

I have noticed that the lodges in this city having the most saloon-keepers as members, have the most funerals. The remains are kept several days, and the obsequies usually very elaborate and therefore expensive. So from the standpoint of financial economy, it might seem that saloon-keepers are not desirable members.[36]

Six years later, in 1893, Tony faced a judge in a St. Louis courtroom. He had been sued by the State Insurance Superintendent for not continuing to pay dues to the Masonic Benefits Association of the Masonic Lodge after he left the organization. The judge declared him not liable for any dues assessed against him after his resignation. Three days later, the same judge allowed an appeal by the State Insurance Superintendent. The case went to the Missouri Supreme Court. Tony Faust won.[37]

Chapter 4
THE 1904 WORLD'S FAIR

St. Louisans desperately wanted to host an exposition. The city hoped to be awarded the honor of hosting the 1892 Columbian Exposition, which would celebrate the four hundredth anniversary of Columbus's discovery of America. For this, St. Louisans raised more than $4 million. The *St. Louis Post-Dispatch* posted an updated list of subscriptions in 1889. Tony Faust and restaurateur Peter O'Neil each gave $10,000 – by far the most. Only four others gave $5,000 or more toward the cause, out of 72 donations. But alas, Chicago was awarded the honor, and that city produced a grand celebration in 1893.[1]

The Missouri Historical Society proposed the erection of a building in 1896 to memorialize Thomas Jefferson and to house Louisiana Purchase documents. Thus, the idea of a celebration of the anniversary of the Louisiana Purchase was conceived. For this celebration, St. Louis was chosen as host. The Louisiana Purchase Exposition Corporation was born in 1900. St. Louisans again enthusiastically raised money. In addition to private subscriptions that raised $5 million, corporate subscribers purchased stock at $10 a share in the new company, totaling another $5 million. Congress pledged $5 million after the original $10 million was spent. Stockholders elected a board of directors for the Louisiana Purchase Exposition, 118 elite society and businessmen. Only a few Germans were named, including Adolphus Busch.[2]

The disappointment of losing the Columbian Exposition and the fervor for the upcoming Louisiana Purchase Exposition shed light on the *much needed* reform in St. Louis. Circuit Attorney Joseph Folk went after corruption in the city government. He represented workers in the streetcar strike of 1900, investigated election fraud, and prosecuted those involved in bribery and perjury.[3] Rolla Wells was elected mayor in 1901 on the platform of reform. He touted his themes of "New St. Louis" and "City Beautiful." The mayor set out to address an embarrassment: city services. To fund his ambitious goal of cleaning up the streets and public buildings, he proposed "prudent borrowing, reassessments, and economical administration."[4] These were new concepts to the corrupt St. Louis city government.

Mayor Wells saw to it that rail service led to Forest Park (the site of the upcoming Exposition), St. Louis's muddy tap water was purified, and the polluted air was cleared of smoke. Citizens of St. Louis got into the act with the formation of the Civic Improvement League. The League asked citizens to acknowledge if they witnessed criminal activity and offered awards for the most improved front yard.[5]

Construction of the Louisiana Purchase Exposition, also called the St. Louis World's Fair, was a massive undertaking. The Fair included 12 palaces, with only one, the Palace of Fine Arts, a permanent structure. The massive ivory-colored buildings were surrounded by magnificent landscaping complete with gardens, fountains, and lagoons.[6] Hotels were built to accommodate the anticipated influx of people. Some were permanent, some temporary; the temporary hotels contractually agreed to keep their room rates at pre-Fair levels. Only one hotel was built within the fairgrounds at Forest Park, the Inside Inn.[7]

A great number of men from around the world worked on

the construction site. To feed those crews, board member Adolphus Busch sent the following telegrams to the Executive Committee of the Louisiana Purchase Exposition:

> March 18, 1902
> The best, safest, most deserving and most experienced man for the restaurant privileges on grounds during erection of buildings is Tony Faust and I shall appreciate it highly if you will interest yourself in my old friend.
> Adolphus Busch

> March 18, 1902
> I request the sole bar and restaurant privileges during construction of fair buildings for my friend Tony Faust, the most experienced man in the business, who will lend it dignity and give thorough satisfaction to all. That he will sell the only beer it is needless for me to say.
> Adolphus Busch[8]

When construction was under way, a worldwide marketing campaign for the Exposition was launched. Sensing that foreign countries had grown tired of expositions, the untiring president of the Louisiana Purchase Exposition Company, David R. Francis, traveled the world. He touted the great fair to be held in St. Louis, and he secured support from around the globe.[9]

The Exposition's grounds and buildings were dedicated in 1903 in a huge ceremony with President Theodore Roosevelt as a speaker. One year later, on April 30, 1904, the Louisiana Purchase Exposition officially opened.[10] One month into the fair, Tony's daughter, Mollie Faust Giannini, wrote a letter to her brother Anthony R. from Europe, "You have no idea how extensively the Exposition is advertised over here in Italy. We see the pictures in all railroad and steamship offices, hotel, stations, book stores, etc. Europeans are having a regular St. Louis Exposition fever."[11] Hundreds of thousands of people visited the fair from around the world. One of the biggest hits of the World's Fair was the Pike.

The Pike was an east-west street that stretched across the northern edge of Forest Park. It was home to great entertainments and concessions. A little rowdy at times, the Pike would remain open long after the rest of the fairgrounds closed for the day. Its carnival-like atmosphere featured concessions, marching bands, exhibits of foreign peoples, and violent reenactments of events like the Boer War and the Galveston Flood.[12]

One of the biggest attractions was the Tyrolean Alps. Located at the East entrance of the Pike, the Tyrolean Alps was a re-creation of a mountainous German village. Fairgoers could take a tram ride through the German village in the snowcapped Alps, complete with gabled houses and churches. Visitors could see the Magic Grotto and tour the beautiful the Royal Castle. Peasant girls worked and sang native songs, and 100-piece orchestras performed in a large outdoor gazebo on a plaza.[13] Each attraction cost extra, but the biggest draw of the Tyrolean Alps was the Lüchow-Faust Restaurant.

August Guido Lüchow immigrated to the United States from Germany and purchased a restaurant and bar in New York City. There he established the famous Lüchow's restaurant in 1882. The restaurant was located on East 14th street in the heart of the theatrical, musical, literary, and political life of New York. Lüchow's restaurant drew in many famous people. The three-story brownstone contained seven dining rooms with high ceilings, dark hardwood-paneled walls decorated with mirrors, oil paintings, and skylights. And, of course, an outdoor beer garden was located in the back. Lüchow served typical German fare like schnitzel and sauerbraten. His restaurant was known for his weeklong festivals and his imported German beer.[14]

August Lüchow and Tony Faust teamed up to make what was touted as the largest restaurant in the world at the 1904 World's Fair. The Lüchow-Faust Restaurant seated 4,000 people in the outdoor plaza, 1,700 in the grand dining hall, and 1,800 in the four banquet halls. Reportedly serving 20,000 people per day, 500 waiters were employed to accommodate the crowds.[15]

Dining area of Lüchow-Faust's Restaurant, in the Tyrolean Alps at the 1904 World's Fair. Courtesy of St. Louis Public Library

Outdoor dining area of Lüchow-Faust's Restaurant, in the Tyrolean Alps at the 1904 World's Fair. Courtesy of St. Louis Public Library

The restaurant's state-of-the art kitchen was roomy and light, with 15 large windows and triple rows of skylights, as well as electric fans, and sawdust on the floor. The 84-foot by 175-foot kitchen was scrubbed three times per day, and was arranged to accommodate the flow of traffic of its 110 staff members. Staff included eight fry cooks, six sauce cooks, eight entrée and soup cooks, seven vegetable cooks, two fish and poultry butchers, three meat carvers, two 2 bread and butter men, and four coffee makers. Pastry chefs, salad makers, linen girls, and dishwashers all worked in the kitchen. A bookkeeper stood at each kitchen exit to supervise the wait staff. Many men were employed in the large cold-storage basement to monitor the refrigeration and the beer kegs, tapped for the 40 bartenders serving in the bar above. The *St. Louis Post-Dispatch* printed a list of what was used in the Lüchow-Faust Restaurant kitchen each day:

        25 to 30 cattle
        12 hogs
        12 sheep
        12 lambs
        6 calves
        1,000 lbs of poultry
        20 barrels of potatoes
        600 to 1,000 loaves of bread
        400 lbs of butter
        75 lbs of coffee
        20 lbs of tea
        150 gallons of milk and cream
        10 to 15 tons of ice[16]

The Lüchow-Faust menu was diverse and lengthy, offering already-prepared foods such as *bratwurst, weinkraut* and *kartoffelbrei,* turkey croquettes, and roast ribs of prime beef, as well as foods made to order, such as tenderloin steak, mutton chops, and *wiener schnitzel.* Customers could order cheeses, breads, fresh vegetables, and omelets. To drink, customers chose from wines, champagnes, German brew and, obviously, Anheuser-Busch beer.[17]

A lengthy list of St. Louis brewers invested $800,000 in the Tyrolean Alps. It grossed more than $1 million by the end of the fair, the second-highest-grossing venue, eclipsed only by the Inside Inn.[18]

Chapter 5
TONY'S FAMILY

Anton Eduard Faust was 28 when he married a fellow German, 19-year-old Elizabeth Bischoff, in St. Louis in 1864. He was naturalized as a United States citizen in 1865. His name was Americanized several times, from Anton to Antony to Anthony to A.E. Faust, (the use of initials was common in the last half of the nineteenth century) to Tony. "Tony" was the name that best represented the jovial man and was the name by which he was most commonly called by his large group of friends and those who wished to be his friend.[1]

Elizabeth Bischoff Faust, wife of Tony Faust, ca. 1880.
Courtesy of Missouri History Museum, St. Louis

Four children came along; three survived into adulthood. Amalia "Mollie" arrived first in 1866, then Edward in 1869, and Anthony R. in 1871. The family lived in St. Louis' 2nd Ward on Carondelet Avenue along with a barkeeper and two teenaged domestic servants, both German. By 1880, the family had moved to 517 Walnut Street, and the Fausts enrolled their boys in Smith Academy.[2]

Mollie & "Eddie" Faust.
Courtesy of Missouri History Museum, St. Louis

A boys' preparatory school for Washington University in St. Louis, Smith Academy provided a far better education than public schools at that time. Tony and Elizabeth paid $30 per son for each 20-week term that little Edward and Anthony R. attended at Smith Academy's Primary School. According to the school catalog,

> To meet the wishes of a number of parents, a Primary School has been organized for boys under eleven years of age. It is placed under the immediate charge of a competent lady, but is under the general supervision of the Principal of the Academy.[3]

Tuition had increased to $40 per son by the time Edward finished Smith Academy at age 18 in 1887.[4]

Edward, the serious one, continued his education in New York City at Packard's Business College. Described at the time as

> ..one of the most important educational institutions in a commercial city…in which the best methods of conducting business of every kind and of keeping accounts may be thoroughly learned, theoretically and practically.[5]

The school had been founded by Silas S. Packard in 1858. Before founding his business school, Packard managed the Bryant & Stratton business schools in Chicago and Buffalo, New York. Edward Faust attended classes at Packard's Business College in the big building at 805 Broadway in New York City while interning at a delicatessen owned by the Tode brothers around 1887-1890.[6]

Adolph Tode and John Wulling comprised the Tode Brothers Company. They owned one delicatessen at 272 Bowery and 3rd Street, and another on 59th Street in New York City. A third shop, located in Monroe, New York, was called the Monroe Cheese Company. In 1882, the Tode Brothers signed a five-year lease on the shop at Bowery and 3rd. Luckily, Edward finished his work with the Tode Brothers just in time. He was not affiliated with them when their stores were closed by the sheriff in 1891. At that time, the Tode Brothers were $60,000 in debt. Adolph Tode and John Wulling officially declared bankruptcy in 1899.[7]

After Edward returned to St. Louis, Tony proudly changed his company's name from "Tony Faust Oyster House & Saloon" to "Tony Faust & Sons Oyster & Restaurant

Company" in 1892. Edward became the vice president, while his brother Anthony R. served as secretary/treasurer. Anthony R. also presided over all affairs of the Fulton Market. A contemporary author wrote, "The two sons combine, like their father, German perseverance and industry with American enterprise and business tact, and are just as well liked as the famous 'Tony Faust' himself."[8]

Newly established as vice president, Edward was no-nonsense. He stepped in to make Tony's restaurant more efficient, first by cracking down on theft. In 1894, an 80-year-old employee was arrested for systemically burglarizing Tony Faust's Fulton Market for two-and-a-half years. He'd been planning to sell the goods for cash and keep the money.[9] One year later, the *St. Louis Post-Dispatch* ran an article about Fred Wellhoff, the man who worked as a fireman for the restaurant:

> Faust's waiters buy checks at the bar and turn them in as they give their orders, receiving cash from the customers. These checks are of different denominations and are of brass. They are deposited in boxes through slots.
>
> Wellhoff, who gets to the place about 3 o'clock in the morning, has been in the habit of extracting checks from the 25 cent box. He used a long needle with a slit in the end, slipping it through the slot and catching the checks in the slit. Wellhoff was arrested…and had twenty-five checks on his person and confessed his guilt. He said he sold the checks to the waiters at cut rates. It is estimated that the Fausts have lost hundreds of dollars this way.[10]

The biggest thief to take advantage of Tony's good nature was his waiter Joseph Weber, the favored waiter of the hard-to-please wealthy set. Expensive items belonging to customers began to disappear in 1900: fans, opera glasses, umbrellas, and shawls. Little by little, the restaurant's silver, linens, beer steins, and champagne went missing as well. Living with her parents in their lavish apartment next door to the restaurant, Edward's sister Mollie made a list of items missing from their home: a powder box, jewelry, cutlery, a silver whisky flask, a silk umbrella, gloves, and handkerchiefs. Table linens crafted by Mollie also disappeared. Mollie marched the list several times to the Four Courts building in St. Louis, before and after the police searched another waiter's home, finding nothing. Finally, when several men stopped in for a beer en route from Pittsburgh to San Francisco, they recognized the popular waiter as a guy who had served time in the Pennsylvania State Penitentiary for restaurant robbing. Edward had him arrested.[11]

Unlike his father, Edward was strict. He placed the financial well-being of the restaurant before his popularity with the employees. The *St. Louis Post-Dispatch* reported,

> Saturday was a trying day for Tony Faust's waiters. An order was issued by Vice President Edward A. Faust Friday, withdrawing the usual privilege enjoyed for many years by all the employees of drinking all they desired. In consequence there was much grumbling among the waiters and other employes [*sic*], and two porters of Socialistic tendencies advocated a strike and, if necessary the use of bombs and dynamite. Their riotous tendencies were checked by prompt dismissal.
>
> In explanation Mr. Edward Faust said: "For many years we have given our people their drinkables free. We began to figure and found that our 100 employes [*sic*] were drinking about $15 worth per day or about

$5,000 a year, so we concluded to shut down on the custom. It may seem a trifle hard on individuals, but it cut a big hole in our profits, so we stopped it."[12]

Edward's brother, Anthony R., was the fun one. He was known for "his urbanity, his fine manners and fine presence" and was a favorite in the German South Side society of St. Louis. His nickname was "Beau Brummell," the moniker given to him for his suave mannerisms, his style, his good looks, and his popularity. Beau Brummell referred to George Bryan Brummell, the fashionable, elegant playboy of early nineteenth-century England.[13]

Anthony R. Faust.
Courtesy of Missouri History Museum, St. Louis

Luckily the playboy of late-nineteenth-century St. Louis had his style, panache, and friends, because he clearly did not have the business sense of his brother. In 1897, when fellow oyster dealer Monsieur S. Gallais suggested that perhaps the Fausts were part of an oyster trust in St. Louis, Anthony R. publically refuted this claim. He offensively called Gallais an "Italian" and a "cheap screw." Gallais gallantly replied that "he could stand the competition, but he could not stand Faust's personal allusions." He "has nothing against the Italians, but he is not one of them. He is of French descent…but is an American citizen." He "denies being a 'cheap screw' and says he will hold Faust accountable for his words." The *St. Louis Post-Dispatch* delighted in printing a three-part caricature of Anthony R. sword-dueling with Monsieur Gallais, with oysters dressed in shoes and top hats in the audience. The captions, mocking the contenders, translated from German for Anthony R. and French for Monsieur Gallais, read like this, "You silly fellow, take that then" and "Rascal, only with your life, shall I be satisfied." How embarrassing.[14]

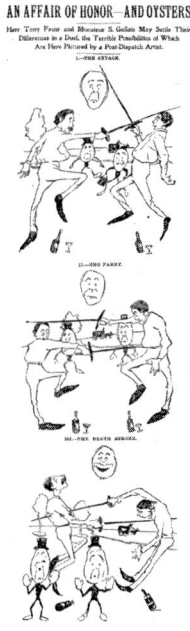

Using their oyster trade as fodder, both men are mocked, each in his native language, in the article accompanying this September 25, 1897 St. Louis Post-Dispatch cartoon.

Like his father, Anthony R. enjoyed entertainment and was known for throwing his money around. He was a constant fixture at the "millionaires' table" at his father's restaurant. He, his father, Adolphus Busch, and some Busch sons became stockholders of the Delmar Jockey Club in 1901, home to the "Gentlemen Riders" of the horse races.[15]

Edward, a lover of the arts, enjoyed a tamer type of fun. At the age of 20, Edward played a part in the performance of Shakespeare's *King Henry IV* staged by the Liederkranz Club (an elite club for Germans).[16] In 1897, Edward threw an elegant bachelor dinner for his friend Ernest Holm. He compiled a 10-page souvenir book that read, "I dedicate to my friend Ernest Holm 'My last bachelor dinner' may you peruse same and ever think of this day March thirteenth 1897" signed "E.A. Faust." Other pages included famous literary quotes, the dinner menu, the list of the evening's music, signatures of the guests, and a group photograph.[17]

Edward, the ambitious, bright businessman who worked for his father, also began working for family friend Adolphus Busch. He stepped into the office of second vice-president of Anheuser-Busch while still in his twenties. And after a long engagement full of parties and celebrations, 28-year-old Edward married 23-year-old Anna Busch, Adolphus's daughter, in March 1897.[18]

The wedding was fantastic. Police controlled the crowds pressing the door of the Church of the Messiah, hoping to catch a glimpse of the sanctuary, lavishly bedecked with flowers covering the altar, the pews, and even the ceiling. A choir and an orchestral quartet provided the music while the wedding procession included two bridesmaids, six ushers, ten "little girls," and ten "little pages," a maid of honor, and four little flower girls. Anthony R. stood as his brother's best man. Seven hundred guests attended. One hundred of them were invited to proceed to the Busch mansion for the reception. The bride and groom took a six-month honeymoon to Europe and Africa. The trip was a wedding gift from Tony Faust. While away, the couple spent a few months with Adolphus and Lilly Busch in their villa on the Rhine.[19]

Edward and Anna (she was called "Tolie" by her father and friends) set up housekeeping in the lovely home given to them by Adolphus Busch on Lafayette Avenue in South St. Louis. They welcomed their son, Leicester Busch Faust (pronounced "Lester"), who was born nine months and two days after their glamorous nuptials.[20] Little Audrey Busch Faust came along in 1902. The household was complete with three female domestic servants to care for the home and children. The family moved to 4630 Lindell Boulevard in the West End, where they lived for a time. But by 1910, Edward's family, two servants, and a valet had moved into the Busch family mansion at One Busch Place. That household included: Edward's family; Adolphus and Lilly Busch; Adolphus's son Carl Busch; Adolphus's son August A. Busch, his wife, and their five children; and six servants.[21] It was surely a wonderful home for young Leicester and Audrey, as the closely knit Busches were known for their devotion to family. No expenses were spared for leisure activities and amusement. The children in the home had each other for playmates, including 13-year-old Leicester and his 11-year-old cousin, August A., Jr., called "Gussie."

In the meantime, Edward's brother Anthony R. used his own approach for finding a mate. When attending the theater in New York, Anthony R. fell in love with Adine Louise Bouvier, the beautiful opera singer. He managed to score an introduction, and then he followed her from city to city. He filled her dressing room with flowers and courted her between performances. Beau Brummell-style, he won her heart. Adine agreed to marry Anthony R. and leave the stage forever. The quick courtship and marriage in 1902 were not announced. The secret wedding of the 31-year-old bachelor took most by surprise, even his parents. Upon returning from a European trip, Tony and Elizabeth met the newlyweds on their honeymoon trip in New York. Anthony R., who had been splitting his time between living with his parents in their apartment next to the restaurant and residing in a boarding house on Vandeventer Street, moved with his new bride into the Southern Hotel.[22]

Marriage settled Anthony R., the former playboy of South St. Louis. Like his brother, he turned his interests toward business ventures. He wisely invested in the Tyrolean Alps of the World's Fair, served as president of the St. Louis Catering Company, and accepted a job as the manager of the new Marquette Hotel on Washington Avenue in St. Louis. The 400-room, fireproof hotel opened for business in 1907. Anthony R. and Adine moved into an apartment there. The couple also built a lovely home on the corner of Shady and Church streets in Webster Groves, a suburb 12 miles southwest of St. Louis along the Pacific Railroad line. It was an affluent community with a country feel.[23]

And what of Anthony R. and Edward's older sister Mollie? She, too, received an excellent education as a child. She attended Mary Institute, a girls' school established by William Greenleaf Eliot, the man who also founded the Smith Academy for boys. At 15, she entered the freshman class at Lindenwood College for Young Ladies in St. Charles, Missouri. She excelled in German, written arithmetic, writing, instrumental music, drawing, geography, and grammar.[24]

When Mollie was 12 years old, her mother gave her a leather-bound scrapbook, inscribed with gold letters, "A Birthday Gift to Mollie Faust, from her Mama. May 31, 1875." For the rest of her life, Mollie filled the pages in her scrapbook with articles about her father and his oyster business; their dear friends the Busches; travel souvenirs like passenger lists, steamship stubs, and menus; and theater playbills. She clipped articles about herself from the society pages that glorified her beauty as a debutante of the "German set." The scrapbook contained articles about her engagement and wedding as well.[25]

Mollie Faust Giannini.
Courtesy of Missouri History Museum, St. Louis

Nineteen-year-old Mollie wed thirty-two-year-old Arthur David (A.D.) Giannini in 1886. In the weeks preceding the nuptials, several dinner and theater parties were thrown in honor of her engagement, yet Mollie's wedding was a small affair in her parents' home at 517 Walnut Street. Though small, it was a beautiful ceremony with an orchestra and imported flowers. The bride carried lilies and wore a gown of "white ottoman" with duchesse lace. Her veil was decorated with orange blossoms. According to German custom, she wore a *myrthen* wreath on her head, imported from Germany for her special day.[26] Mollie's brothers ushered, and several members of the Busch family rounded out the bridal party. No members of A.D.'s family attended the ceremony. The reception dinner for an invited 500 guests was catered by Mollie's father, Tony Faust. After their wedding, the couple moved to A.D's home state of New York. A.D. Giannini worked as a clerk, and Mollie furnished their new home with the $5,000 given to her as a wedding gift from her parents.[27]

Mollie and A.D.'s daughter, Vera, was born in 1887. The family lived in New York City for nine years. During this time, Mollie and Vera spent months at a time staying with her parents in St. Louis or traveling with her parents overseas while A.D. continued to work as a clerk and a salesman in New York.[28] In March 1896, the *St. Louis Post-Dispatch* announced that Mollie and Vera had moved to St. Louis; A.D. would follow in April. He remained in New York to close "his business interests." However, A.D. was still in New York working as a manager of the Wilcox Silver Plate Company's cut glass department on May 27, 1896, during the St. Louis tornado. He received a telegram explaining that his family was safe.[29] But by 1898, A.D. seemed to have disappeared from their lives. Mollie and

Vera were living full-time at 419 Elm Street in St. Louis with her parents.[30] Mollie helped in the restaurant, decorating it for its New Year's Eve parties.[31] A newspaper reported in 1901 that 14-year-old Vera traveled to Minneapolis to visit her father. Then, while traveling with her mother in Germany, Vera sent her father a postcard. She wrote, "Received your short note this morning. [You] can not understand why you have not heard from me for so long. I felt the same way about you." Some time later, a newspaper reported that A.D. Giannini was circulating around the West, selling the Sunbeam Draft Burner. He felt lucky, as a salesman, to have access to all agents of Anheuser-Busch's various locations.[32]

During their formative years, the well-educated and worldly Mollie, Edward, and Anthony R. traveled extensively. As though those in the upper ranks of society were royalty, the local newspapers carefully chronicled their comings and goings. When the Faust children were ages nine, six, and four, they accompanied Tony and Elizabeth to Europe for three months. Upon their return, the *St. Louis Globe-Democrat* noted, "Tony Faust has returned from a three months' visit to Fatherland, whither he was accompanied by his family."[33] The next summer, the family vacationed on Coney Island. During the early years of the 1880s, in addition to their trips abroad, the Faust family took summer vacations on the East Coast, where Tony also conducted business. Mollie was in her first year of marriage by 1887. Only Edward and Anthony R. accompanied their parents to Europe for that summer, and they stayed for a few weeks with Mollie in New York when they returned. They repeated their travel agenda the following year.[34]

By 1891, Mollie and her little girl, Vera, joined her parents on their trips overseas. Nearly all of their visits to Germany included time spent with the Busches at their home on the Rhine, called "Villa Lilly." The two families traveled together in the States, too. Tony and Elizabeth Faust joined Adolphus and Lilly Busch, and some other friends in the Busches' new, private, luxurious railroad car "Adolphus." The group trekked to the Busch home in California in celebration of the Busches' anniversary. By the time Edward married Anna Busch in 1897, the Fausts were well established as guests at the Busch estates.[35]

A popular practice for those of means during the late nineteenth century was to "take the waters" in resorts that popped up over natural hot springs all over the United States, Europe, and Asia. Believing that the minerals in the waters held healing powers, the wealthy often journeyed to such resorts for their health and relaxation. Hot Springs, Arkansas, provided such a spot for the Fausts and other St. Louisans who frequented the resort town. Several luxury hotels sprouted up in the town. In 1899, Tony, Elizabeth and Mollie attended an invitation-only ball in one of the hotels. There, they hobnobbed with same St. Louisans they hobnobbed with at home.[36]

As the turn of the century approached, the travel became easier. The Fausts likely secured private railroad cars for their trips to the East. The family slept in luxurious suites on the steamships that took them overseas. They probably took along a domestic servant or two to assist with the children, their baggage, and their personal needs while traveling and after they arrived at their vacation home or hotel.

The newspapers kept tabs on the Fausts while they were away, reporting their goings-on for St. Louisans back home.

One instance was in 1883, when 17-year-old Mollie was in London with her family. She took a cab to go shopping:
> The driver was either drunk or careless, and overturned the vehicle, breaking his own neck, but hardly bruising Miss Faust; but she was so badly frightened that she fainted, and when she recovered found herself supported by a gentleman whom she at once recognized as John T. Raymond, the actor, who happened to be in London at the time. She made herself known to him, and he was overjoyed to know that she was a daughter of an old friend of his. A very happy coincidence.[37]

When the St. Louis Cardinals played the Brooklyn Superbas in baseball in 1901, the Fausts attended the game in New York. In its game write-up, the *St. Louis Post-Dispatch* sadly reported, "Mr. and Mrs. Tony Faust [and] Mrs. Giannini…attended the game, but their presence failed to inspire the Cardinals to win."[38]

The *St. Louis Post-Dispatch* reported a disturbing incident in 1902 when Tony, Elizabeth, and Mollie were in Germany. Tony had been invited to the home of one of his German friends for a card party when, en route, the horse was spooked and the driver thrown. Tony jumped out of the carriage and landed on his right side. He broke his shoulder. Despite his age, then 66, Tony recovered fully.[39]

Though he was home for about eight months during the World's Fair, Tony made a point of traveling through Europe for long periods during the next few years. One of his passport applications even cited "retired" as his occupation. His wife, Mollie, and Vera accompanied him in 1904 and again in 1905. Tony and his group were still in Europe in May 1906 when Adolphus and Lilly Busch, and

Edward and Anna Faust and their children, Leicester and Audrey, set off in the private railroad car "Adolphus" for New York. The party boarded a steamer bound for Europe. Edward Faust accompanied his wife and children only as far as New York, but Anthony R. bid them farewell from St. Louis – he rarely traveled. Once in Europe, the Busches met up with the Fausts at Villa Lilly and the group spent the summer traveling around Europe in several of Adolphus Busch's French touring cars.[40]

During that summer of 1906, Tony was involved in an accident nearly exactly like the one in 1902: he was in a carriage when the horses were spooked and bolted. Tony again made the decision to jump. This time, at age 70, his injuries were more serious. The sun began to set on his life. The group planned to return to St. Louis in the fall and booked tickets aboard the steamer *Kronprinz Wilhelm* for October 16. However, in the late afternoon of September 28, 1906, the Fausts cabled Anthony R. in St. Louis, advising him that Tony had fallen gravely ill. An hour later, Anthony R. received the message that his father had died.[41]

Elizabeth, Mollie, Vera, and the Busch clan surrounded the Oyster King as his eyes closed in Wiesbaden. Then, once again, Tony Faust left Germany to make a permanent home in St. Louis, 53 years after his first departure as a 17-year-old striking out for a new life in America. Anthony R. met his family in New York and accompanied them back to St. Louis.

The funeral was held at the 1605 Missouri Avenue home where Mollie and Vera lived with Tony and Elizabeth Faust. Though the funeral was meant to be a private affair, members of the public filled the front lawn. The funeral service was conducted in German. The home was filled with flowers sent to the family by mourners, including a prominently displayed, enormous arrangement of flowers that spelled *Unser Freund* (Our Friend) from Tony's employees. A string quartet played throughout the service, opening with *Es ist bestimmt in Gottes Rath* (It is Determined in God's Advice).

The day was Saturday, October 27, 1906, and it was cold. A large crowd gathered at the lovely Bellefontaine Cemetery for the burial. Thirty-five honorary pallbearers included dear friends Adolphus Busch and August Lüchow, Tony's partner in their World's Fair restaurant. The active pallbearers were all long-time employees of Tony Faust's beloved restaurant. Nearly a month after his death, the family buried Tony Faust.[42]

BOOK TWO

Edward A. Faust.
Courtesy of Missouri History Museum, St. Louis

Chapter 1
LIFE AND DEATH

The business of death kept life humming along. Tony Faust had designated Elizabeth Faust and Edward as executors of his carefully planned will in 1905. Tony's estate was valued at $260,000 and consisted entirely of personal property. He left Edward, Anthony R., and Mollie each $10,000. Edward's children, Leicester and Audrey, received no inheritance. With Edward's head for business and Adolphus Busch's patronage, the financial future of Tony's two youngest grandchildren was assured. Mollie's daughter Vera, on the other hand, received $5,000. She was 19 and unmarried. She was living with her mother and grandmother, and the three women's provider was now deceased.

Mollie received one-ninth of the remainder of the estate. Elizabeth received two-ninths, which was stipulated by Tony to go to Mollie upon her death. The remaining six-ninths of the estate went solely to Elizabeth. Interestingly, Tony clearly stated in his will that the bequests to his widow and daughter deprived any present or future husband from any interest in the property. This stipulation suggests that Tony was protecting Mollie's inheritance from her absentee husband, A.D. Giannini.[1]

During the next few years the family threw themselves into their activities. In spite of Edward's busy career, he made time for his outside interests, specifically the St. Louis Aero Club. With its roster described as the "richest" and "most venturesome," the club's secretary reported in 1908 that the club consisted of 100 millionaires and 350 "near ones." The *St. Louis Post-Dispatch* wrote a satirical article about the club, at times mocking the members for being afraid to go up in one of its member's balloons or flight machines. The newspaper suggested it was not the members' fear of death, but of losing their wealth upon death. The editorial cited the bravery and success of the Wright Brothers' brief flights a few years earlier. It egged on the members of the club to take some risks. The newspaper mocked Bud Dozier, president of the Aero Club. Mr. Dozier sent a postcard from Paris, writing that the ride in the elevator to the top of the Eiffel Tower was "worse than a balloon." The editorial challenged its readers, "Don't say, 'How do YOU know?'"

However, the article acknowledged the difficulties facing aeronautics in 1908. It was respectful of the efforts of those working to discover how to best make a heavier-than-air machine successfully take flight. Aeronautics was indeed an exciting prospect, and St. Louis got into the spirit. Similar to other competitions around the world, pilots were offered $1,000 by the city to fly 300 miles in any direction from St. Louis. London, by comparison, offered $50,000 to fly across the English Channel.

Though he did not take flight, Edward was active in the club, and he served as chairman of its Entertainment & House Committee in 1909. In 1910, Edward Faust's name was batted around as a potential presidential candidate of the club along with Albert Bond Lambert, a genuine mover and shaker in the St. Louis aeronautics world. Neither wanted the position. Dozier, fearless rider of the Eiffel Tower elevator, was reelected.[2]

As expected of society women, Anna Faust occupied her

time with charity work. In 1908, she served as a patroness of the Knights of Columbus Choral Club, and she was in charge of the club's German Village Concessions at the Charity Carnival. Anna and her committee made a radical change to the usual arrangement. They declared that, rather than hiring waiters, young men and women of German society would dress as Heidelberg students and serve the food themselves. Those men on the Heidelberg student committee included Anthony R. Faust and a couple of Busches. Lovely Vera Giannini, a waitress, was voted the "Most Popular Young Woman Waitress" of the event. It was a great success, with a reported attendance of 50,000. The wait-staff plan was repeated at the St. Louis Altenheim Spring Festival charity event the following month. That time Anna, Mollie, and Vera helped to run the Wheel of Fortune.[3]

Anna Louise "Tolie" Busch Faust.
From the Collections of the St. Louis Mercantile Library
at the University of Missouri-St. Louis

It was by design that a busy social life intertwined with philanthropy. Anna Busch Faust had vast amounts of money to give and the social standing to raise awareness of causes. She also had the domestic service staff to maintain her home and raise her children. When she served as a patroness of a charity ball in 1904, the *St. Louis Post-Dispatch* wrote a flowery column on how brilliant the event was expected to be, stating, "The fact that philanthropy plays a large part in the function adds to its merits and should bring society out in force."[4]

In May 1911, Anna and a group of society women set up booths on designated street corners in busy downtown St. Louis. They sold theater tickets to raise money for the St. Louis Pure Milk Commission, which "provided healthful milk to the babies of the city's congested quarters."[5] This seemingly small fund-raising event is one example of many that shaped reform in the early twentieth century. Anna represented empowered women of the Progressive Era, leaving the house for reasons other than making a social call. Women of means banded together to aid women in need. They unintentionally made smaller the chasm that separated them and gave way to one female voice. They built the foundation for the political voice that would come later with suffrage.

Anna often saw her name in the headlines. The *St. Louis Post-Dispatch* printed a large picture of her in 1910. The newspaper praised her and her mother for giving $10,000 collectively toward the new building fund for the Y.W.C.A. To raise more money for the cause, the *St. Louis Post-Dispatch* printed the names of 55 St. Louisans who gave $1,000 or more, shamelessly attempting to guilt others into getting on that list.[6] Taking advantage of the marriage between philanthropy and society, the newspaper playfully printed,

> Young society beaux who do not contribute generously to the Y.W.C.A campaign…are likely to find themselves in the black books of the prettiest belles for the remainder of the social season… Those who give the largest amounts are to be repaid, it is said, with dance favors, invitations to balls and house parties, and first calls for theater and dinner parties, while the piggardly ones will find themselves temporarily in eclipse.[7]

That was a huge threat! An eventful social life was an accomplishment. The newspapers relished printing the details of the upper-crust men's and women's goings-on in the society pages. The *St. Louis Post-Dispatch* printed a list of "carefully selected …ladies who will keep open house" on New Year's Day, 1886. The list was "A Guide for Gentlemen Who Make Calls." Mollie's name appeared. Interestingly, she was to be married in less than two months.[8]

Daytime functions were often segregated by gender. The women gathered for teas and luncheons during the day while the men had the excuse of their jobs. Rather than gathering for the sake of gathering, a lady held a get-together in honor of another for a myriad of reasons: to celebrate an engagement, a graduation, a lady's visit from another town, or simply as a gesture of friendship.

Euchres were an extremely popular form of entertainment in the late nineteenth and early twentieth centuries. Euchre was a card game played with four people in two partnerships with a deck of 24 playing cards. The Joker was introduced through euchre as the best bower, from the

German word "Bauer" or farmer, denoting the Jack. "Progressive euchre" is a tournament format of Euchre:

> Play begins when the lead table rings a bell. The lead table plays eight hands, the deal revolving to the left with each hand, so that each player has dealt twice, then rings the bell again. When the bell rings, players at each table finish their current hand, record their team score on an individual tally. The losing team at the head table moves to the tail table; otherwise the winning team at each table advances to the next table, and one member of the losing team changes seat so that partners in one game are opponents in the next game. Play begins on the next game immediately without waiting for another signal. After ten games, players total their tally sheets, to determine high score and low score for the tournament.[9]

Progressive euchre parties were thrown in Mollie's honor in 1893 and 1896. The first was during one of her long visits from New York, and the second when she moved home for good. Mollie threw a progressive euchre to celebrate Anna Busch's engagement to her brother in 1897. Anna honored graduates of Mary Institute with a euchre at her starter home on Lafayette in 1900. Such parties, some with as many as 100 guests, were elaborate, with decorations, food, and expensive gifts for the winners. Men joined in the fun when euchres were held in the evenings, such as the party in 1889 attended by Tony and Elizabeth Faust, Adolphus and Lilly Busch, several Busch brothers and sisters, 18-year-old Anthony R. Faust, and 20-year-old Edward Faust. Edward won the gentlemen's consolation prize of a "gent's traveling companion." A lunch was served at midnight, followed by dancing.[10]

These social gatherings, particularly the daytime events, indicate the closeness between the Faust women. In March 1898, Anna and her sister-in-law Mollie threw a koffee klatch together (*koffee klatch* is the German phrase for a gathering at which ladies drink coffee and gossip). Mollie and her mother, Elizabeth Faust, threw their own koffee klatch together. That same month, Anna and her mother, Lilly Busch, hosted a euchre described as "the most elegant and elaborate progressive euchre party of the season."[11]

Several theaters in town kept busy night after night. Mollie hosted a theater party to celebrate her engagement in 1886. In 1896, Edward hosted a party of 12 at the theater. In keeping with the closeness of the families, Adolphus and Lilly Busch invited their daughter Anna and her fiancé, Edward Faust, and his sister Mollie to join them in their theater box for a concert by famous singer Lillian Nordica. The newspaper reported, "The Nordica concert brought out a beautiful audience of well-known society people..." Edward, Mollie, and Vera attended the Boston Opera Company's performance at the Olympic theater in 1910. Mollie had her own box at the Odeon theater (where the St. Louis Symphony performed) and was accompanied by Vera, Anthony R., and his wife, Adine, in 1908.[12]

The new Marquette Hotel opened up in late 1907 with Anthony R. as its manager. And though he had neither the business sense nor the opportunities that blessed his brother, Anthony R. made plans to build a lavish restaurant of his own in New York City. But as early as 1909 his health began to fail him. In May 1911, he and Adine arrived in New York to meet his mother, but he suffered what contemporaries called a "nervous breakdown." He was sent to a sanitarium. Edward immediately traveled to New York to be with his brother, and the prognosis was grim. Anthony R. spent the summer at a sanitarium with varying degrees of paralysis and insanity. He was then brought back to St. Louis by his family, where he holed up in his Webster Groves home. In November Adine petitioned the Probate Court to have her husband declared incompetent.

In a hearing that lasted only 12 minutes, a jury in the Probate Court declared Anthony R. insane. Edward, the only relative at the hearing, was granted guardianship of his brother. Anthony R. languished at his lovely Webster Groves home on the corner of Shady and Church streets for two more years.[13]

Life continued on around him. Mollie, her mother, and her daughter traveled year after year. They spent time in spas in Colorado, visited the Busches in California, or traveled through Europe. Then came Vera's nuptials.[14]

Mollie, alone, announced the engagement of her daughter. Vera had traveled to Europe with Mr. and Mrs. August A. Busch. She enjoyed the summer with Adolphus and Lilly Busch at Villa Lilly on the Rhine. It was there that Vera's longtime acquaintance, Eugene Angert, became her love.

Eugene was born to a prominent family in St. Charles, Missouri. He attended college at St. Louis University, then graduated from Harvard Law School in 1899. After working in New York for a time, Eugene returned to St. Louis and enjoyed life as a well-respected lawyer and bachelor. He wrote humorous articles and plays and took on speaking engagements. He courted Vera Giannini that summer in Germany. She was a beautiful blonde who spoke French, German, and English. The two planned their wedding for December 14, 1912.

Speculation swirled that they planned to marry in August A. Busch's enormous home, once it was completed, outside of St. Louis on the old Ulysses S. Grant property. But instead, Vera chose to have her wedding at the new home of her uncle and aunt, Edward and Anna Faust. Edward and his family were still living with Adolphus and Lilly Busch at 1 Busch Place. Their new home at 1 Portland Place was scheduled to be finished and ready for occupation soon before Vera's December 14th wedding. However, a hitch arose when Adolphus Busch grew ill while at his estate in Pasadena, California, and Anna rushed to California to be with her father.

Instead, 25-year-old Vera and 35-year-old Eugene married on December 14th as planned, but in the Waterman Avenue home of Mollie and Elizabeth Faust. The couple's first baby, Eugene Angert, Jr., was born the next year, in October, only a few hours after Adolphus Busch was buried.[15]

Vera Giannini.
Courtesy of Missouri History Museum, St. Louis

Tony Faust's dearest friend was laid to rest in the fashion which most suited him – elaborately. Like Tony, he died in Germany and his body was shipped home to St. Louis. An estimated 30,000 people viewed his body at the 1 Busch Place mansion. Dignitaries from St. Louis, Washington, and Germany paid homage to Adolphus Busch at his funeral service. Members of the St. Louis Symphony provided the music. Florists were hard pressed to find enough flowers to fill the orders for the funeral, some from as far away as New York. It took 25 automobiles to carry the arrangements from the Busch home to the cemetery. Thousands lined the streets along the funeral procession route from the Busch mansion to Bellefontaine cemetery. The parade solemnly began its route around the circumference of the Anheuser-Busch brewery before heading to the cemetery.[16]

Just a month later, Elizabeth died. Elizabeth Bischoff Faust had quietly receded from her social circles a couple of years before she passed away in 1913 at the age of 68. She was laid to rest next to her husband at Bellefontaine Cemetery after a funeral in her home on Waterman Avenue, without fanfare.

Attorney Eugene Angert assisted Edward as executor of Elizabeth's will. Each grandchild, Vera, Leicester, and Audrey, received $5,000 from their grandmother. Mollie and Edward each received 1/3 of their mother's estate. They were named trustees of the final third, a trust in the name of Anthony R. In her will, Elizabeth specified that Mollie and Edward were to use that trust money to "procure the best medical attention which can be obtained" for Anthony R. The money would pay for all his wants and needs, as well as his wife's wants and needs while he was in ill health. Finally, what remained of the trust was to pay for Anthony R.'s inevitable funeral, $1,000 to Adine, and the rest to revert to Mollie and Edward.

Like Tony's will, Elizabeth's also specified that the bequests to her daughter and granddaughter bar any present or future husband from any interest in the property. Again, Mollie's inheritance was protected from her absentee husband, as was Vera's from her new husband.[17]

Still of unsound mind in 1913, Anthony R. did not have the capacity to process the rapid-fire events of the previous year. In 1914, Edward found it necessary to place him in a sanitarium in St. Louis, where Anthony R. died within a month.

He was buried in Bellefontaine Cemetery with his mother and father. His one-third of the inheritance from Elizabeth amounted to $43,000. After Adine received her stipulated $1,000 from the trust, the rest reverted to Mollie and Edward. Adine also collected $18,000, which was how much Anthony R. was worth when he was declared insane.[18]

It was a horrible death for Anthony R., the once suave, stylish playboy. He was only 43 years old. His illness? Paresis: "neuromuscular disturbances progressing to generalized paralysis occurring 10-20 years after initial infection with syphilis."[19]

Beau Brummel's past had come back to haunt him.

Chapter 2
A MEMBER OF THE POSSE

Sometime around 1914, Edward, Anna, 16-year-old Leicester, and 11-year-old Audrey moved out of 1 Busch Place, the mansion on the brewery grounds in South St. Louis. The family moved into their new home at 1 Portland Place in St. Louis's West End. Edward had hired Tom Barnett, formerly of the architecture group Barnett, Haynes & Barnett to design his new home. The lot at 17 Portland Place was originally surveyed for Edward Faust in 1903, when Tom Barnett likely conceived the house's design. However, construction did not begin then or there. In 1909, the lot at 1 Portland Place was surveyed for Edward Faust, and the building permit for the home at 1 Portland Place was issued in 1910. The masterpiece was completed in 1912, and Tom Barnett added 1 Portland Place to his growing list of highly acclaimed buildings in St. Louis and beyond.

Edward's movement away from the heart of the city was typical for a man of his wealth and position.[1] Unlike the urban poor, who required their homes to be near their places of work, Edward was part of the elite who had the means to live in an area with fresh air, privacy, and breathing room. He also had the leisure time to travel to and from his workplace. His new neighborhood in the West End of St. Louis was a preference, not a necessity.

St. Louis was no different than any other American city whose streetcar lines gave way to suburbanization. St. Louis's West End typified other turn-of-the century cities in that the further away from the city center, the more magnificent the homes and the better the services. Those services allowed for indoor plumbing, hot water, and electricity.[2]

Portland Place belonged to a new section of St. Louis's West End called the Forest Park Addition. In 1887, the Forest Park Improvement Association acquired 78 acres bound on the east by Kingshighway. The real-estate venture group set out to perfect the St. Louis phenomenon of private "places." They established Forest Park Terrace (which later became part of Lindell Avenue), Westmoreland Place, and Portland Place. Wide streets were laid out with park-like medians. Sewers, gas, and water pipes were installed in 1888. The Missouri Cable Railroad laid a cable from Grand to Kingshighway, making it easy for residents to travel to the city. Building restrictions limited the properties to the wealthy, including covenants requiring that each home cost more than $7,000. As actually built, none cost less than $25,000.[3]

With a chronology of architectural styles, the Forest Park Addition was a "concentration of architectural merit."[4] Edward Faust's new home at 1 Portland Place rivaled any of its neighbors in size and grandeur. The palazzo-style home was carefully constructed with minimal ornamentation. Its massive proportions, complemented by its clean lines and symmetry, gave the home an imposing dignity.[5] Edward himself was reflected in the design of 1 Portland Place: austere, uniform and crisp.

1 Portland Place, ca. 1930.
Courtesy of Missouri History Museum, St. Louis

The eastern façade of the mansion opened up with a loggia with a frescoed ceiling and white columns. It overlooked a circular reflecting pool in the garden. A sleeping veranda atop a porte cochère on the west gave the home its balance. The wide front terrace of Carthage stone was simply ornamented with a balustrade and two Italianate vases on either side of the steps.

Unlike its exterior, the interior demonstrated pure opulence. Upon entering the home one was greeted by two huge yet graceful staircases, each winding up the circular walls of the rotunda. A living room sat in view off to one side, and a French drawing room off to the other. White columns continued throughout the home. No expense was spared in the décor. The *St. Louis Post-Dispatch* ran an article about the Fausts' new home. It described the home's interior and furnishings in detail, including the front hall:

The walls of the main entrance hall are of imported

Caen stone and Breccia Violette marble. The columns of its colonnade are Breccia Violette monoliths....In the center hangs a huge bronze lamp, a duplicate of one which hangs in the baptistery of the cathedral at Pisa.... In the four lunettes of the arches supporting the dome of the grand hall are mural paintings by Thomas.[6]

Silk wall coverings, gilded hardware, intricate vaulted ceilings, and tapestries and furniture from around the world gave the home its richness. Edward and Anna decorated their home with magnificent works of art. They proudly displayed a massive portrait of Anna's father, Adolphus Busch, in their living room.[7]

The home was filled with servants. Again, no expense was spared in the domestic service portions of the home. It included quarters for live-in help and a light, airy basement with a state-of-the art kitchen and laundry.[8] Without the hassles of housework, Anna jumped right into the work of philanthropy as soon as she had moved into her new home. After spending the summer in Europe in 1914, she opened up her home to sponsor a benefit for orphans. She charged admission to the public, served tea, and gave the proceeds to the St. Louis Protestant Home.[9]

The Fausts' new home was indeed awe inspiring. Adolphus Busch, Edward's father-in-law, was rumored to have given lavish homes to each of his children, including Anna's at 1 Portland Place. Another was August A. Busch's (according to Edward Faust, "pretentious") mansion outside of St. Louis on Gravois road. It was built on the farmland of former president Ulysses S. Grant (August A. called his home "Grant's Farm"). The brewer's other children lived in Chicago, New York, and Germany.[10]

87

Edward's father, Tony, and his father-in-law, Adolphus, were the closest of friends. They traveled the world together, celebrated their families' joys and sorrows together, and built their businesses together. Adolphus Busch lunched at Tony's restaurant nearly every day. In his saloon Tony sold Faust Beer, an Anheuser-Busch product made especially for him. Their children, of course, grew up together. So when Edward married his childhood friend Anna Busch, the Faust / Busch relationship moved to another level.

Edward's closeness to Adolphus Busch was evident. Adolphus and Lilly Anheuser Busch celebrated their fiftieth wedding anniversary on March 7, 1911. The brewery was decorated with 100 American flags between its smokestacks. Anheuser-Busch officials shut down production to honor the occasion. A brass cannon at the brewery fired off a 50-gun salute. Employees, their families, and party-goers (as many as 13,000 people) gathered at the Coliseum in St. Louis to celebrate the couple by drinking Budweiser and dancing into the night. Banks decorated their façades with bunting. Gifts were sent to the Busches from the likes of President Taft and Kaiser Wilhelm II of Germany. The honored couple, however, received their well-wishes at their home in Pasadena – it was Edward and Anna Faust who represented them at the festivities in St. Louis.[11]

Edward's position of vice president at the Anheuser-Busch brewery placed him in charge of all grain and raw materials purchases. He also served his first stint on Anheuser-Busch's board of directors from 1898 to 1914. Edward often served as a voice for the brewer:

My dear Mr. Francis-

Mr. Busch desires me to acknowledge receipt of your invitation of the 22nd to be present at the annual meeting of the World's Fair Directors. He takes this means of thanking you for your kindness, but while he is in fairly good health, his present condition does not permit of his participation in the program as outlined.

Mr. Busch and the writer extend their kind regards.

Very truly yours,
Edward Faust[12]

Adolphus Busch debuts his elaborate railroad car, flanked by August A. Busch and Edward Faust, in this Nov. 3, 1901 picture in the St. Louis Post-Dispatch

Edward's roles in the company and the family allowed him to act as Adolphus's right-hand-man as much as his own son and fellow vice president, August A. Busch. Edward, along with August A., stood with Adolphus as he presented his luxurious, private railroad car, the "Adolphus," to the *St. Louis Post-Dispatch*. Edward, along with August A., stood by the brewer's side on the veranda of the brewery as Adolphus was serenaded by 100 members of the Liederkranz Society. It honored him for his $100,000 donation to San Francisco earthquake survivors in 1906. It was Edward, though, whom Adolphus tapped to supervise the construction of the great Adolphus Hotel in Dallas, Texas, in 1910. It was Edward whom Adolphus labeled in his will as the second-in-line to the entire Anheuser-Busch enterprise, after August A. When Adolphus Busch died in 1913, August A. took the helm of Anheuser-Busch. Edward was named one of the executors of the brewer's will.[13]

Edward's choice of location for his home was pivotal. The West End was already a well-established enclave by the time Edward moved there in 1914. The relocation of his family to that particular neighborhood, in that particular part of the city, was deliberate. Many of those who built their houses in Portland Place were men like Edward: men with higher educations, men who were directors of corporations, and men whose business networks benefitted each other. Like the others, Edward had multiple business interests, including his positions as a banker. As early as 1902 he had served as vice president of the Fourth National Bank. Later, he became director of the Mercantile Commerce Trust Company. Though his primary occupation was vice president at Anheuser-Busch, his banking interests made him a valuable member of his highfalutin' neighborhood.[14]

The West End wealthy joined social and country clubs. Edward was one of the early members of Glen Echo Country Club, founded in 1901. He joined Bellerive in about 1910. By 1912, Edward belonged to both the St. Louis Club and the Noonday Club, two of the most prestigious downtown luncheon clubs. He also joined the St. Louis Country Club around 1914, Sunset Country Club in 1916, and Riverview in 1917. At one point, Edward belonged to as many as nine social and golf clubs.

These clubs offered a place to relax and socialize, enjoy recreation and exercise, and make business and political deals. Like others in his circle, Edward joined some clubs for their elite factor. He joined others as a courtesy to friends. Edward joined Glen Echo for his fellow aeronautics enthusiast (and two-time Olympic golf competitor) Albert Bond Lambert, and Sunset Country Club for his brother-in-law August A. Busch.[15]

Adolphus Busch conceived the idea of a social club in the rolling land of south St. Louis County. His son August A. made it a reality. He established the exclusive Sunset Inn (which served only Anheuser-Busch products) in 1910. In 1916, he added a golf course designed by Robert Foulis, a course architect and native of Saint Andrews, Scotland.[16] The construction of the Sunset Country Club was the Busches' response, it is said, to having their membership requests turned down by other clubs in St. Louis, including the most elite St. Louis Country Club.[17]

No amount of money could buy the Busches' way into the hearts of St. Louis society. Though the Busches and the Fausts had obtained popularity in their own right, they had two strikes against them: they were German, and they were in the beer business. An article was printed at the time of

Edward's engagement to Anna Busch. The writer defended the couple who sat on the fringe of society. He wrote:

> The newspapers that have commented upon the engagement of Mr. Ed Faust and Miss Busch...appear to me to have missed the lesson which that engagement conveys. The lesson is that society cannot be kept exclusive of any profession that is not *malum per se*.

That is, as long as the couple comes from professions that are not absolute crimes against humanity, they should not be excluded from the inner circles of society. The writer continued, "It is a finer thing for a man to brew good beer than it is for a man to idle his life away and be remarkable only for keeping out of jails and scandals." His argument was that brewing beer was better than being a criminal – and why didn't society recognize that?

> As for the lady in the case, she is beautiful...I am sure that all the world loves the lovely, and it cares little whether loveliness be adorned by the profits in beer or by the exactions of an aristocrat from a piteous peasantry.

The writer blamed nativism, suggesting that Americans set standards too high for entrance into society. "It seems rather ridiculous to me that some people in society here should profess to look with some scoffing upon the announcement of the engagement in question." He suggested that the fame and wealth of the brewer and saloon keeper spelled success, and, "The alliance is one that shows a hearty contempt for all the false distinctions that certain foolish people have endeavored to establish in American life." The writer passionately concluded:

> The Busches are true democrats and deserving of all the interest they create, while "Ed." Faust is the

clever son of a very clever father, whose character stands as proof that catering to the hunger and the thirst of the people is not opposed to the development of a fine, broad, free manliness and genuine worth as a citizen.[18]

That Edward's "manliness" and "genuine worth as a citizen" needed to be defended probably made him cringe.

Yet, Germans and brewers continued to be set apart. Anna Faust threw a party a few years later, in 1900, and the *St. Louis Post-Dispatch* added its description to its "The News in Society" section, "A beautiful and elaborate affair in the most exclusive of the German circles was the entertainment which Mrs. Eddie Faust (formerly Miss Busch), gave yesterday afternoon…."[19]

A few years later, the tide turned. The *St. Louis Post-Dispatch* ran an article in 1903 featuring Edward Faust, titled, "Some Things Concerning the 'Somebodies' in St. Louis." The article showered Edward, son of the restaurateur and son-in-law of the brewer, with adulation.

> Most everybody in St. Louis knows Eddie Faust, who is handsome, rich, in the prime of life, the second vice-president of the Anheuser-Busch Brewing Co., vice-president of the Fourth National Bank of St. Louis and the manager of that celebrated Broadway oasis – Tony Faust's place…. Edward A. Faust is one of the rising young men of St. Louis. It keeps his distinguished father busy getting up early enough to see the son rise.

After describing Tony Faust's and Adolphus Busch's immigration from Germany and economic rise in St. Louis, the article's writer stated, "Mr. Faust made the hungry world a big luscious sandwich, and Mr. Busch made beer with which to wash it down." The article concluded, "Edward A. Faust exhibits all the business acumen characteristic of his father."[20]

This article was run the same year Edward first surveyed property for his future home at 1 Portland Place. Nevertheless, the Busches continued to find themselves on the perimeter of St. Louis's social scene. This mentality fueled the Busches' independence. They resided not in elite neighborhoods but in St. Louis's South Side on the grounds of their brewery. And (except for Anna) all of Adolphus Busch's children built their homes in the country or in other cities.

Judging by his choice of neighborhood, Edward clearly wanted in. And he got in.[21] In 1914, the year after the death of Adolphus Busch, he no longer sat on the board of directors for Anheuser-Busch. Sometime between 1914 and 1916, Edward left his position of vice president at Anheuser-Busch. He stayed connected to the brewery only by the retention of his general manager position of the St. Louis Refrigerator Car Company, the railroad line established by Adolphus Busch in 1878. Instead, Edward founded his own corporation, the St. Louis Boat and Engineering Company.[22]

Why the change? Upon Adolphus' death, August A. took the reins at Anheuser-Busch. Did August A. bring too much change to the old establishment of Anheuser-Busch, displeasing Edward? Perhaps more likely, Edward's departure from the brewing industry was in keeping with the temperate nature of his new neighborhood.

Edward did not officially move into his West End home until 1914. The neighborhood, laden with the city's business leaders, already had a reputation when Edward's architect began his home design in 1903. St. Louis had a geographical divide: the city's large German population inhabited the periphery of the city to the north and, particularly, the south, while the wealthy "Americans" built their homes in the sanctuary of the West End.[23] The location of his new residence was an ambition, an *intentional choice*, for Edward, son of a German immigrant.

A myth (or perhaps a conspiracy theory) developed about those men who lived in the West End at the turn of the century. They were the *Big Cinch* – a "few rich and powerful men" who "controlled the political life and economic destiny of St. Louis."[24] But perhaps these magnates of business were also scapegoats for the average citizen who had grown wary of national monopolies and corrupt politics. Maybe those "members" of the Big Cinch were branded unfairly. Instead, perhaps they should have been given accolades for their savvy economic prowess that made St. Louis a thriving city.

Many of the men who comprised the Big Cinch were bank officials. Their professional lives lent credence to the accusation that they, and they alone, controlled the financial resources of the city, as well as the financial destinies of the average citizen. Edward was vice president of the Fourth National Bank when the blueprints were being drawn for 1 Portland Place. He later became a director and investor of the National Bank of Commerce. It was the largest St. Louis bank and a pure example of the "concentration of bank ownership within the business elite."[25]

Fourth Street was the heart of St. Louis's financial district. Banks in that vicinity boasted American stockholders. Banks tucked into residential neighborhoods served German-American clientele. A few German-American businessmen proved to be exceptions, like Adolphus Busch, who had stock in both types of banks. Nevertheless, he founded the South Side Bank, a financial institution in his German-American community. Meanwhile, Edward Faust proved his clout when he became director of the Mercantile Commerce Trust Company, an institution largely comprised of elite stockholders of the Big Cinch. The connection between the bank stockholders and the West End businessmen made St. Louisans suspicious of an ongoing monopoly. It fueled the notion that the Big Cinch pumped the economic heartbeat of St. Louis.[26]

At the turn of the century, the city was ill equipped to meet the ever-growing need for improved public services demanded by the public. To meet those demands, the city turned to political machines at the ward level. Though undemocratic with their bribes and patronage, they got the jobs done. The city also looked to private enterprise. The powerful downtown business leaders who invested in the city's infrastructure were credited with providing those services for St. Louis. The city government also created franchises. "The franchise was essentially a grant of special privileges and access to public property in exchange for the provision of the service. Through the franchise the city encouraged essential private investment while retaining ultimate control of its property."[27]

This relationship between the wealthy private investors and politicians propagated the distrust of St. Louis citizens, especially since "boodle" was often involved. "Boodle" was the term for bribing city officials for franchises, low tax assessments, contracts, and other privileges. The interlocking relationships among industry, banks, and public services made it impossible for the Big Cinch to conduct its business without the presence of boodle. It was cheaper to bribe a franchise from city officials than to pay fair price and be taxed accordingly.[28]

Nevertheless, the downtown business leaders and the people of St. Louis cooperated well with each other as the city prepared for the 1904 World's Fair. This was achieved through the leadership of a non-excessive mayor and a city attorney who cracked down on corruption. The Fair was a worldwide success. The city's powerful circle of businessmen and the citizens of St. Louis had high hopes for a prosperous, democratic, and progressive civic future.

Though construction was years away, the design of Edward's home at 1 Portland Place was well underway in 1905, a year after the World's Fair. Perhaps he hoped that the successes of the Fair had eased negativity and would persuade St. Louisans to drop the moniker "Big Cinch." The *St. Louis Post-Dispatch* published an article about the Big Cinch that year, looking back over the first few years of the new century that led up to the Fair,

> The top of the business heap was a nebulous sort of an amalgamation known locally as the Big Cinch. It was composed of the bank presidents and others of high standing.... When the Big Cinch handed down an opinion or made a suggestion, that opinion and that suggestion were the word of the prophet, to be obeyed.
> The Big Cinch is made up, principally, of the men who organized and carried through the World's Fair. Still, there developed ...a spirit of revolt. Some men with ideas of their own stood out...against the

97

opinions handed down by those all-powerful business organizations. This was treason…but the bold spirits told the Big Cinch to make the most of it.
That is one sign of the awakening of St. Louis. Another is the partial purification of the politics of the place. No city in the country was so rotten politically, as St. Louis, but the people, aided by a fearless newspaper, have done a good deal toward cleaning up. Germicides have been scattered in some of the festering sores.
There was to be a new St. Louis one of these days…. The old St. Louis is working to that end, slowly, cautiously, handicapped by that spirit of self-sufficiency that prevails, but it will come.[29]

But alas, the Big Cinch's power held firm for three decades into the new century. Edward Faust was firmly entrenched as one of the coterie. Nor was public opinion to improve, especially with the election of Mayor Henry W. Kiel, who served from 1913 to 1925, the "leader of a corrupt machine" and "the best entrenched municipal machine in the country."[30] And no amount of optimism could erase the anger and hatred that erupted from the streetcar strike of 1900.

William Marion Reedy, the outspoken editor of *The Mirror*, felt the primary source of Big Cinch power was "monopolistic control of certain public services."[31] Of course, change was essential in public transportation as horsecars converted to cable, then cable converted to electricity. Consolidation of local streetcar lines to city-wide systems under one corporate entity was necessary. But it intensified the friction among the streetcar companies, the government, and the public. Consolidation was incredibly complex, heavily relying on outside capital yet maintaining reliance on local financiers. Many of the local financiers became the subject of bribery investigations in 1902, tarnishing the entire process in the eyes of the St. Louis general public. The new unified streetcar system became the United Railways in 1899. The St. Louis Transit Company managed it. A man named Edward Whitaker headed the new management company. He became a key player in the streetcar strike of 1900.[32]

With the consolidation, the union workers had less leverage. They reorganized into Local 131 of the Street Railway Employees of America. They asked for shorter workdays, higher wages, and recognition of their union. Whitaker agreed, then reneged. On May 8, 1900, 3,325 streetcar workers walked out, and the strike began.[33]

The St. Louis Transit Company held firm. On the other side, Adolphus Busch, the president of the Central Trades and Labor Union, and other strike sympathizers met with the mayor to assess the needs of the streetcar union. Other types of support poured in: both the St. Louis Type and Founders' Union and the Switchmen's Union endorsed the strike. They pledged to fine their members if they should be caught riding on the streetcars. The Beerdrivers and Stablemen's Union, among many other groups, pledged ongoing financial support for the streetcar strikers.[34]

When Whitaker brought in strikebreakers from Cleveland, the strikers escalated their revolt from protests to violence. Strikers lit bonfires and placed dynamite on the rail tracks. Strikers and their sympathizers mobbed streetcars, beating passengers and scabs. Policemen found themselves firing into angry crowds.[35]

On May 19, Judge Elmer B. Adams of the United States Circuit Court issued an injunction restraining the strikers and their sympathizers from interfering with the streetcars in any way. He cited tactics such as cutting cable wires, piling rocks and rubble on the tracks, and gathering near streetcar power stations to block the tracks. All of this activity was deemed criminal by the Judge in that it "obstructed, interfered with and prevented the operation of the mail cars of the United States."[36]

The Judge authorized the St. Louis police to form a *posse comitatus*. This sheriff's posse, a citizen's army drawn from the "better elements" of St. Louis, highlighted the dissection of St. Louis society. Many of the posse members were downtown businessmen who lived in the West End. Edward Faust, of the West End, was a proud member of the sheriff's posse. Meanwhile, the strike was strongly supported by the citizens of the south side of the city – the German population.

Members of the posse, also called sheriff's deputies, were tasked with patrolling rail lines. They also prevented the use of alternative (creative, but unlicensed) types of vehicles by strikers and strike sympathizers. The deputies found themselves unwelcome in strikers' neighborhoods. In a letter to Col. J.H. Cavender, commander of the posse, the chief of police wrote,
> Regarding the detail along the Sixth St. Line last night, I would suggest that you have some deputies placed in the vicinity of the Anheuser-Busch Brewery, say between Arsenal and Sidney St., as there was some trouble in that territory last evening.[37]

Fear of the lawlessness changed to disgust toward the,

according to one posse member, "lower class of Germans at the South End."[38]

Members of the sheriff's posse, St. Louis Streetcar Strike, 1900.
Edward Faust is second from left.
Courtesy of Missouri History Museum, St. Louis

Twenty-five hundred businessmen were called upon to serve in the posse. Some, unused to physical rigors in their daily lives, found inventive reasons to be excused from duty. However, many gallantly took up their weapons, including one who wrote to a posse leader on June 8, 1900,

> My business engagements are such that I can not volunteer to join the Posse without any serious financial sacrifice, but I will hold myself in readiness to respond at any time of day or night to a telephone call if I can be of any service – I will have proper arms both at my residence and at my office and will report with them on the shortest notice, and can probably bring with me one or two good men, so fast as bicycles or horses can carry us.[39]

Treated like an army, members of the posse were assigned regions of the city and were provided with barracks, provisions and weapons. Lists of supplies delivered to the barracks in June and July included 504 canvas cots, 566 blankets, 108 tin cups, 52 lanterns, and 30 boxes of matches. And on June 30, a list of bills was submitted to the posse commander for meals given the posse members. Of the total $17,300, nearly $200 was to go to Faust & Sons.[40]

The commanders of the sheriff's posse detachments were given their orders:
> Your men will pay no attention to trifling annoyances from citizens, but will submit to no abuse, promptly arresting any offender. In [containing] any riot or disturbance, and in dispersing any unlawful and threatening assemblages of persons, you will use your utmost endeavor to arrest the ring leaders and instigators, turning them over to the Police for incarceration. You will use only the necessary force in the performance of such duty, but will match violence with violence, and if fired upon, you are expected, with due regard for the safety of innocent bystanders, to make sure that the criminals reach the jail, or the morgue if necessary.[41]

A letter of warning to the citizens of St. Louis was distributed from the *posse comitatus:*
> When we came out here on last Friday night, privately and publicly we begged and ...implored you to keep the peace and refrain from destroying the public and private property, and many of you promised to do so, and we are sorry to say many have failed to keep their word with us.
> ...This then is to notify you that the next person

caught destroying property will be arrested and if he resists arrest will be shot on the spot. ...Such assemblies will be commanded in the name of the State of Missouri to disperse, and in failing to do so strong force will be used to move them on. Good citizens are warned to keep within doors, for fear they may be shot. This is positively the last warning.[42]

Though St. Louis was not the only American city beleaguered by strikes, the nation kept watch on the violence. Pulitzer's New York City newspaper *The World* requested a wire from Col. Cavender, commander of the posse, asking if "everything is being done that should be done to prevent the outrages upon women and street killings...."[43] As does the media, *Collier's Weekly* sensationalized the streetcar strike, reporting,

In St. Louis a concerted movement seemed to have been made to humiliate women who patronized the street cars in the grossest possible manner. No less than three of them were stripped entirely of their clothing upon the public street and hunted and kicked and buffeted about like wild animals.[44]

Harper's Weekly, however, intuitively picked up on the heart of the dispute,

The first day was a decisive triumph for the strikers. They succeeded in blocking all lines of street cars and produced a tremendous feeling of indignation on the part of the citizens because of the unpleasant situation. Public sentiment was strongly...on their side. But their obstinacy in insisting upon the letter of their demands turned this sentiment against them, and the capitalists, not being disadvantaged by having to provide today for to-morrow's dinner-pail, are about to score another victory.[45]

Nearly two months after the strike began, Whitaker agreed not to fire strikebreakers and to fill vacancies with union streetcar workers. He lied. The strike continued until September when the hungry and weary strikers gave up. It was not all for naught, however. The strike raised awareness of the dire need for better public services, exposed corrupt politicians, and highlighted the strength of the Big Cinch.[46]

By serving on the *posse comitatus* and building a home in the West End, Edward Faust had made his intentions clear, despite his German roots, his childhood footsteps in his father's German restaurant, and his time spent rearing his children in the city's South Side amongst the proud towers of a brewery.

Chapter 3
THE AMERICAN
GERMAN-AMERICAN

And what of Edward Faust's German heritage? The history of German immigrants in St. Louis began well before his father, Tony, made his way there in 1853. One of the earliest Germans to entice others to emigrate was Gottfried Duden. He had been a prosecuting attorney in Mulheim on the Ruhr. He traveled to America in 1824 and settled in a rural area of Missouri beyond St. Louis. After he lived on the land for three years, Duden returned to Germany with a detailed written account of Missouri's landscape, wildlife, and fertile ground. He also carefully recorded a history of America's laws and form of government. Duden published a book, encouraging immigration to Missouri. He pushed his philosophy that the German people could settle the land together and make a "New Germany" – a better version of the Fatherland.[1]

As a result of his wildly popular book (as well as overpopulation, poverty, and economic and political upheaval), Germans formed societies, or companies, and began to emigrate in groups. There were enough Germans in St. Louis by 1835 to found the first German newspaper, *Anzeiger des Westens.* In 1837, a German school opened in St. Louis (before the city established its first public school). The largest wave of immigrants came from Germany after the failed Revolution of 1848.[2]

Tony Faust lived through that fateful event in 1848 at the impressionable age of 12. In 1853, he boarded the steamer *Baltimore* for New York. The year Tony arrived in the

United States, the St. Louis City Directory boasted the publication of six German newspapers and seven German Societies. These organizations smoothed the transition for newly arrived Germans:
>   German Emigrant Society
>   German Benefit Society
>   German Workingmen's Society
>   The Society of Freemen (German)
>   German Savings Institution
>   German Roman Catholic Benevolent Society
>   St. Vincent's German Orphan Association[3]

The Germans were not necessarily welcome as they moved into the fabric of St. Louis society. In April 1852, the municipal elections produced riots between German and non-German citizens around Soulard Market, Seventh Street, and Park Avenue. The violence continued the entire day. The hostilities climaxed when a home that was serving as a refuge to a large number of German immigrants was set on fire and burned down. An angry mob then stormed the office of *Anzeiger des Westens*. They were turned back by a military company.[4]

Two years later, the Know-Nothings, a political movement comprising anti-immigrant, "native" Americans, directed their aggression toward Germans, Irish, and Catholics. The hoodlums attacked homes and stores for two days. The Know-Nothings were finally suppressed by military units and an armed citizens' posse.[5]

In spite of the unrest, by the time Tony opened his first café on Carondelet Avenue in the early 1860s, South St. Louis was largely inhabited by Germans. His business quickly became a hit:
>   Tony Faust had his tavern, in which one could also

get meals, where "oysters in style" were served. Tony obtained his supply of oysters direct. It was a happy idea to combine the tavern with the oyster business, a business in which he practically held a monopoly in that part of the city. It was the only business of this kind south of Market Street.[6]

Tony seemed to fit the mold of the hard-working German. By the time Tony's children were small, a contemporary author wrote glowingly about the German immigrants, "the Americans rejoiced at their coming, and extended to them a hearty welcome, for they...proved to be honest, industrious, thrifty citizens."[7]

By 1860, there were 38 private German schools in both North and South St. Louis. The school board of the public schools began adding German studies into their curriculum in 1864. By 1881, when the second wave of immigrants from Germany descended upon St. Louis, 54 public schools offered German classes. This instruction of the German language in school was meant to "hasten the assimilation" of the immigrant children into society.[8] Edward and his brother were required to study German language and literature during their tenure at the elite Smith Academy.[9]

The German newspapers provided the means for German immigrants to keep up with all things American in their own tongue. But the children of immigrants brought the English language home. They weaned themselves away from the language of their parents. Like other first-generation Americans, Tony's children fluently spoke German (and even French), but English was their first language. In the 1880s, English-language newspapers began to encourage the public schools to omit the German language from their curriculum. The *Anzeiger des Westens* and the *Westliche*

107

Post put up a fight, attempting to rouse the German population into solidarity. The issue was put to a vote by the public school board and, as a strong indicator of the lack of cohesion of the German population, the Germans did not turn out to vote. In 1887, German language was removed from St. Louis schools.[10]

St. Louis was unlike rural American communities and pockets in some American cities where Germans collected and maintained a cohesive society. The large number of Germans in St. Louis scattered around the city. They settled both in the northern and, especially, the southern parts of the city. The geography of St. Louis spread its population along the river, making unified German neighborhoods nearly impossible.

Nonetheless, Germans enthusiastically embraced their culture by forming an astounding number of social clubs, or *Vereine,* in St. Louis, using America's hospitable environment to create organizations just as they had in the Fatherland. In fact, "…it seemed that anywhere there were at least three Germans they formed a society…"[11] Edward and his brother were proud members of the Liederkranz society, the club for elite German citizens, known in part for its elaborate masquerade balls. The *Vereine* covered every possible interest of the diverse German population. The great numbers of them (hundreds!) superficially "reflected a bond of cultural unity."[12] In fact, however, the large numbers of *Vereine* further separated the German-Americans from each other and hindered the creation of a cohesive ethnic group. The many *Vereine* in St. Louis mirrored the geographical and even cultural diversity among St. Louisans.[13]

Other characteristics of German culture took hold. Interest

in German theater in St. Louis began before the Civil War. Heinrich Börnstein was editor of the *Anzeiger Des Westens*. He founded the Philodramatische Gesellschaft, an amateur theater, in 1853, the year Tony arrived in America. In 1859, Börnstein managed an Opera House and established the first successful professional theater in St. Louis. Both were short lived. Interest in the German theater ebbed and flowed in the decades after the Civil War. Success was hindered by arrests of its actors for appearing on stage on Sundays, and it also was difficult for the theater to compete with the ever popular German beer gardens.[14]

Still teeming with a large first-generation German population in 1885, the city held a four-day festival for the German-American veterans of the late German wars. The event included fireworks and concerts by the many singing *Vereine*. A celebration at Schnaider's Garden, one of the most popular beer gardens in St. Louis, capped the festivities. This one-time event invited a rare show of unity among the German-Americans of St. Louis. Other American cities, however, managed to coordinate annual German days.[15]

The tension leading up to America's entry into World War I provided opportunities for unity in St. Louis German-Americans. The United States claimed neutrality early in the war, yet seemed to favor the stance of the Allies. This placed the German-Americans in a difficult position. The Fatherland was at war with France and England. France was the "historic enemy of Germany," while German-Americans associated England with Puritans – those who fueled the temperance movement in the US.[16]

The first opportunity for cohesion capitalized upon by St. Louis German-Americans came in August 1914. The *St.*

Louis Post-Dispatch, the *Republic,* and the *Star* had published anti-German editorials. Most of the German societies of the city were represented as several thousand German-Americans gathered at the Central Turner Hall. The rally successfully achieved a show of solidarity. It protested against the newspapers for advocating war against the German Emperor. The rally-goers requested that Germany not be given any favors, but appealed that Germany be given a fair shake.[17]

Only once more did St. Louis German-Americans congregate in a unified effort. After several paltry attempts at fund-raising, the committee of the Citizens' Relief Fund planned a bazaar, always a sure way to garner attendance. After eight months of planning, the Bazaar, a fund-raiser for relief of war widows and orphans in Germany and Austria, opened its doors in the Coliseum in October 1915. The Bazaar was a "gigantic undertaking," extraordinary in its size, number of booths, and outstanding décor. Visitors beheld a "panoramic view" of St. Louis, Berlin's Brandenburg Gate and Unter den Linden, and New York's Statue of Liberty. Cafés were scattered among the areas also set up for music, theatrical performances, and dancing. Fifty booths sat under a canopy made up of huge American flags.[18]

One of the most elaborate booths was managed by the Busch family. August A. had arranged for their booth to occupy the "entire southwest corner of the building." They displayed several types of his prize farm animals and a miniature of his estate, Grant's Farm. One of August A.'s employees, in full uniform of the 66th Alsace artillery, saluted visitors as they entered. Another, attired in the uniform of a hussar of the Strasburg regiments, sat horseback on one of August A.'s Arabian stallions. Most of the members of the Busch family participated in the booth.[19]

Prior to the Bazaar's opening, the *Post-Dispatch* hyped the event. It called for all St. Louis citizens to attend. The newspaper claimed that sympathy for war victims should be nonpartisan. Indeed, the event was a huge success. The goal of $100,000 was attained and sent to the German and Austro-Hungarian Red Cross immediately. The Bazaar was the last cohesive effort of St. Louis German-Americans.[20]

As the war raged in Europe, German-Americans found themselves in a desperate situation. They pressed for the neutrality of the United States in an attempt to keep the peace between the US and Germany. Across America, leagues were formed for the cause. In December 1914, the Neutrality League was formed in St. Louis. Comprising largely German- and Irish-Americans, the League held a demonstration in January 1915 to protest the shipments of arms to nations at war. More than 12,000 St. Louisans turned up. Unfortunately, the meeting turned into a "display of pro-German sympathy."[21] Speakers heralded the cause of Germany and railed against England. Amidst the cheering the crowd broke out in singing *"Deutschland Über Alles."*

This demonstration was alarming for "native" St. Louisans, and the League found itself in damage-control mode. The next few rallies (American flag-waving attempts at regaining the focus on peace and neutrality) were each called a "colossal flop" and did little to regain the public's trust.[22]

Pro-German demonstrations made headlines around the country. In August 1914, the *New York Times* reported on a large group of native Germans who lived in New York and had cheered the Kaiser as they marched down Broadway.

The group entered the German Consulate General's office to request joining the fight in the Fatherland. The marchers were joined by pro-German passersby, who stopped traffic while singing *Die Wacht am Rhine*. Several other "parades" followed. One notable march included several hundred Germans who paraded down Broadway while waving the German flag and singing German anthems. The demonstrators turned East at 14th Street and entered Lüchow's Restaurant (owned by August Lüchow, Tony Faust's friend and partner in their World's Fair restaurant), where they gave speeches and sang some more.[23] Such events irked "native" Americans and fostered the growing anger toward German-Americans.

By the time the United States entered the war in 1917, allegiance toward anything German was considered disloyal, especially in American cities with large German populations. To sanitize itself of the enemy, St. Louis schools pulled German language classes as an elective from their curriculum, removed books written in German from the public library shelves, and changed street names. The biggest offender, Berlin Avenue, was changed to Pershing Avenue. German-language newspapers were required to submit their articles to the postmaster for censorship. The *Westliche Post* proclaimed its loyalty by printing, under a waving American flag on the first page, "An American Newspaper Standing for American Ideals and Principles."[24]

The campaign against German-Americans was not limited to St. Louis. A few high-profile incidents involving German loyalists marred the psyche of Americans.

> On a summer night in New York City in 1916, a pier laden with a thousand tons of munitions destined for Britain, France, and Russia in their war against Imperial Germany suddenly caught fire and

exploded with a force that scarred the Statue of Liberty with shrapnel, shattered windows in Times Square, rocked the Brooklyn Bridge, and woke sleepers as far away as Maryland. Within days, local authorities had concluded that the blasts at "Black Tom" pier were the work of German saboteurs seeking to destroy supplies headed from neutral America to Germany's enemies.[25]

In its effort to curb the flow of supplies and arms to its enemies, the German General Staff in Washington, D.C. authorized a military attaché to "mount sabotage operations against" "every kind of factory for supplying munitions of war." In 1915, one of the 80-odd blockaded German ships that languished in New York harbor was turned into a bomb factory. After several "accidents" on Allied ships, President Wilson ordered the Secret Service to watch German diplomats. One diplomat's briefcase (snatched from him on a streetcar) yielded several leads to the sabotage campaign. It gave a new reality to German espionage on American soil.

That discovery shed light on the fact that local and national agencies were completely ill-equipped to handle Germany's secret activities. The United States had no national intelligence service, no code-breaking agency, nor any federal statutes forbidding peacetime espionage. With no integration of authority and a lack of communication among agencies, it took innovation to stop the saboteurs. For example, the bomb squad of the New York Police Department employed German-speaking German-Americans. The imbedded informants were stationed in dockside taverns, where they engaged in gossip. The police then rounded up German sailors who divulged the plots.

A few saboteurs managed to sneak into America's heartland

and plant bombs in factories. But the overall German efforts in sabotage and espionage hardly made a dent in the American economy and the Allied war effort. They were detrimental to the American consciousness, however, and effectively poisoned public opinion against German-Americans.[26] As elsewhere, German newspapers in St. Louis cautioned German-Americans to watch what they said, especially on the streets and in public places. This warning included patrons and employees of Faust's Fulton Market, of which Edward was president. Citizens of German descent who simply discussed war news ran the risk of being accused of breaking the new Federal Espionage Act.[27]

A fanaticism accompanied patriotic furor. The foolish acts of a few engendered suspicion of the rest. A great many German-Americans were accused of some sort of treason, but, according to Secretary of State Robert Lansing,
> Certainly nine out of ten, and probably ninety-nine out of a hundred, of these suspects were guiltless of any wrongful act or intention, but much time had to be wasted by our Secret Service in providing their innocence and satisfying their accusers that they were mistaken."[28]

Everyday German-American citizens of St. Louis suddenly found themselves accused of treason or worse. Disbelieving, they asked, Wasn't it they who saved Missouri for the Union during the Civil War? Didn't they, too, have sons fighting overseas for the Allies? Hadn't they proved their patriotism by purchasing Liberty Bonds and flying the American flag?[29]

One of the biggest targets was the Busch family. After Adolphus Busch died in 1913 in Germany, Lilly Busch and her family returned to Germany the following May. She sought solace in the company of two of her daughters who were married to German army officers and resided in the Fatherland. Lilly was still in Germany when the war in Europe began. Edward Faust wired $25,000 for the family's return; however, Lilly stayed. Back in St. Louis, her son, August A. Busch, was heavily persecuted. The Busch family had openly supported the Kaiser when the war began in Europe, and August A. found himself frantically backpedaling. He was forced to answer questions regarding everything from his mother's situation to the portraits of Germans hanging in his brewery. He repeatedly proclaimed his loyalty and that of his family to America. He cited their years of building their brewing industry in the United States. He attempted to prove their dedication to their country by providing evidence of their Liberty Bond subscription purchases totaling $400,000. The Busches also made a $50,000 contribution to the YMCA fund for soldiers, as well as donations to the Red Cross.[30]

While in Germany, Lilly Busch and her daughters aided war victims and wounded soldiers in a hospital in Munich. By November 1917, her attorney, Harry Hawes, had obtained United States passports. He began his trip to neutral Switzerland to collect Lilly and escort her home to St. Louis.[31]

In December 1917, before her return, the United States government seized all of Lilly Busch's property. This included her mansion at 1 Busch Place, her stock in the Anheuser-Busch Brewery, and her stock in other Busch holdings around the United States. In all, it was reportedly worth $15,000,000. The government cited the Alien Property Law, which was enacted to protect the United States against the use of property by an enemy country.[32]

With the help of her attorney, Lilly managed to exit Germany in early 1918. The logistics of war dictated that they take a convoluted route to the United States. She met Hawes in Switzerland, then via Spain and Cuba the pair returned to America. Her ship was met by United States Immigration and Department of Justice agents in the Florida Keys. Lilly was searched and detained for hours. After being allowed to stay overnight, she made her way back to St. Louis, accompanied by August A. Upon arrival, Lilly was greeted at the train station by many members of her large family. Her first hug was with her grandson Leicester Busch Faust. August A. whisked her home to 1 Busch Place. A year later the government of the United States returned her property.[33]

Edward Faust had as much German blood flowing through his veins as did his brother-in-law August A. But Edward's keen eye and discretion served him well. Except for his management of the St. Louis Refrigerator Car Company, he had completely disengaged himself from the management of Anheuser-Busch by the time the United States entered the war in 1917. Edward had also intentionally distanced himself, his wife, and his children geographically from the Busch family residence in the heavily German-American populated South Side of St. Louis. He resided in the West End, in an "American" neighborhood. So American, in fact, that the West End was held up as *the* example of patriotism by those defending themselves in the South Side:

> Charles Nagel, a prominent second generation German-American, former secretary of Commerce and Labor in Taft's cabinet, had stated in 1916, when German-American loyalty was questioned, that there was more patriotism on the South Side than in the West End. Every Fourth of July there was scarcely a house in the German neighborhoods

that did not display the flag, while in the West End "you could go a long way without seeing a flag."[34]

Anna was sheltered in the West End but stayed true to her character. She continued to busy herself with philanthropic work and geared her interests toward the war effort. She worked alongside her sisters-in-law, Alice (Mrs. August A.) Busch and Mollie Giannini. The ladies hosted a lecture sponsored by the Liederkranz Club to benefit the St. Louis Unit of American Physicians' Expedition to the Central Powers. They worked a Red Cross pledge drive and a theater event to raise money for the American Hospital No. 1 in Neuilly, France, for wounded soldiers. In 1919, the women helped throw a charity "Victory Ball." As late as 1921, they sponsored a fund-raising event to aid starving children in war-ravaged Europe.[35]

Wartime fundraising generated a Who's Who list in St. Louis. Anna helped staff a booth during Liberty Bond Rally Day. She personally pledged $1,000 toward the United War Work Campaign Fund. The Fausts attended an elegant dinner on the roof garden of the Statler Hotel in 1918. The dinner was called a "social-patriotic affair," and it benefited the Italian War Relief Fund. The couple, box holders at the Odeon Theater in St. Louis, graciously agreed to attend a performance of the St. Louis Italian Grand Opera Company to again raise money for Italian war sufferers. Edward even tried his hand at philanthropy when he agreed to sit on the Men's Committee of the American Fund for French Wounded. One of his duties was to attend a two-day event that included horse racing, an automobile fashion parade, and even - believe it or not - auto polo. It was billed as "too fast for even the movies" and considered an "expensive game."[36]

117

In December 1921, the Fausts hosted a "reception" at 1 Portland Place for former soldiers with head wounds that resulted in the inability to speak. The Fausts also invited students from the Central Institute for the Deaf. The wounded soldiers and the deaf students gave demonstrations on how to use their other senses so they might have alternative methods of communication. One hopes that this form of entertainment for 150 of the Fausts' friends was tastefully done.[37]

Chapter 4
THE ART OF MAKING MONEY

It was easy for Anna Faust to busy herself with her social calendar. Domestic servants handled the housework duties and nannies took care of Leicester and Audrey. As Audrey entered her teen years, she was shipped off to boarding school. Her mother had the pleasant task of celebrating her daughter when she was home. When Audrey was 14, Anna planned a matinee party for her and her school friends. When Audrey was 16, her mother gave her a tea with 200 guests. Every year, Anna threw her daughter and son a Christmas bash when they were home for the holidays.[1]

Audrey graduated from her boarding school, Miss Wright's School in Bryn Mawr, Pennsylvania, in 1919 at the age of 17. She settled into the life of an incipient debutante at 1 Portland Place, attending many parties and dinner-dances in her honor. The society pages of the *St. Louis Post-Dispatch* tirelessly listed the comings and goings of young society. In August 1921, Audrey's nineteenth year, the newspaper announced her debut four months in advance.[2]

Audrey's debut was absolutely fantastic. The theme was "Spring Garden." The Fausts erected an enormous tent in their yard, enclosing the balcony and portico of the eastern façade of their home, as well as their garden wall along Kingshighway. The enclosed fountain, the portico, and the garden wall, reproductions of those in the Boboli Gardens of Florence, Italy, were banked with flowers. The tent, lighted from the top and heated in the cold night, was filled with tropical plants, fresh flowers, and branches delicately adorned in pink and white tissue paper simulating cherry and apple blossoms.

Moving between the ballroom and the tent, Audrey's 400 guests dined and danced. At midnight Audrey was introduced to society. She and 25 other debutantes took their seats with their escorts. Louis Kreidler, baritone for the Chicago Opera Company, performed, and another professional singer entertained later in the night as a dance troupe swirled around the fountain. It was magical.[3]

The *Post-Dispatch* gushed in 1922, "Miss Faust's debut ball of last year is still fresh in the minds of the St. Louisans who remember it as one of the most elaborate of recent years." The article then suggested that the young maidens would hardly have time to catch their "beauty sleep until the Busch party is held."

> It will be a ball given by Mr. and Mrs. August A. Busch for the formal debut of their daughter, Miss Alice Busch, and will take place at Grant's Farm, the home of the Busch family. . . . Expectations of a setting just as beautiful for the formal dance are justified when one calls to mind the attractive affairs given by the Busch family in the past."[4]

The Fausts continued to throw fabulous parties. In December 1922, Anna and Edward threw an East Indian durbar in their ballroom at 1 Portland Place in honor of Audrey and two of her debutante friends. The actual durbar was a celebration in India in honor of the coronation of the King and Queen of the United Kingdom, who were also Emperor and Empress of India. In St. Louis, over 200 guests, dressed and bejeweled in (their version of) East Indian garb, were greeted at the door by the *maharaja*, "the great king," played by Edward Faust. The ballroom's décor reflected the Fausts' version of the "Orient," complete with a Buddha. A sketch artist drew illustrations of the revelers that the *St. Louis Post- Dispatch* eagerly printed.[5]

Days were a busy social time, with card parties, teas, and lunches. A particularly unusual event took place one day in May 1922. The St. Louis Cardinals played Pittsburgh in a benefit game at Sportsman's Park, with the proceeds earmarked for more playgrounds around St. Louis. Audrey Faust and 17 other debutantes, dressed in their finest daytime wear, formed a semi-circle on the field. The girls threw baseballs autographed by the players into the stands (they had practiced throwing the previous afternoon while gathered for a tea). One of the debutantes presented the honored guest, federal judge and Baseball Commissioner Kenesaw Mountain Landis, with a baseball autographed by President Harding. Then, the lovely ladies presented each of the Pittsburgh players with a rose. All of the Cardinals players received a four-leaf clover for good luck. Edward Faust, a host for the event, stood on the field with his daughter and her friends.[6]

Like her mother, Audrey busied herself philanthropically. She was a member of the Red Cross Knitting Club and joined the Junior League, actively working to raise money through the Junior League's dance group called the "Follies." Audrey, who later proved she had more grit than many men, no doubt watched her mother work for suffrage; Anna was a member of the Women's Equal Suffrage League. Once the Nineteenth Amendment was ratified in 1920, Anna became an active member of the League of Women Voters.[7]

It is notable that a large number of Anna's charities benefitted women and children. A great deal of her time between 1918 and 1922 was spent helping organize events to fund the St. Louis Children's Hospital. In 1920, Anna did her part to raise money for the St. Louis Protestant Orphans' Home, hosting a box party at a benefit theater performance followed by a ball at a fine St. Louis Hotel. Two years later she helped preside over a theater full of poor children at a Christmas performance of "Tip Top," dedicated solely to that audience. That same year Anna was elected director of the Missouri Welfare League.[8] Its agenda included addressing:

> ...proper care and instruction of children as a crime preventative, an intermediate reformatory for young men, adequate provisions for the dangerously insane and for tubercular prisoners, and adequate facilities for the institutional care of the feeble-minded.[9]

Edward did his part, too. He sat on a committee to distribute funds to hospitals in 1922. He gave $5,000 toward a Washington University salary endowment, and he helped a friend campaign for Senate. While his wife chose civic charities that directly benefitted the less fortunate, Edward preferred those that satisfied his interest in the arts while hobnobbing with his capitalist pals. He served on the board of directors for the Municipal Theater Association along with Eugene Angert, the attorney husband of his niece, Vera; his home's architect Tom Barnett; and his less-than-scrupulous friend, Mayor Kiel.[10]

Edward was passionate about the symphony. The Fausts attended frequently. Like the other couples in their "set," they socialized with friends over dinner before the symphony (or the theater) and afterward danced deep into the night.[11] As early as 1914, Edward became more than a patron. The St. Louis Symphony Society solicited his Business Men's League to campaign for an endowment for the Orchestra. The society proposed a longer symphony season, a permanent schedule of concerts at the popular Coliseum, and 25 more musicians. At that meeting, Edward applauded the concept and committed fully to supporting the symphony in more ways than occupying a seat. He became a member of the Symphony Society.[12]

The Business Men's League agreed to provide as much as $45,000 annually for four years. The symphony used the money: it added new musicians during the 1916-1917 season; however, it still faced a deficit of $36,000 that year. Edward Faust, August A. Busch, and 23 other members of the Symphony Society donated $1,000 each toward the debt. Edward agreed to serve on a committee to raise the remaining funds to prevent closing the season in debt.[13]

Going into the 1917-1918 season, the symphony speculated that it would cost $100,000 to maintain the season. The Symphony Society guaranteed $40,000 of the total. After exhausting its account of $28,000, the group solicited donors for the final $12,000. Edward and several others pledged $1,000 each toward that amount. Advanced ticket sales promised great revenue while providing optimism during the darkness of war: "Music is expected to be the principal diversion, when many Americans will not care for gayer amusements."[14]

In 1919, Edward was elected a vice president of the St. Louis Symphony Society. But by 1920, the estimated cost to maintain the orchestra was $155,000. The society needed to raise a whopping $30,000. The symphony carried a growing $13,000 deficit from previous seasons. Clearly, the orchestra was in dire straits,
> Attributed chiefly to the competition of moving picture houses that are featuring their orchestras and which have raided the ranks of the Symphony

Orchestra for good musicians by offering better contracts and wages.[15] The St. Louis Symphony Orchestra lost 20 musicians that year to the moving pictures.[16]

In 1922, Edward was elected to the Board of Management of the St. Louis Symphony Society. Once again, he and his fellow symphony devotees pledged $22,000 of their own money. But they were once again tasked with raising more money to cover the $15,000 deficit that year.

The symphony limped along through the early 1920s. Edward continued to serve as an officer of the society. He continued to pour his money into his passion. He and those in his circle found the symphony, in spite of its financial struggles, to be an excellent advertisement for their fair city. They realized that as the symphony embarked on its yearly concert tour, the better quality of its musicians produced a better sound that favorably represented St. Louis. Perhaps, then, capitalists like themselves in other cities would see St. Louis not just as a cultural center, but as a financial beacon as well.[17]

In 1911, Andreas Dippel, general manager of the Chicago-Philadelphia Grand Opera Company, felt troubled. Although the United States had the "greatest operatic forces in the world," the opera singers were not American. "They are developed in Europe and imported into this country along with Camembert and Roquefort cheese."[18] His desire was to make an American opera, sung in English and "produced by our own forces." This would
    1) provide opportunities for American youth
    2) develop local talent
    3) allow for long opera seasons for the cost of short seasons

4) keep money spent on opera at home

Agreeing with this concept, Edward Faust enthusiastically suggested that St. Louis build an opera house. He envisioned a beautiful structure built solely for the purpose of staging great operas. A year later, Adolphus Busch pledged $50,000 toward his son-in-law's dream.[19]

In 1914, Edward served as vice chairman of the newly formed St. Louis Grand Opera Committee. He announced that the Chicago-Philadelphia Opera Company, directed by his friend Cleofonte Campanini, would give several performances during the opera season in St. Louis. He, August A. Busch, and 20 others provided $2,000 each to bring the opera company to St. Louis. The performances were to be held in the Odeon Theater (where Edward had a box for the season). It was a lovely theater, but it was not an opera house.[20]

By 1917, Edward was closer to realizing his dream. He put together a "syndicate of wealthy St. Louisans."[21] The group called themselves the Thirty-Six Fifty Lindell Corporation. In January of that year, they purchased an old mansion and lot at 3650 Lindell Boulevard for $100. The group planned to build an opera house on the property. Edward, the group's president, raved, "I believe the splendid idea of a St. Louis grand opera house is soon to be realized."[22] The *St. Louis Post-Dispatch* reminded readers that the late Adolphus Busch had pledged $50,000 toward the project, and "it is understood that the Busch heirs are willing to renew the offer."[23] The offer, however, was on the condition that the remaining proposed costs of $450,000 would be raised within six months.

The *St. Louis Post-Dispatch* promoted the project. Edward

Faust was heralded as the "prime mover" in the venture. The newspaper chided its readers, "These men have acted. They have come forward with a definite plan. They have put their own money into it. They are seeking help and they should get it." The newspaper did suggest, however, "There is a diversity of opinion as to whether the location chosen is the most desirable for the purpose."[24]

Those on the nay-saying side of the "diversity of opinion" correctly assumed that the opera house project would not materialize. In July 1918, the Thirty-Six Fifty Lindell Corporation sold the property to Edward Faust and another investor for $9,229.05. Two years later, Edward and the other owner sold the property, officially giving up on the idea. The opera house venture may have failed, but, ever the shrewd businessman, Edward and his partner sold the old mansion and lot to the Missouri Province Educational Institute (of the Jesuits) for $35,000.[25]

In the years after Tony died, Edward and Anna continued their yearly summer sojourns to Europe. Their servants went along, with Leicester and Audrey in tow. The group often stayed in the Busch home on the Rhine. During the winters in St. Louis, Leicester and Audrey boarded a train to Pasadena, where they again stayed at length with Adolphus and Lilly Busch.

As the rumblings of war began in Europe, Edward wisely kept his family stateside. He began a tradition of taking his family to a summer home they rented. In 1916, his sister Mollie, her daughter Vera, and son-in-law Eugene Angert visited Edward's family in Greenwich, Connecticut. The next summer the Fausts stayed a month in Estes Park, Colorado, and then finished the "season" in New London,

Connecticut. Like many of their friends from St. Louis, the Fausts spent the summers of 1920 and 1921 in Rye Beach, New Hampshire. In 1922, Edward and Anna spent September and October in Hot Springs, Virginia, then wintered with Lilly Busch in Pasadena. It wasn't until February 1923 that the family again ventured overseas. That year, Edward, Anna, and Audrey traveled to Egypt and then toured Europe.[26]

Often, Edward stayed with his vacationing family for a short time, or he would not travel at all. Anna and Audrey were at ease traveling by themselves. Edward stayed in St. Louis to tackle his busy work schedule.

In 1915, Edward served as director of the Kinloch Telephone Company, one of two rival companies serving St. Louis. He found himself cleaning up a years-long mess. The convoluted fiasco began in 1905 in Rochester, New York. The people of New York had tired of the monopolistic Bell Company's long-distance rates. So, with a plan for a franchise in New York City, the United States Independent Telephone Company was born in Rochester. Breckinridge Jones, president of the Mississippi Valley Trust of St. Louis, was approached by the entrepreneurs from Rochester. They struck a deal. He signed a syndicate agreement and invested $25,000. Breckinridge Jones then sold the concept to a large number of St. Louis capitalists, including Adolphus Busch, who purchased the bonds at par. The investments were received in the office of the Mississippi Valley Trust Company. Both the Mississippi Valley Trust Company and Jones received a commission.

Apparently, the United States Independent Telephone Company's principal asset was a burglar-alarm franchise. It would supposedly allow stockholders the right to run telephone wires through the streets of New York. This concept was not only flawed but unfeasible. In 1907, the valueless company went under. Edward Faust and his friend Edward Goltra, a leading St. Louis capitalist, made a valiant attempt to purchase the foundering company and thus save the heavily invested St. Louisans. The two put together a syndicate of independent telephone companies. It included Kinloch of St. Louis, which raised $6 million toward the purchase of the United States Telephone Company of Rochester, New York, and a telephone supply plant. Hoping to raise $6 million more for the corporate reorganization of the foundering company, the purchase would give the independents control of about 75 percent of the country's 1907 telephone mileage. Adolphus Busch invested in the syndicate of independents.

The hopeful purchase fell through. In 1908, the Supreme Court of New York declared a "judgment and decree of foreclosure" against the United States Independent Telephone Company. The St. Louis investors lost millions; a slew of lawsuits followed. In 1912, the stockholders of the defunct company sued the voting trustees for $2 million. Breckinridge Jones was one of those named in the lawsuit. A year later, Adolphus Busch was sued for $750,000 on the grounds that Busch "induced" the plaintiffs to purchase stock in the defunct telephone company by "misrepresentations." Busch's New York properties were at stake. In 1913, Busch lost a lawsuit filed against him by the Rochester telephone supply plant, which was nearly taken down with the defunct telephone company. A judge ordered Busch to pay $27,636 in that suit. He died later that year. Two years later, Edward Faust and the Busch attorney, both executors of the estate of Adolphus Busch, were continuing to fight that lawsuit. Busch relatives told reporters that his purchase of stock in the United States

Independent Telephone Company was the "worst investment he ever made."[27]

On May 19, 1918, the Mississippi Valley Waterways Association decided to send a delegation to Washington, DC, to "urge upon the Government the taking of the lower Mississippi as part of the Federal transportation system."[28] The US government had already taken control of the Erie Canal for the war effort. The St. Louis group felt that such action on the Mississippi River would enhance river traffic, and thus the economy. Edward Faust was selected as delegate.

When the St. Louis committee arrived in Washington, DC, they joined delegations from the entire Mississippi River Valley. The representatives took their case to Secretary of the Treasury William Gibbs McAdoo, Director General of the United States Railroad Administration. The United States government had nationalized American railroads in 1917 for the war effort. The Inland Waterways Committee was created to ease congestion of railroad shipping. Edward Faust and other delegates explained to the officials that barges and powerboats could be built in St. Louis quickly and easily. The city stood ready to do its part. The delegation of men explained that not just St. Louis, but every city up and down the Mississippi River would benefit from the economy brought by river traffic.

In July, McAdoo gave the go-ahead and assigned M.J. Sanders, a New Orleans shipman, to head the operation called *Mississippi Warrior Waterways* by the United States government. The government would conscript available boats and barges for use on the upper Mississippi and planned to contract for a fleet to be built for use on the lower Mississippi (St. Louis to New Orleans). The Inland Waterways Committee recommended the construction of seven towboats (used to propel barges) and 50 steel barges. The government would cover the costs and production of some of the boats. The Committee requested that the St. Louis representatives prepare information as to what St. Louis could contribute toward the speedy construction of the barge line. Edward Faust spoke to the inquiry, recommending the immediate organization of a shipbuilding company and the construction of shipyards. He estimated that "St. Louis could complete within 12 months all seven towboats and 24 of the barges of material obtained within the city" at the rate of one towboat and two barges a month.[29] Edward announced that a company in Granite City, Illinois, near St. Louis, planned to set aside 1,000 tons of steel monthly. Edward also reported that St. Louis engine companies would manufacture the towboat engines and St. Louis boiler companies stood ready to manufacture the boilers.

The president of the Mississippi Valley Waterways Association pressed for urgency. "We must at once organize the shippers of St. Louis, so that when the Government boats are ready to move St. Louis will be the first city to offer a full cargo."[30] The shippers were the key. Sanders optimistically reported that St. Louis shippers promised to ship all southbound freight by water. He encouraged the merchants and manufacturers to stand by their word. He reminded them, "The Treasury of the United States stands back of any deficits we might have." To further entice shippers and to relieve the strained railroads, freight tariffs were issued "on the basis of 20 per cent less than railroad traffic."[31]

By September, the Government had assembled 30 steel

barges and seven towboats for immediate use on the lower Mississippi River. On September 28, 1918, the operation officially began when one towboat pushed three loaded barges away from St. Louis on their way to New Orleans. The *St. Louis Post-Dispatch* pronounced,

> The day and hour is accounted of moment in the commercial prosperity of the city and one that portends the revival of the use of the Mississippi River as a great shipping highway.[32]

The businessmen of St. Louis rejoiced. After a celebratory luncheon at the Planter's Hotel filled with congratulatory speeches, the group walked to the water to watch the mayor's daughter break a bottle of Mississippi River water over the bow of the towboat before it pushed off.

In October, the newspaper declared, "The permanency of the St. Louis-New Orleans barge line is assured."[33] This proclamation was due to McAdoo's announcement that the United States was contracting for six steamers and 40 steel barges. All would be permanent vessels in the barge fleet of the lower Mississippi River. These contracts were announced after the War Industries Board indicated that there was an adequate steel supply in the United States to begin building the watercraft. St. Louis businessmen again exulted. The war ended less than three weeks later.[34]

Edward made another trip to Washington, DC, in February 1919. His St. Louis Boat and Engineering Company had been awarded a contract by the government for the construction of four barges. Edward negotiated the terms of the agreement. He returned to St. Louis and proudly announced the $1 million deal, making plans for the construction of a shipyard at the end of Franklin Street on the Mississippi River. Edward proclaimed that the project would employ 300 to 400 people. He planned to offer St. Louis companies the opportunity to bid on the making of the boilers, engines, and other components of the vessels. The building of the river craft in St. Louis, he said, [will be a] "stimulus to the project of waterways development" and "an important addition to the city industrially."[35]

Four months later, Major General William M. Black, Chief of Engineers of the United States Army, made an important visit to St. Louis. He awarded Edward Faust and his St. Louis Boat and Engineering Company a contract for the construction of four towboats to be used to propel barges on the upper Mississippi. The project was another coup for St. Louis manufacturers:

> The barges were authorized as a war measure and leased to the Mississippi Iron Co. of St. Louis to bring ore from the Minnesota iron ranges to St. Louis, returning with coal from Illinois fields.[36]

As a member of the executive committee of the Mississippi Valley Association, Edward continued to travel to Washington, DC. He tirelessly lobbied for the use of inland waterways for shipping. In April 1921, two years after Edward began construction of his shipyard, he celebrated the completion of the third of the four barges. He was joined by an impressive coterie of dignitaries, including such military brass as Brigadier General W.W. Harts, Colonel E.J. Dent, and Major J.S. Schley; as well as Colonel John H. Parker, commandant of Jefferson Barracks; Colonel T.J. Ashburn of the division of Inland and Coastwise Waterways of the War Department; and Colonel Potter of the US Army Engineering Corps. The Jefferson Barracks band played, and several thousand people lined the docks and cheered as the champagne bottle broke over the bow and the barge was launched.[37]

Edward's strenuous business agenda did not include management of his late father's famous restaurant. Before his illness and death, Anthony R. kept the place humming and, in keeping with tradition, threw a fantastic New Year's party to usher in 1909. The *St. Louis Post-Dispatch* recorded the event, noting that tables had been reserved for years. An orchestra played to a packed house. Each table received a complimentary bottle of wine to accompany their oysters. *Faust* red devil hats and noisemakers were passed around, and electric lights spelling "1909" lit up the room at midnight.

> In the center of the room, as has been the New Year's custom for a quarter of a century, sat the Faust family. Most plainly gowned woman in the hall was Mrs. Elizabeth Faust, widow of A.E. Faust, founder of the restaurant. Facing her was Mrs. Mollie Giannini, her daughter, and ranged about them were other Fausts…[38]

This was the last hurrah of Tony Faust's restaurant.

When Anthony R. fell ill, the St. Louis Catering Company assumed ownership of the restaurant. The Southern Hotel closed its great doors in 1912. In 1915, Henry C. Dietz, Tony Faust's former chef, purchased the struggling restaurant. The St. James Hotel, located across from the old Southern Hotel, announced its closing one year later. The Olympic Theater, across from Faust's restaurant, would not open its doors for the coming theater season. Once part of the thriving city center, the iconic restaurant now stood hopelessly tranquil while the flourishing commercial district moved westward…and onward.

On the last day that Faust's restaurant opened its doors for business, a sign hung over the bar: "Au revoir, but not goodby." Lately, there had been crowds only for lunch, and the establishment stood empty during the once-busy dinner and night shifts. The waiters, some of whom had worked at Faust's for 30 years, wept as they carried steins to customers for the last time. As they worked, the wait staff sang German songs in farewell to the restaurant that once was the Delmonico's of the West. Then, it was over.

An auction of the contents of the restaurant was held in July 1916. The sale was a success for the entertainment value, but not the monetary value. Everything was sold. Men purchased beer steins with the Faust trademark for mementos. Wine, champagne, and liquor sold by the bottle. German linens, silver, china, cash registers, and even the Elm Street window awnings were sold.

At the start of the auction the auctioneer explained that "the contents of the restaurant in their present condition [were] worth at least $30,000. Their original cost was much greater." After the sale, the gross receipts tallied to a measly $4,000. A cut crystal chandelier from the second-floor dining room sold for $25, not the anticipated value of $600. A $660 mirror sold for $15.50. The mahogany furniture sold for $1.20 per chair, $1.25 to $2.40 per table, and $11 for the massive mahogany sideboard. Mural paintings and tapestries, purchased by the Fausts for thousands, sold for a pittance.[39]

Edward was a forward-thinking business man. He probably saw this coming. No matter. As his father's torch went out, his son Leicester Faust's fire began to burn.

BOOK THREE

Leicester Busch Faust.
Courtesy of Missouri History Museum, St. Louis

Chapter 1
THE JOYS OF YOUTH

Leicester Faust received an excellent education. As a child, he first attended a little school that had been transformed from a fine home on Washington Avenue. He was one of a select group of students, and was driven to school by the family's chauffeur.[1] Leicester then followed in his father's footsteps by attending Smith Academy, along with August A.'s son August Anheuser Busch, Jr. (Gussie). Like his father, Leicester took academics seriously. In fact, he entered Smith Academy one grade level ahead of his age group. Gussie, on the other hand, geared his attention toward athletics, particularly Smith Academy's football team (Leicester was never accused of being athletic). Gussie also had a passion for boxing. He perhaps took after *his* father, who had been in several barroom brawls at Tony Faust's saloon.[2]

Leicester Busch Faust.
Courtesy of Missouri History Museum, St. Louis

As children, Leicester and Gussie were raised together for a time at 1 Busch Place. Gussie's address changed to 2 Busch Place, the newly built second mansion on the grounds of the brewery, in 1911. However, the two cousins did not truly live apart until 1914, when Leicester, at age 16, moved with his family to 1 Portland Place and Gussie, at age 14, moved with his family to Grant's Farm.³

Leicester attended Smith Academy in St. Louis until he was 15 or 16 years old. Then, like other kids from the West End, his parents sent him off to boarding school. Leicester traveled to New York to attend the Lake Placid School, a college preparatory school set in the Adirondack Mountains. The school offered year-round "out-of-door life" made possible by transferring the entire school population to sunny Florida during the winter months.

Anna wanted Leicester to attend Yale, but his grades from Lake Placid School were not good enough to gain him admission. Anna knew her son's dream was to be a farmer, so they struck a deal. If he could get into Yale, she would buy him a farm. Leicester moved to Cambridge, Massachusetts, and attended preparatory classes with several other young men. Soon, he passed the entrance exams for Yale.⁴

Anna spent a month in 1917 touring St. Louis County in search of a picturesque property. She found it about 14 miles west of Clayton and about a half-mile south of the Missouri River, near the tiny rural town of Chesterfield. In July 1917, Edward Faust paid $16,400 for the first 80 acres of his son's dream. That December, on the day before his twenty-first birthday, Edward and Anna sold the country property to Leicester for $1, with "love and affection."⁵

In September 1918, when Leicester was 20 years old, he began his first semester as an undergraduate at Yale. He also registered for the draft and was inducted into the Army one month later. The World War I ended in November. Private Faust was honorably discharged from the United States Army in December 1918. That fall at Yale, Leicester enrolled in the Student Army Training Corps. He proudly kept his uniform from that stint for years.[6]

While living in New Haven, Leicester fell victim to the 1918 flu pandemic. Because he had nearly died after contracting typhoid fever in Europe when he was younger, Anna was frightened. She and her personal maid bravely visited Leicester and other Yale students in a hospital in Connecticut. After only a year at the Ivy League school, Leicester came home. He recovered and continued his education in his hometown of St. Louis at the esteemed Washington University. In 1921, in his junior year, Leicester posed for a yearbook photo with the rest of his Law Class of 1922.[7]

Back in St. Louis, Leicester began to develop his farm. The heirs of Henry Jackson, an African-American, had sold the property to the Fausts. The deed of sale specified that though they would retain possession of the land until November of that year, 19-year-old Leicester could begin making improvements right away. By 1919, his farm had a new house and at least three outbuildings. They were designed by none other than Tom Barnett, architect of 1 Portland Place.[8]

The house and outbuildings were built in the Pueblo Revival style, "derived from the Native American pueblos and early Spanish Colonial buildings of the American Southwest." The American Southwest and its culture became popular in the early 1900s as wealthy Americans "rediscovered" it through art and travel, particularly to Santa Fe and Taos. Leicester's farm buildings fully reflected the Pueblo Revival style:

> ...characterized by earth-colored stucco walls, battered buttresses, flat roofs with parapet walls, projecting wooden roof beams (called vigas) deepset openings and slightly irregular rounded edges."[9]

Fittingly, Leicester named his estate "Swastika Farms" after the "broken cross pattern found in Hopi and Pueblo art."[10] Leicester emblazoned the swastika symbol and the name "Swastika Farms" on everything, including playing cards, stationery, his cutlery, and the grandiose entrance gates to his property.

Entrance to Swastika Farms.
Courtesy of Jane Keough

Now and then, Leicester spent weekends living in the new bachelor house on his farm. However, he continued to permanently live with his parents (and their five German servants) at 1 Portland Place while he attended Washington University. In 1918, 21-year-old Leicester hired 18-year-old Fred Sellenriek to work as a hired man at Swastika Farms. The young man was tasked with managing the Farm in Leicester's absence. Fred was raised on his family's farm on White Road, across Olive Street Road, the gravel road that bordered Leicester's property. Fred loved farm life and hated school; he was allowed to drop out in the fourth grade. Though he was only a couple of years younger than Leicester and "slow with his numbers," young Fred proved to be a great asset.[11]

Leicester fully understood the agricultural industry. He recognized the need for a grain elevator in the Chesterfield region. At that time, the area's farmers took their grain, by wagon and mule, all the way into St. Louis. In 1919, Leicester organized the Chesterfield Farmers Elevator and Supply Company, with a prime location along a rail line. As the primary stockholder, Leicester became president. Area farmers became stockholders of the elevator and its store, which sold farm goods. "The plant numbers among its various products the high-grade and popular Swastika Brand Flour." Leicester had become a successful entrepreneur.[12]

Neither his schooling nor his business interests kept Leicester Faust from a lively social life. He was one of the original 80 "beaux" to organize the dancing club *Le Minuet* in 1920. The group sent invitations to belles and debutantes of St. Louis society. The couples danced to orchestral music at the St. Louis Woman's Club on the second and fourth Fridays of the month.[13]

The *St. Louis Post-Dispatch*, ever delighted to report on the social life of the elite, listed two accounts of Leicester's parties in its society pages in 1921 and 1922:

> Leicester Faust of 1 Portland place will be a host at a tea Sunday afternoon at his farm on the Olive street road.[14]

> Miss Audrey Faust, daughter of Mr. and Mrs. Edward A. Faust, 1 Portland place, will entertain with a house party over the next week-end at Leicester Faust's farm, the "Swastika," on Olive Street road.[15]

The Bachelor House.
Courtesy of Jane Keough

Leicester Faust's aunt, Mollie Giannini, lived with her daughter and son-in-law, Vera and Eugene Angert. Vera and Eugene had purchased a home on Kent Road in Ladue where they raised their young family, Eugene Jr., Vera, and Claire. In the winter of 1917, 51-year-old Mollie had surgery at Barnes Hospital for a "cancer." Mollie passed away a year later, on March 9, 1918. Edward Faust buried his sister Mollie in the Faust family plot at Bellefontaine

Cemetery with his father, mother, and brother.[16]

Vera held a Christmas Party at her home in 1918, her first Christmas without her mother. She asked Samuel Plant, a friend of her husband, to dress up as Santa Claus to surprise her children. Samuel brought along his wife and his daughter, Mary. There Mary visited with Vera's cousin, Audrey Faust. She also met Audrey's brother, Leicester Faust, home from Yale. Mary and Leicester chatted while looking at ornaments on the Christmas tree. When Vera asked them to locate a particular ornament, Leicester and Mary crawled under the tree. Under the cover of the fragrant branches, the two stole a kiss and began a courtship.[17]

Mary Plant was born November 4, 1900, to Clara and Samuel Plant in St. Louis, Missouri. She was born into prominence on both her mother's and her father's side. Samuel Plant carried on his family's milling interests. His great-uncle, George P. Plant, had built the Franklin Flour Mill at Franklin and Broadway in 1840. George P.'s nephew George H. Plant built a new flour mill at Chouteau and Main in 1884. "By the turn of the century, annual production was about 400,000 barrels of flour, which were shipped to all parts of the United States, Europe, and particularly the West Indies." Mary Plant's father, Samuel Plant, succeeded his father, George H., in 1918.[18]

Her mother, Clara Ewing Plant, was a direct descendent of Marie Thérèse Chouteau and Pierre Laclede, the founder of St. Louis. Her family, wholesale grocers, were truly "native" St. Louisans of French descent.[19] Clara, quiet and reserved, grew up in a large French- and English-speaking family. Clara's mother passed away when she was still a young woman. Clara helped to raise her youngest two brothers. She had the assistance of a houseful of Irish maids "fresh off the boat." The privileged Ewing family had an African-American coachman who drove the spirited team of horses and lived above the stables with his wife.[20]

Mary Plant's parents, Samuel and Clara, married at the Ewing family home on Locust Street. After a honeymoon in Havana, not long after the Spanish-American War, little Mary Plant was born. Mary's mother "didn't know a saucepan from a skillet." Mary, an only child, knew of nothing else than to be surrounded by a houseful of Irish servants. Mary knew she was different from the other children of her social class. Her mother took her places while the others stayed home with their nurses and nannies. Mary was just a little girl when she accompanied her mother on many trips to the 1904 World's Fair. There they dined at the Lüchow-Faust Restaurant in the Tyrolean Alps.

Mary grew up making an exodus every summer to her mother's family's vacation home in Minnesota. Her grandfather vacationed with them. Her mother's sister's family joined them from New Orleans. Her father, Samuel, had a demanding business schedule and would join the family only for a couple of weeks, if at all. Servants would pack the family's bags and load them onto the train at Union Station in St. Louis. Mary and her family would follow in her grandfather's Victoria, a lovely carriage, pulled by four horses driven by her grandfather's coachman. The coachman would drive under the porte cochère at Union Station, and the family would step onto the train. After a day and a half, Mary's family arrived in Minnesota. Their coachman would join the family with the carriage and horses, having journeyed up the Mississippi River using river transportation.[21]

In 1912, 12-year-old Mary moved with her family out of St. Louis into the country. Settling on six acres on Cella Road, Samuel Plant was one of the first to build a home in that part of St. Louis County. Called "Easton Farms," Samuel Plant's brick home was magnificent. The red brick, Georgian Revival home was huge, with outstanding architectural features and elaborate interior décor. Mary adored life there, and she learned to love gardening from her mother. She and her mother were each given their own horse. Mary loved to explore their little farm, where they raised horses, cattle, hogs, chickens, and ducks. Her father, described by Mary as a "man's man," had many caretakers for their property. He was free to tinker with his cars (he was one of the first to own a car in St. Louis, a Stanley Steamer) or go on one of his many hunting trips in Nebraska. He was also a "good, strong, God-loving man" who became Catholic, to the pleasure of Mary's deeply religious mother, who took Mary to church every Sunday.[22]

Mary attended school at Sacred Heart Convent in St. Louis, also called "City House."[23] Samuel Plant drove his daughter to school in his Packard, dropping Mary off at school on his way to work. After school, Mary took the streetcar home. From the time she was 12, she rode the 04 home alone. When Mary was 14, her parents sent her to boarding school.

Mary attended Miss Wright's School in Bryn Mawr, Pennsylvania. Founded by Eliza Mary Wright, the school sat on seven acres of land that housed a stable, gym, basketball court, and infirmary. Mary attended Miss Wright's with a number of St. Louis girls, including Audrey Faust. She had a large circle of friends. Like the others, Mary's mother hosted garden parties and teas at Easton Farms when her daughter was home during school breaks. In spite of her friends and the lovely school grounds, Mary loathed school. Her one bright spot was her economics classes. She found herself tutoring other students. The subject came naturally to her: she'd had economics lessons from her father at the dinner table for years. Mary quit school in 1916 at the age of 16 and never returned to a classroom again.[24]

Life was gay when one needn't take a job. Back in St. Louis, Mary was a socialite. The *St. Louis Post-Dispatch* printed a picture of her with a group of girlfriends lounging in their bathing suits, swim caps and stockings next to the high dive at the Sunset Hill Country Club swimming pool. Socializing became even better when the Doughboys returned from the war.[25]

Just after she turned 20, Mary Plant made her bow to society at her debutante ball, thrown for her by her parents at the St. Louis Country Club. Four hundred guests attended the lavish soirée. The club was decorated with flowers; pink roses decorated the tables. Mary wore "a gown of silver cloth" and carried a bouquet of pink roses.[26]

As socialites do, Mary involved herself in philanthropy. When she left Miss Wright's School in 1916, Mary threw herself into the war effort. She learned to drive, taught first by her family's chauffer (fun), then by her father ("painful"). Mary drove herself around St. Louis in a Dodge, helping to wrap bandages and attending fund-raisers.[27]

Mary was a suffragette. Preceding a suffrage demonstration, she played a role in a tableau on the steps of the "old Art Museum" on Nineteenth and Locust Streets. Reported the local newspaper:
> In the tableau each state in which the women are

allowed to vote will be represented by a woman attired in white. Each nation in which women are enfranchised will be represented by… women attired in the national colors, while each state in which partial suffrage has been granted will be represented by a woman attired in gray. The states in which women are denied the vote will be represented by women in black.[28]

Mary Plant also was deeply involved in the Junior League. By the time she was 21 years old, she was vice president of the St. Louis chapter of the Junior League. The *St. Louis Post-Dispatch* interviewed Mary and the chapter's president in December 1921. The reporter sought comment on the criticisms of American society girls by an English writer, Elinor Glyn. Ms. Glyn, with disgust, attested that American women "in her hour of ease" never "had a seriously occupied moment." The *Post-Dispatch* reporter acknowledged that the very class of girl chastised in Ms. Glyn's article comprised the membership ranks of the Junior League.

> The members of this organization are all girls or young matrons of the leisure class. Its ranks are recruited from those groups who figure most prominently in the society news. Most of the members have made their formal debuts with all that implies of deliberate pleasure seeking.

Revealing her powerful personality, Mary Plant scoffed at Ms. Glyn's allegations that "nothing seems sacred to them; nothing satisfies them. They are like vampires sucking blood" and "morality among American girls is at a low level." Mary took offense, especially, to the "morality" comment. She quoted from Ms. Glyn's list of moral offenses, "Lipstick, eyebrow pencils and rouge." Mary asked, "Well, what of it? What has painting your face got to do with morality?" Mary jeered at the notion that American girls' lack of corsets and shorter skirts were seductive. Rather, she proclaimed, they were liberating.

A more telling defense, however, was in the list of activities conducted by the Junior League. Members of the group served as waitresses at a public school lunchroom serving some of the city's poorest children. They assisted nurses in the city's "baby clinics." The League split into committees: one committee offered aid to blind women; another delivered a daily batch of flowers to the hospital; while yet another mobilized "motor cars" to transport ill people to doctors and wounded soldiers on outings. The society girls hosted carnivals and balls, and they put on plays to raise funds. In essence, they worked.[29]

Mary Plant and Leicester Faust announced their engagement on June 15, 1921. As their January wedding day approached, the *St. Louis Post-Dispatch* announced, "Because of the prominence of both families, the Faust-Plant nuptials will be one of the most important of the season."[30] In the days before the wedding, the couple attended numerous engagement parties thrown in their honor, including a lavish celebration at the St. Louis Country Club and dinner parties in West End homes. Finally, six days before the wedding, Leicester hosted his "farewell bachelor dinner" at Swastika Farms, while Mary invited the ladies of her bridal party for a gathering at her parents' home, Easton Farms.[31]

The couple was married on January 14, 1922, at 5:00 p.m. in the living room at Easton Farms. The home was decked with palms and banked with lilies. Six bridesmaids and six groomsmen stood up for the couple. Audrey Faust was the bride's maid of honor. Following the ceremony, the wedding party and guests (including Lilly Busch, who traveled from Pasadena, California, to attend) celebrated with a dinner and a reception. Leicester and his new bride sailed for Europe soon after. They embarked on a honeymoon during which they visited Paris, Rome, Milan, and of course, Busch relatives in Germany. After three months, the newlyweds came home to Swastika Farms.[32]

Wedding of Leicester Faust and Mary Plant, January 14, 1922.
Courtesy of Missouri History Museum, St. Louis

Chapter 2
GOLF, TULIPS, ANGUS, AND FINALLY, BEER

During the 1920s, there were 10 or so golf clubs in St. Louis. Each club had women who competed, but only a few were exceptional. Audrey Faust was one was St. Louis Country Club's finest.

The St. Louis Country Club was relocated to the intersection of Price Road and Ladue Road in 1913. When it officially opened in 1914, the year the Fausts moved into 1 Portland Place, the club offered golf, polo, tennis, and swimming. Although the club was in the country on the outskirts of St. Louis, members soon surrounded the property with large, lovely homes.[1]

In 1921, 19-year-old Audrey was coached by Stewart Maiden, the professional golfer from Atlanta who also mentored the legendary Bobby Jones. In women's golf, Audrey rose to the rank of seventh in the world. Though opportunities for women to compete were far fewer than for men, Audrey traveled the country to play golf. The *New York Times* reported on golf tournaments in which Audrey played, including the 1922 tournament at White Sulfur Springs, West Virginia. Citing that 1922 golf tournament, *Golf Illustrated* wrote that Audrey was "one of America's strongest players, and has a fighting spirit excelled by none."[2] And in 1923, *The American Golfer* described Audrey as a player "of nerve and skill. . .to be reckoned with."[3] Audrey made history in 1924 in one of the greatest matches of all time, proclaimed by the *St. Louis Globe-Democrat* to be "one of if not the most grueling final matches that has ever attended a women's tournament in St. Louis."[4]   In the exciting duel, Audrey barely beat her nemesis and friend, Virginia Pepp.[5]

Audrey Faust.
September 7, 1922, St. Louis Post-Dispatch

Audrey and Virginia traded turns at winning titles through the 1920s and 1930s. Unlike Audrey, Virginia was a "public player from Triple A-Forest Park."[6] Audrey was known to send a car to fetch Virginia so she could practice at the St. Louis Country Club. This typified Audrey's reputation in the golf community. She was known as classy: "Audrey retained the qualities that made her a champion on and off the course."[7]

In 1924, the newspapers no longer reported her golf scores under the name of "Miss Audrey Faust." She was called her by her new married name, "Mrs. Mahlon Brookings Wallace, Jr." Audrey had married the son of Mahlon Brookings Wallace, a contemporary of Edward Faust's. After their wedding, Audrey and Mahlon Jr. took a hunting-trip honeymoon in Canada. Edward Faust hired the architectural firm of Maritz, Young & Dusard to build his daughter a home. Audrey's "Casa Audlon" became one of the lovely homes surrounding the St. Louis Country Club golf course.[8]

Leicester's sister had married into a well-bred family. Mahlon Jr.'s grandfather served as the United States assistant treasurer under President Taft. His grandmother was Mary Jane Brookings, whose brother Robert helped establish both Washington University and the Brookings Institute in Washington, DC.[9] Mahlon Jr.'s father purchased the Standard Pencil Company in 1915. He moved it from Kansas City to Locust Street in St. Louis. The company printed advertisements on pencils. When pencils became hard to obtain from manufacturers during World War I, the senior Wallace began the Wallace Pencil Company and manufactured his own pencils. By 1928, he had moved the plant to South Hanley Road, a country road through farmland. Audrey's husband soon rose to vice president of the company. In addition, he bought out Hugh Steele, owner of a clothespin- and toothpick-making company in 1928. He renamed his new company the Steele-Wallace Corporation and maintained plants in West Virginia and Wisconsin.[10]

Audrey and Mahlon Jr. began their family in 1934 when they adopted the first of their two children, Mahlon Busch Wallace III (called "Lonnie"). Audrey Faust Wallace (called "Tolie") joined the family in 1936. Anna Hohn, an immigrant from Germany, had worked for Audrey and Mahlon Jr. since 1924. It was she who primarily raised little Lonnie and Tolie. Audrey "was more interested in doing things outside." Ms. Hohn was an "enormous" part of Audrey's children's lives, and was forever dear to them. She worked for the family for 60 years.[11]

Leicester's cousin Vera and her husband, Eugene Angert, enjoyed their life on Kent Road in Ladue. Eugene, the attorney who loved gardening, founded and became president of the St. Louis Horticultural Society. He developed a glorious garden on their property along Kent Road,
> To him the day for potting seedlings or for going to a rural wood to seek wild flora, was more sacred than any other. [He was] dressed in old faded clothes and a weather-beaten hat, his characteristic pipe clenched between his teeth, digging deep into the ground and placing there an infant plant, or stooping in ecstasy before a little starlike flower pushing its way up among a mass of rock.[12]

Each spring the family opened their garden for the public to enjoy the wonderland of tulips, wild flowers, and blossoming shrubs. Said one visitor, "It's as near to heaven as I ever expect to get."[13]

As crowds thronged amongst his tulips in May 1929, 51-year-old Eugene Angert died at a hospital in St. Louis. He had succumbed to "septic poisoning" that followed the removal of a hair from his nose.[14] Fifteen-year-old Eugene memorialized his father, who was known as a devoted family man,

> To me, my father was first of all a companion. No finer, no more frank understanding could exist between father and son. He gave as much attention to remedying my minor difficulties as to his important business affairs. To him business and family life were two things apart; and he gave unselfishly to both.[15]

Eugene Angert was laid to rest at the ever-growing Faust family plot in the Bellefontaine Cemetery.

Sixteen months after her first husband's death, 43-year-old Vera Giannini Angert married Dr. Borden S. Veeder. The groom, who had served as a Lieutenant Colonel of a Base Hospital unit in France in World War I, was a nationally recognized authority on children's diseases who served on the teaching staff at Washington University Medical School. After their wedding, Dr. Veeder moved in with Vera, her children, and their governess in the home with the lovely garden on Kent Road.[16]

Mary and Leicester returned from their honeymoon in April 1922. They lived at Swastika Farms only in the summers. They first resided in the little bachelor house originally built for Leicester. Soon, though, they moved into the 'big house' upon its completion. Leicester loved the southwest Indian style and filled their home with that décor. Outside, both Leicester and Mary gardened. She employed the skills she learned from her mother at Easton Farms.[17]

Leicester and Mary lived in St. Louis when the weather turned cold. Their trusted farm manager, Fred Sellenriek, and his new bride, Myrtle, ran the place in their absence. The first winter, the Fausts lived on Lake Avenue, where their daughter Lily Claire (called "Claire") was born in

1923. Ann came along three winters later, when the couple lived on Waterman Avenue. The family then purchased an apartment on Lindell Avenue, and the girls attended school at City House (Sacred Heart Convent), as their mother had. At the Farm (the casual name given to Swastika Farms by the farmhands) in the summers, Mary determined that the big house was just too crowded with their entire family and their servants. So Leicester and Mary lived in the big house with two maids and a cook, while little Claire, Ann, and their nannies lived in the guesthouse next door.[18]

The Big House.
Courtesy of Jane Keough

By the end of its first decade, Swastika Farms had become a showplace. Leicester supervised the planting of more than 25 different species of evergreens on his property. The trees were cultivated in the farm's greenhouse. In his evergreen "forest," Leicester created what he called a "deer preserve." Along a hillside and into a valley, a spring-fed stream flowed through the heavily wooded, 35-acre area. Leicester explained:

In this forest are eight deer. I began with only two. You can see that the preserve is fenced in with a low wire fence, thus allowing the deer a larger range than the enclosure, as they can easily jump the fence, and at the same time keeping my other stock out, as wild life production would be a failure if not segregated from domesticated animals.[19]

The Farm.
Courtesy of Jane Keough

Leicester fully trusted his farm manager, Fred Sellenriek, to carry out the ambitious dreams he had for the Farm. Fred, who was a stickler for detail, did well in fulfilling Leicester's goal of creating a self-sustaining farm. Besides the milk and butter from the Jersey cows, eggs from the chickens, pork from the hogs, and produce from the gardens, Leicester's farm produced strawberries, wheat, corn, and alfalfa. Fred used mules to plow and plant the wheat and corn. Threshing crews would move from farm to farm, and all the farmhands pitched in. Fred was in charge, and his wife, Myrtle, was tasked with feeding the crew.

Fred oversaw the livestock production. Two hundred head of sheep dotted the pastures of the Farm. Leicester was incredibly proud of his flock of White Rock chickens, 200 strong and prize winners at poultry shows. Thanks to architect Tom Barnett, the chickens were housed in a state-of-the art chicken coop, nay, a chicken *house* built to furnish all the creature comforts a prize chicken might need. Yet that does not compare to the barn provided for Leicester's greater pride and joy, his Angus cattle.[20]

The Chicken House.
Courtesy of Jane Keough

Leicester owned about 100 head of registered Black Angus cattle. There were papers for every cow. The Farm usually had one, no more than two breeding bulls. The pastures were divided, and the cattle were rotated through. As each catch pasture was grazed down, they moved the cattle to the next, and the first would recover. Each cow had an ear tag as well as a chain around her neck with a corresponding number.

Leicester used a breeding program. Each cow was put in with the bull on a schedule. Fred's wife, Myrtle, was in charge of the papers. She kept a big ledger-type book with the detailed bloodlines. Fred separated the cows that were good breeders. The others were fattened for market or sold via ads in the newspaper. Generally, though, neither was necessary. People became eager to purchase the Fausts' cattle just by word of mouth. Leicester belonged to the Angus Association of Missouri, and Fred showed the cattle in the County Fair.[21]

In 1925, Leicester's father, Edward, hosted a group of businessmen, engineers, and architects at his home at 1 Portland Place. The men gathered for a lecture with movies. Edward introduced a building structure called "lamella." It was thought that a housing official in Dessau, Germany, invented the design, which consisted of wooden ribs "curved on one edge, beveled at both ends, and connected into a continuous network, having the appearance of a fish net and the effect of an arch. They are short, easily handled, and when set into a curved roof have great strength, due to their mutual bracing."[22] The concept worked in Germany: the economical lamella design easily increased attic space when the country was faced with housing shortages and construction restrictions.[23]

The lamella technique was patented. In the mid-1920s, the Lamella Roof Syndicate, Inc., was set up in New York. Franchises were set up in 20 cities in the United States and Canada. Edward Faust invested in the local firm, called the Missouri Lamella Roof Company. He invited the company's construction officer, 23-year-old German immigrant Gustel R. Kiewitt, to build a barn with the lamella construction on Leicester's farm. The spectacular barn, 50 by 100 feet and 36 feet high at the roof's apex, was built in 1925. The Farm's pure-bred Angus cattle were housed there.[24]

Interior of the Lamella barn. The architectural design provided space, strength, and beauty. (This photo was taken during 1996 repairs).
Courtesy of St. Louis County Parks

Edward proclaimed Leicester's lamella barn to be the first sample of the lamella construction style in the United States. Three years later, Ben G. Brinkman, a Miami promoter, encouraged Edward Faust and other St. Louis capitalists to bankroll an arena on Oakland Avenue in St. Louis. The wealthy industrialists hoped to lure the National Dairy Show to St. Louis. Kiewitt's Arena was one of many lamella buildings subsequently built in St. Louis.[25]

At the Farm, the lamella barn had a concrete floor, calf pens, hay mows, and steer pens. The ceiling had a track in the center, and a trolley ran the track with a series of ropes that an operator would use. Then a claw would go into the hay wagon and lift up the loose hay into the hay mow. It was a five-man operation.

Leicester's Angus cows calved in the spring. At weaning time, the calves were put into an area in the lamella barn with their feed: an area in which the cows wouldn't fit. Calving pens, complete with sheds, lined up along the west broadside of the lamella barn and were called the "Maternity Ward." The two friendly Angus bulls lounged beyond the maternity ward's confines.[26] By 1936, Edward had been president of the Missouri Lamella Roof Company for several years. Leicester served as his vice president.[27]

Lamella barn.
Courtesy of St. Louis County Parks

During the years of Prohibition, the cost of beer increased 600 percent from 1916. As a result, the ban was more readily violated by those in the upper class rather than those in the working class.[28] The Fausts probably imbibed. In fact,
> In 1925, a federal grand jury in New York began investigating a nationwide bootleg syndicate that shipped liquor in truckload lots to twenty thousand customers in seventy large cities in twenty-nine

states. Every member of the St. Louis Country Club was on the ring's prospective customer list...Tracing the buyers was difficult, because it was common practice for the buyers to use fictitious names and addresses.[29]

Prohibition had been a long time coming. The soft rumblings of Prohibition kept brewers and saloon keepers alert throughout the late nineteenth century. In 1881, a group of brewers, including Adolphus Busch and William J. Lemp, sat around a table at Tony Faust's discussing the issue with their host. What would happen should it come to pass? Said one,

> It would prove disastrous to the prosperity of the city and State; it would be disastrous to our tax lists. The brewers and malsters of this city alone pay about $720,000 annually in State, city and Government taxes. There is more than $6,000,000 capital invested in brewing in St. Louis, and the money interest involved, when you take into consideration the manufacture of glass bottles, the cooper trade, the ice business, and other dependent branches of industry, will amount to over $8,000,000.

And it wasn't just the financial factor...

> Then, besides, there are about 5,000 men employed in our breweries, all Germans, and each having a family, making more than 20,000 people whose bread is earned in this business.[30]

Like the brewers who convened at Tony Faust's in 1881, the government was aware of the immense revenue supplied by the alcohol industry. In fact, until 1913 liquor taxes supplied as much as 40 percent of the federal government's annual revenue. But with the ratification of the Sixteenth Amendment in 1913, the new source revenue from income taxes was seen as a replacement for the liquor levy. This provided the impetus to move toward enacting Prohibition.[31]

The movement made for unlikely bedfellows. Clergy, motivated by their faith, sided with reformers, led by Jane Addams, who saw "the devastating effect that drunkenness had on the urban poor." The Ku Klux Klan, whose anti-liquor sentiment stemmed from their hatred of immigrants, bedded with the Industrial Workers of the World, who believed that "liquor was a capitalist weapon used to keep the working classes in a stupor."[32]

If the brewers (who often owned saloons in towns and cities) and the saloon keepers had been more forward thinking, perhaps Prohibition could have been avoided. Perhaps they might have enforced earlier closing times, placed limits on the number of alcoholic beverages served, and so forth, rather than taking the all-or-nothing stance. They dug in their heels. It wasn't until a few years before Prohibition became law that they softened their position. By then, moderates who wished for temperance, not a complete ban on alcohol, had been forced to take the side of prohibitionists.

Finally, in a last-ditch effort, August A. Busch tried to please everyone. In 1917, he built Bevo Mill, a restaurant at Gravois Avenue and Morganford Road in South St. Louis. The restaurant, built to look like a Dutch windmill, was meant to inspire citizens to dine in a classy restaurant, drink alcohol served at the table, and enjoy themselves without a bar. The place was incredibly popular; Leicester and Mary Faust dined there often.[33]

But nothing could stop the freight train that was Prohibition. On January 16, 1919, the thirty-sixth state ratified the

Eighteenth Amendment to the Constitution, prohibiting the sale, production, importation, and transportation of alcoholic products. In anticipation of the ban, August A. Busch instructed the department heads at Anheuser-Busch to prepare for conversion of the plant to non-alcoholic beer and other products. While other St. Louis breweries foundered, including the great Lemp Brewery, August A. braced Anheuser-Busch for the fight. The brewery marketed "near beer, malt tonic, soda, ice malt, wagons, refrigerated cabinets, and diesel engines."[34] August A., who gave up his salary, leased some of the factory space and equipment to other industries to keep the income rolling in. In 1927, Anheuser-Busch converted its idle stockhouse #3 into a plant to produce baker's yeast. It proved to be the greatest profit-maker for Anheuser-Busch during Prohibition. August A. also tore down his family's mansions at 1 Busch Place and 2 Busch Place. There he built a switching yard and factory that produced non-alcoholic products during the last years of Prohibition.[35]

When Prohibition was repealed in 1933, St. Louis' South Side celebrated. Great crowds of people jubilantly gathered around the brewery's gates at midnight on April 7, 1933, as the Anheuser-Busch trucks rolled out to deliver beer. That same year, Leicester Faust joined Anheuser-Busch's board of directors. He was loyal to his familial duties and loyal to his mother, who quietly urged him to go "keep an eye on things over there."[36]

Chapter 3
THE GREAT DEPRESSION

The stock market crash of 1929 ushered in the Great Depression. The country plunged into despair while banks failed. The unemployed moved about the US in search of work and food. Hoovervilles cropped up around America, even in St. Louis; desperate people pieced together ramshackle shelters and shacks along the riverfront.

The Depression robbed Leicester of a tangible legacy of his grandfather, Tony. The Fulton Market lived on long after Tony's death in 1906. Leicester's father, Edward, was president of the Fulton Market's through the prosperous 1920s. In 1933, the Fausts became incorporated. They were called Tony Faust's Sons, Inc., of St. Louis. The incorporators were listed as Edward A. Faust, A.B. Faust [Anna], L.B. Faust [Leicester], and A. Faust Wallace [Audrey] along with another businessman.[1]

But the Depression choked business at the Fulton Market, and in January 1935 Edward filed for bankruptcy. The building that housed the former Fulton Market for decades, 408-410 Elm Street, directly across from where Tony Faust's restaurant used to be, was finally torn down in 1941.[2]

Edward and Anna boarded up 1 Portland Place and lived at Leicester and Mary's Lindell Boulevard apartment during the winter of 1930. The following year, Edward and Anna again boarded up the mansion and spent the winter abroad. It was then that Leicester's family spent their first winter at the Farm. Grateful for their fireplaces, they hung their clothes near the flames to dry and warm them. Claire and Ann began attending the newly opened Villa Duchesne, a Catholic school for girls and a sister institution to City House, on Spoede Road. Leicester concentrated on keeping his farm afloat.[3] Leicester was proud that his farm was self-sustaining, and his hobby had become a necessity during the dark years.

Fred Sellenriek, Leicester's farm manager, and his wife Myrtle, did not have the luxury of spending winters in St. Louis. They lived in a tiny, white frame house near the duck pond on the Farm, and there they began their family. Baby Donald was born in 1928, and their second baby, Allen, came along in 1935, during the heart of the Great Depression.

In the early 1930s, Leicester's help included multiple farmhands and gardeners, many of whom lived on the property, rent free. Leicester offered a deal. He informed them that because of the Depression he could not pay them, but if they would stay and continue working for him, he'd turn the Farm over to them. They could have their own parcels of land to farm as they saw fit, then keep the produce as their own. This deal remained in place until the conclusion of the Depression. At times, Fred Sellenriek and the other employees made more money during the Depression years than before, a result of the sale of their grain.[4]

Leicester kept his options open. In addition to serving as vice president of his father's Lamella Roof franchise, he had a brief stint as president of the Rio Grande Agricultural Company. Then, in 1933, Leicester became a director at Anheuser-Busch. In 1935, he went to work at the brewery in the Grain Department, where he purchased barley, rice, and corn.[5]

Leicester Faust's business sense was as acute as his father's. The hard times shed light on the differences between father and son, however. Edward was furious at his son after Leicester took a trip to Germany, a country also in the depths of the Depression. While in Germany, he visited "the old homeplace." The caretaker showed him around. Before he left, Leicester gave him $50. The caretaker fell to his knees, cried, and hugged Leicester's legs. Now, the man explained, he'd have enough to pay his bills. Leicester's father was angry because Leicester "corrupted him so now he wouldn't work."[6]

Leicester and Mary added bedrooms onto their home for their children around 1936. Leicester hired the architectural firm of Maritz, Young & Dusard (the same architects of Audrey's home on the St. Louis Country Club) to design the addition. During construction, Leicester moved his family into 1 Portland Place. He, Mary, and the girls occupied one part while Edward and Anna occupied another section of the home. Leicester and Mary and their children had lived with Edward and Anna over the years, during various times when they wintered in the city. The arrangement worked well; Mary deeply respected her mother-in-law. Though Mary was known to have a similar personality as the austere, even stern, Edward, she disliked him. Much to her relief, her father-in-law was rarely around. By the time the addition of their daughter's bedrooms (one blue and one pink) to the big house was complete, Claire and Ann had only a couple of years before they were sent off to boarding school at Greenwood Academy in Maryland.[7]

Because Claire and Ann attended private schools, Fred

Sellenriek's boys saw relatively little of the boss's daughters. Nevertheless, the children of the Farm had a fondness for each other. Claire seemed to adopt little Donald, the Farm manager's oldest boy, giving him the pet name of "Henry." She'd say to his mother, "Myrt, I'm going to take Henry," and would whisk the toddler off to play. Occasionally the girls would invite the boys into the big house when Mary was not home. The children would use the Indian rugs to slide across the floor, then frantically put the house back together as Mary's driver returned with their mother.

Claire and Ann were excellent with horses. Their trophies from horse shows and competitions lined the walls of the stable. Claire, in particular, was outdoorsy. She earned the respect of the hardworking farm manager's boys. They liked that she had a free spirit like her father. She'd call, "Hey, Boots!" Leicester, wearing cowboy boots, happily responded. The boys' admiration for her deepened when Claire once joined the hay crew in the field. She walked alongside the baler, fascinated. Finally, she announced that she wanted to tie the bales. She worked with the men and tied the bales for hours. She retreated to the big house only to nurse her blistered hands.[8]

On April 16, 1936, Anna Busch Faust died. Less than three months later, on July 5, 1936, Edward A. Faust died.[9] Edward's funeral mirrored his wife's: like hers, his funeral service was held at 1 Portland Place. And, like hers, the music at Edward's funeral was provided by a string quartet consisting of members of the St. Louis Symphony Orchestra. The music included the Fausts' favorites, "Dreams" from Wagner's *Tristan and Isolde* as well as the largo movement from Dvorak's *New World Symphony*.[10]

Because the Faust family plot was nearly full, Edward was buried next to his wife in a new Faust family plot in Bellefontaine Cemetery.[11] It was not far from his father, mother, brother, and sister.

Anna's estate was valued $1,908,139, while Edward's was valued $296,982. He owed $45,000 for the Lamella Roof Company, which was declared bankrupt. The St. Louis Boat and Engineering Company was appraised at $1. And Edward owed $185,000 in unpaid debts. The remaining wealth was divided evenly between their children, Leicester and Audrey.[12] This included Anheuser-Busch stock, stock in a great number of investments, various real estate properties, their Portland Place mansion, and three cars: a 1933 Pierce Arrow Sedan, a 1929 Lincoln Touring car, and a 1923 Mercedes Touring car, located in Pasadena. Audrey was bequeathed the Fausts' summer home at Harbor Point, Michigan, with all of its furnishings.[13] And Audrey was specifically mentioned in her mother's will:

> It is my desire that my daughter AUDREY FAUST WALLACE shall continue to live in the station of life which she has enjoyed during my lifetime, and in the event that the income produced from her share of my estate is not sufficient to so maintain her, I instruct and direct my Trustees to augment the income by encroachments upon the principal to such extent that always my said daughter shall enjoy an income sufficient to maintain herself. A request by her in writing, addressed to the Trustees for any sum or sums in excess of the income payable to her under the provisions of this trust shall be full and complete authority to my Trustees to make such payments.[14]

Leicester was a trustee. As the years passed, he voiced his concern about Audrey's spending.[15]

Anna did not forget about the family's longtime maid, Dora Asher, whom the children fondly referred to as "Aunt Dora." Though Dora was living in Germany by the time Anna died, Anna dictated in her will that Dora receive $600 per year for the rest of her life. So loved, Dora was one day buried in the Faust family plot at Bellefontaine cemetery.[16]

The newspapers reported on the public's interest in the whereabouts of Fausts' art collection. Their concern was valid; it was well known that the Fausts had one of the greatest private art collections in the country. Edward had long built his collection. He acquired *Holy Family* by Peter Paul Rubens in 1911. In 1917, he paid a New York dealer $75,000 for a Bartolomé Esteban Murillo painting, *St. Joseph and the Infant Christ*. During those years, Edward also acquired *Virgin and Child* by Joos van Cleve. Around 1921, Edward acquired *St. John the Baptist* by Andrea del Sarto. Del Sarto was an Italian artist called "the faultless painter" and was the subject of one of Robert Browning's poems.[17] The Fausts often lent their works to the St. Louis City Art Museum, and in 1921 the museum announced its exhibition of some of the Fausts' fine works:

Madonna and Child by Rogier van der Weyden
Portrait of an Artist by Sir Anthony van Dyck
Mme. Josina Pyll De Dordrecht by Albert Cuyp
A Venetian Senator by Jacopo Robusti (Tintoretto)
The Banquet of Nastagio by Ercole Roberti
Portrait of a Man by Govaert Flinck [18]

In 1929, Edward added a fifteenth-century Italian painting, a cassone, to his collection. This type of painting was created on a wooden panel from a wedding chest, a common art medium at the time. Edward announced that the artwork, by artist Bernardino Fungai, would be kept at the City Art Museum for public viewing.[19]

A 1936 *St. Louis Star-Times* article reported on the Fausts' art collection, calling a triptych (a three-panel painting) the "most important single piece" in their collection. The newspaper claimed that the triptych called *Crucifixion* was "the only example extant of the painting of Erasmus Desiderius, the most learned man of the fifteenth century."[20]

The Fausts' art collection included more than paintings. When the couple lent a large portion of their collection to the St. Louis City Art Museum in 1931, the museum touted an early eighteenth-century Flemish-Gothic tapestry, *David*, as "the chief gem of the collection." The 21-foot by 11-foot wool and silk tapestry depicted an episode in the history of King David of Israel.[21]

The couple did more than just collect fine art – they immersed themselves in the art world. Edward was elected second vice president of the St. Louis Art League in 1918, an organization in which he and his wife were fully involved for years. He served on the Exposition Committee, a planning group for the National Exposition of Industrial Art, whose purpose was "visualizing the world value of beauty and art in industrial products, and furthering improved design and craftsmanship." And in 1930, Edward was elected president of the Municipal Art Commission.[22]

So, following the deaths of Edward and Anna Faust, the newspapers calmed the public's fear of the collection being lost. After investigating, reporters announced that the art had been given to their children "during the couple's lifetime."[23] Mary chuckled as she integrated the fine art and classical furnishings into their Indian motif at the Farm.[24]

Neither Leicester nor Audrey wanted 1 Portland Place. It

was a burden to rid themselves of the absurdly huge mansion during the Great Depression. Soon after their father's death, Leicester and Audrey offered the home to the St. Louis Art Museum as an ancillary building to be used for the display of fine art. The museum declined, citing the astronomical costs of maintaining the property. Even if the museum had agreed to the deal, strict Portland Place regulations dictated that the homes were to be used only as residences.[25]

Next, the siblings offered 1 Portland Place to the city of St. Louis as the official residence for the Mayor. Again put off by cost of upkeep, the city turned them down. And so the magnificent mansion, with its frescoed ceilings, silk wall coverings, splendid ballroom, and even an enormous pipe organ, sat empty.[26]

At last, Leicester and his sister found a ray of hope. In 1943, they wrote a letter to the St. Louis Academy of Science to offer 1 Portland Place as a museum. Thrilled, the Academy of Science accepted, pending approval from the Portland Place residents. If the residents again snubbed the museum concept, they feared the mansion would be razed and leave a gaping hole in their neighborhood. Nevertheless, they again said no. Except for a caretaker who roamed its lonely rooms, 1 Portland Place remained vacant.[27]

Finally, in 1945, a doctor and his wife purchased the massive home. Once a monument to Edward Faust's wealth and status, the mansion was now only an impersonal piece of Leicester's past.[28]

Little by little, Leicester expanded the Farm. He purchased

adjacent parcels in large and small acreages. He expanded south across Olive Street Road and north toward the Missouri River bottom. In 1930, he acquired land adjoining his property to the west that overlooked the Missouri River. On that land stood Thornhill.[29]

Haying on the Farm, south of Olive Street Road.
Courtesy of Allen Sellenriek

Frederick Bates was serving as Justice of the Territorial Supreme Court for Michigan Territory when President Thomas Jefferson gave him a promotion in 1806. Jefferson, concerned about political hostilities because of the Aaron Burr conspiracy, appointed Bates Secretary of the Louisiana Territory. Bates arrived in St. Louis in 1807 and assembled a code of law for the Louisiana Territory. In 1812, Bates became acting governor of the newly named Missouri Territory. And in 1821, Missouri achieved statehood. Frederick Bates became the second governor of Missouri in 1824.

Around 1809-1810, several years after he arrived in St. Louis, Bates purchased property near the Missouri River. In 1819, he and his new bride, Nancy Opie Ball, the daughter of a wealthy Virginia colonel, built a stately house, a beautiful barn, and fine outbuildings. They called their estate "Thornhill." In 1820, Bates purchased his first slaves, eventually owning 11. Less than a year after taking the position of governor, Frederick Bates died and was buried at Thornhill. The couple's fourth child was born after his death.[30]

Thornhill barns, built in the 1820s by Missouri's Governor Bates. Courtesy of St. Louis County Parks

In the late 1930s, Leicester moved the Sellenriek family out of the tiny white house and into the much larger Bates house. Attentive to its historic importance, Leicester asked that Fred and Myrtle not make any structural changes to the house. Leicester gave Fred permission to build a temporary pantry and an indoor stairway to the basement and to add a concrete floor in the basement. The improvements made the house a home for his farm manager's family.[31]

The Bates house, where Fred Sellenriek raised his family.
Courtesy of St. Louis County Parks

Around that time, with World War II looming on the horizon, Leicester quietly changed the name of his farm from "Swastika Farms" to "Thornhill."

Chapter 4
LIFE ON THE FARM

The years of World War II ushered in prosperity at the Farm. In 1939, Leicester had two greenhouses built that featured a variety of exotic and domestic plants. After years of using two teams of mules for the farm work, Leicester purchased his first tractor, a Case, in the early 1940s. Even Fred Sellenriek's young son, Allen, would drive the tractor on its rounds. Fred was in charge of Leicester's side business of buying and selling vehicles and machinery. He rotated out the old machinery and replaced it with newer and more modern equipment. He traded with neighbors: a baler for a combine, and so forth. Leicester Faust soon owned his own fleet of state-of-the art equipment.

Fred Sellenriek, 1946.
Courtesy of Allen Sellenriek

During the war, farming was deemed a necessary occupation. The draft board "didn't bother" the hired hands on the Farm. Only one hired hand was drafted, but he did not pass his physical. Sugar, meat, and eggs were rationed, but the folks of the Farm had all the food they needed. Because of gas rations, Leicester and Mary lived at the luxurious Park Plaza Hotel in St. Louis during the war. As always, Leicester entrusted the work of his farm to his workers while he continued working at Anheuser-Busch.[1]

The Fausts employed a large number of people. Some stayed for years or decades, others came and went. Eddie Stewart and his wife lived with their two children on the 160 acres across Olive Street Road. The other hired men held Mr. Stewart in high regard; "he was a hard worker, in spite of his club foot."[2] John Maloney was an elderly, illiterate man who lived with the Sellenrieks in the Bates house. Joseph and Hilda Krupp began working for the Fausts around 1946.

The Krupps first lived in the bachelor house. Hilda worked for Mary Faust in the kitchen and also spent many hours working for Leicester in his greenhouses. When the Stewarts left the Farm, the Krupps moved across Olive Street Road, where they raised their three daughters. Hilda walked across Olive Street Road to the big house each day. Joseph Krupp, hindered by his difficult personality, was relegated to chores across Olive Street Road, away from the bustle of the main section of the Farm. The Krupp girls took shelter in the huge entrance pillars at the Farm's gate on Olive Street Road as they waited for their school bus.

Around 1959, Julius and Gerdie Moore moved into the bachelor house. Julius became the Fausts' butler and chauffeur, while Gerdie cooked, cleaned the house, and washed the windows. The domestic help were on call for Mary 24 hours per day. Gerdie, known for her happy nature, became a dear friend to Myrtle, the Farm manager's wife. Their friendship demonstrated the sense of community among the Fausts' employees.

The Farm was a flurry of activity. The land along the Missouri River bottom was the main farming area. The hands drove tractors up and down the road adjacent to the Bates house. The sheds, located by the Bates house, were used for machinery storage. Every two weeks, the hands would grind corn – cobs and all – then take it over to the lamella barn to feed the Angus cattle.

Wheat straw was used for bedding in the barn. The alfalfa fields provided three cuttings (four in a good year) for square bales. Baling became more efficient when Leicester purchased a Case baler. Two men would ride the baler, which had a plunger system, while one man slipped the baling wire around the bale and twisted it. It was back-breaking work.

About 75 of Leicester's prized chickens were used for their eggs, while 100 were used for their meat. Fred Sellenriek chopped off the chickens' heads, then Hilda Krupp stepped in to clean and cook them. When in surplus, the chicken meat was frozen and stored in Glen Konneman's frozen food lockers located next to Leicester's grain elevator in Chesterfield.[3]

Fred would smoke meat in the smokehouse behind the Bates house for the Fausts, including hams and beef sausage. He checked the smokehouse a couple of times daily to ensure that it was smoldering properly. Hams would smoke for days, even for a year. Mary Faust would call for a ham, and

Fred would select the oldest. He'd carry it into the Bates house kitchen. He or Myrtle would cut off the mold, then send it over to the big house. It was tasty!

The Sellenriek children considered the Farm their home. They worked alongside their father, and each had daily chores. They kept up their family's huge garden behind the Bates house and worked in the orchard beyond the garden, as well as the orchard east of the big house. Young Allen mowed the Bates cemetery every week. For that task, Leicester paid him 50 cents.

Eleven year old Allen Sellenriek drives the tractor, pulling the baler.
Courtesy of Allen Sellenriek

While in grade school, the Sellenriek boys attended Lake School. Lake was a small community further east down Olive Street Road, across from Hog Hollow Road. The children would walk two miles each direction to the two-room school each day. In bad weather, Fred used the Farm truck to drive them. Later, the boys attended Eureka High School. They caught the bus at Olive Street Road.[4]

At Christmas, Leicester Faust would go to Rinkel's Market, a country store just down the road, and pay his employees' bills.[5]

Leicester's Chesterfield Farmers Elevator and Supply Company prospered. The original elevator was square and concrete with a large logo that advertised "Ful-O-Pep Feeds" and "Chesterfield Farmers Elevator & Supply Co." In 1922, only three years after Leicester became president of the company, 25-year-old Leicester hired 23-year-old Herbert Autenrieth. Herbert soon became manager, and he ran the elevator for 42 years. Two grain bins were added in front of the original silo and covered up the logo. Though Leicester worked at Anheuser-Busch and lunched at the Merchant's Exchange every day, he usually found time to pop in at the elevator and visit with his workers.[6]

Herbert Autenrieth.
Courtesy of Gloria Ruck

Herbert was raised on a farm just east of the Fausts. Like the Farm, the Autenrieths' farm encompassed land from Olive Street Road to the Missouri River. As his father had, Herbert and his wife raised their family in a little white house next to the Fausts' farm. They had three children, Lionel, Gloria, and Leitha, who attended Lake School with the Sellenriek boys. In fact, the Autenrieths were kin to the Sellenrieks. During the winters, the Autenrieth kids went sledding at the Farm. Gloria Autenrieth even attended parties and dances at the lamella barn. During one of these festivities, her grandfather jumped off a barrel of beer and broke his ankle. Of course, the Fausts never attended the shindigs. They were credited, however, with allowing their help to live full lives on their property.

Herbert smoked three packs of cigarettes a day while working long days at the elevator. Harvests were particularly busy. Every elevator employee stayed until the work was done. The early truck farms of Gumbo Flats (the old name for this part of the Missouri River Valley) had changed to grain by the mid-1940s. Farmers brought mostly wheat to the elevator. In the summers, farmers would arrive with their wheat and get their load weighed on the scale. A worker stuck a probe into the grain and pulled out a sample to check for rocks, weeds, and overall grain quality. The farmer was then given a ticket. He would drive his truck toward the grain bins and an auger would transfer the grain into the appropriate bin, based on the grade of the grain. The farmer would again drive onto the scale to have his empty truck weighed. The grain was later transferred into train cars (the elevator sat next to a rail line) and hauled by rail to St. Louis. People came from as far as Wentzville, and even Buford, to use the elevator. Herbert listened to the stock market reports on the radio every day and paid farmers accordingly. In the earlier years, during threshing, then later during harvest, grain trucks lined up in each direction from the elevator. At times, the trucks lined up as far as the Smokehouse in Chesterfield.

Fred Sellenriek (in the truck) helps two Chesterfield Farmers Elevator and Supply Company employees unload Faust grain.
Courtesy of Allen Sellenriek

The Chesterfield Farmers Elevator and Supply Company was next door to the Co-op grain elevator. The two elevators were very competitive. But unlike Leicester's elevator, the Co-op neither sold nor delivered coal.

The Chesterfield Farmers Elevator and Supply Company had a small fleet of trucks that delivered furnace coal and stoker coal to farmers all over Gumbo Flats. They also delivered feed for poultry, hogs, cattle, and horses. Ganahl Dairy, at Kehr's Mill and Clayton Roads, was one of the elevator's biggest clients for feed. In addition, the elevator's store sold seemingly everything under the sun: fertilizers, seeds, baby chicks, firewood, hog vaccines, tools, furnaces, paints, baling twine, fencing, and roof supplies. The elevator even repaired and sold Case tractors!

Bags for the elevator were purchased from the Bemis Bag Company. The elevator made its own feed and bagged it. Some of the feed sacks came in printed cloth, called a "print sack," and women would often make girls' dresses from these.

Delivery truck and elevator employee.
Courtesy of Gloria Ruck

When Herbert's daughter, Gloria, graduated from Clayton High School in 1942, he instructed her to work at the elevator. She joined a staff of two office workers, two full-time truck drivers, one mechanic, and four warehouse men who mixed feed.[7]

During World War II, the Hellwig Brothers Farm in Chesterfield served as a branch camp for German prisoners of war (POWs). Occasionally, when things got busy at the grain elevator, Herbert requested the use of several POWs to load grain cars and help with the manual labor. A military truck delivered several POWs and a guard. The men worked hard. For a time, Herbert's daughter Gloria dated the army's truck driver who drove the Germans to and from the elevator.[8]

Leicester's experience as a German-American was far different from the animosity faced by his grandfather, the immigrant from Germany. There was far less shame being a third-generation German-American living in the country during the Second World War, unlike the stigma faced by Edward in the years leading up to World War I. Leicester found that most of the residents of Gumbo Flats embraced the POWs living near them in Chesterfield.[9]

In fact, Mary acknowledged that she fell in love with Leicester against the odds at that Christmas party in 1918. Prior to their courtship, her parents intentionally kept their distance from Edward and Anna Faust. They did not "associate" with them because the Fausts were "South Side Germans." Such a comment would likely have been devastating to Edward, had he known.[10]

In 1934, August A. Busch shot himself in his bedroom at Grant's Farm. Upon his death, his son Adolphus Busch III took the reins as President and Chief Operating Officer of Anheuser-Busch. Gussie Busch, August A.'s other son, waited impatiently in the wings. While Adolphus III sat at the helm, Gussie was arguably in charge from the position of General Manager. Gussie left the brewery to serve his country in the Pentagon during World War II and returned from the war a colonel, having won the Legion of Merit medal for his service. In 1946, when Adolphus Busch III died, Gussie became President and Chief Operating Officer of Anheuser-Busch. And Gussie's antics made his cousin

Leicester Faust's job unpleasant.

Gussie and Leicester shared a love of country living. Gussie's wild country lifestyle fit his raucous personality just as Leicester's quiet, staid life on the Farm suited him. Gussie was an excellent shot and indulged in hunting. He was the master of foxhounds at the Bridlespur Hunt Club, which had been established by his father. He replenished his father's menagerie of exotic animals at Grant's Farm (most of which had been sold during Prohibition). Gussie was an excellent horseman. He had begun racing coaches competitively at the age of 14. Additionally, Grant's Farm was one of the locations for his trysts.

Gussie was profane and domineering and had a rotten temper. He was manipulative. Yet Gussie took Anheuser-Busch to the next level. A "consummate salesman and promoter,"[11] Gussie built regional breweries around the country. He had a network of loyal wholesalers with whom he cut deals, insisting that they cut deals with their own clients to sell more beer. Gussie hired his brewmaster from Germany and upheld the highest standards for the quality of his beer. Portrayed by his devoted marketing team as the savior of baseball in St. Louis, Gussie purchased the Cardinals for $3.75 million in 1953. He keenly recognized that the baseball team was a "travelling billboard for the brewery."[12] Like his grandfather, Gussie understood the value of advertising. He made Sportsman's Park in downtown St. Louis a Budweiser extravaganza. Ed McMahon was a spokesman for Anheuser-Busch beer in commercials for the Tonight Show, and Gussie even hired Frank Sinatra to hawk his beer on television. Under Gussie's direction, Anheuser-Busch became the largest brewery in the world.

In keeping with his family's philanthropic nature, Gussie

Busch played a key role in organizing Civic Progress. This group of St. Louis leaders was committed to revitalizing downtown St. Louis. Gussie gained celebrity status, putting St. Louis on the map when his photo appeared on the cover of *Time*. His story was also featured in *Life*.[13]

In 1952, a year before Gussie bought the Cardinals, Leicester sold his and Audrey's stock in Anheuser-Busch. He'd had enough. It was no secret that Gussie was paranoid about relatives who worked for him. It is unclear whether Gussie finally pushed Leicester out or Leicester simply left in disgust. Regardless, it had been a long time coming.[14]

Perhaps the bad blood between the cousins began with their fathers. Edward's successful entry into St. Louis society, the same society that snubbed the Busches, certainly did not go unnoticed. And August A. competed for the affection of his father Adolphus, who lavished attention on Edward. It is inevitable that August A. was irritated that Edward's first position at Anheuser-Busch was as vice president. August A. and his siblings were expected to pay their dues by working their way up. Adolphus even stipulated in his will that, should August A. die prematurely, it was Edward who should take over Anheuser-Busch. After Adolphus died, Edward publically turned his back on South St. Louis and what it represented, including fellow Germans and the Busch family. The grudge between Edward and August A. came to a head in the early 1930s when Anna requested $26,908 from Adolphus' estate to cover expenses incurred in maintaining 1 Portland Place. Since Edward was executor of the estate, the money was not contested.[15]

The differences between the cousins started in childhood. Leicester was well educated. Gussie dropped out of Smith Academy and laughed at his tutors. Leicester, like his father, began his career at Anheuser-Busch as a director and a company officer, while Gussie, like *his* father, began by pushing a broom and making the brew.[16]

On October 28, 1952, Leicester's request to sell his Anheuser-Busch stock was cleared through the Securities and Exchange Commission. The selling price to the public of the 356, 717 shares was $22 per share.[17]

Chapter 5
TIMES ARE CHANGIN'

Though compatible, Leicester and Mary Faust were as different as night and day. Leicester was loved by everyone. Short (5'6" on a good day) and pear shaped, he was called "dapper" because he rarely appeared in work clothes. Leicester greeted all the employees at his grain elevator with equal kindness and respect, a handshake, and a pat on the back. Fred Sellenriek, Leicester's farm manager, was a dear friend and confidante. The fact that Leicester treated him with the same regard as he treated his pals at the Merchant's Exchange was not lost on Fred. Leicester often hosted Fred in his home office, where, over cocktails, the two discussed the Farm's management and enjoyed each other's company.

Leicester and Mary enjoyed traveling the globe. Upon their return to the Farm, Mary would stay in the big house while Leicester packed up his slides and slide projector. He would then head over to the Bates house for popcorn and an evening of revelry.

During the 1930s, Fred Sellenriek owned a Model A Ford. It "came out" only on Sundays. After the war, Fred went to a Dodge dealership in St. Louis and ordered a Plymouth coupe. Before it arrived, Leicester drove to the Bates house and picked up an unsuspecting Fred. The two were gone for several hours. Fred returned home with a brand new car, purchased for him by Leicester. Fred, surprised and grateful, cancelled his order.

One hot summer day in the mid-1940s, Leicester drove over

to the Bates house, sitting on a newspaper in his pickup truck. He arrived soaking wet, hovering and awkwardly making small talk. Finally Leicester admitted to his farm manager's family that, to beat the heat, he had jumped into the lovely fountain outside of the big house. Dripping wet, Leicester did not want to go home to Mary until his clothes were dry.[1]

There was a large pin oak tree on the east side of the big house. Leicester initiated the annual "pin oak true leaf" contest, one of his favorite springtime rituals. Every family member and employee would put a dollar in a pot. Whoever correctly guessed the date of the emergence of the first true leaf on the tree would win the pot. Leicester often studied the pin oak tree out the window with binoculars.[2]

Leicester was raised primarily by nurses and nannies. He, in turn, employed nurses and nannies to raise his daughters. In spite of this, his love for his children was unquestioned. He taught them how to ride horses, and the girls became accomplished horsewomen. When Leicester's daughters had children, fun-loving Leicester romped with his granddaughters in the big house, playing hide and seek in the basement and splashing in the fountain. He was dearly loved by his grandchildren, who called him "Booba."[3]

Mary, on the other hand, was neither fun-loving nor easy-going. Intensely private, her stern, even gruff, personality was off-putting. She was described as the type that would never invite the neighborhood children into her home for cookies. Mary was called "The Madam" by her help – the Madam wants this, the Madam wants that. Though she was fair to her employees (many stayed on for years), her personality was challenging. One cook threw down her apron and walked out.

Mary believed that exhibiting emotion was "tacky and vulgar." The consummate lady, she was as strict with her granddaughters as she had been with her daughters. She constantly corrected their grammar and admonished them to "cultivate repose!" when they became too noisy. But, like their mothers, Mary's granddaughters saw beyond Mary's strict demeanor. They appreciated her intelligence and generosity. They called her "Cici" and enjoyed her great sense of humor. As Mary grew into the dusk of her life, she allowed more people to love her as her family always had.[4]

Both Leicester and Mary loved horticulture. Mary had shelves of vases for her daily arrangements of fresh flowers. She and Leicester each had their own gardens; hers by the fountain and his beyond the orchard on the east side of the big house. Leicester, however, was more likely to actually dirty his hands by working in his garden. He loved it when his plant catalogs came in the mail, and he pored over them. Around 1950, Leicester had a new greenhouse built next to his previous two. This greenhouse dwarfed the others. It was designed by Lord & Burnham, the premier greenhouse maker in the country. In 1948, 1950, and 1952, Leicester and Mary sailed to Hawaii. They not only vacationed, but they found exotic plants to bring back to their greenhouses on the Farm. Leicester's retirement from Anheuser-Busch allowed him to foster his love of horticulture. He and Mary began donating a great deal of time to the Missouri Botanical Garden.[5]

By 1954, Mary was a member of the St. Louis Garden Club. That same year, Leicester accepted a position on the Missouri Botanical Garden's Board of Trustees. He remained a Garden Trustee for the next 25 years. He also served on the Garden's Historical Committee. Through a generous donation from the Fausts, the Garden's main entrance area received a face-lift in 1964, with new plantings and lily pools. The Fausts gave generously toward the construction of the Climatron in 1959 as well as a greenhouse in 1968. The new greenhouse was dedicated in memory of Anna Busch Faust.[6]

The Missouri Botanical Garden remained close to his heart. In 1973, Leicester was celebrated by the garden, which named him an Honorary Trustee. It was a great honor.[7]

Leicester devoted time and money to philanthropic ventures that interested him, including history. He was involved in the Missouri Historical Society and served on the Board of Trustees in 1947 and 1949. Mary was elected a member of the Board of Directors of the Missouri Historical Society's Women's Association in 1953.[8]

Once, Leicester even dabbled in politics. In 1934, he became president of the newly organized Sane Laws Association of Missouri. The group's purpose was to foster "legislation for the good of the people at large, as compared to legislation favoring special interests." Leicester explained that the association would "work for modification or repeal of laws now on our statute books that are antiquated and hypocritical." The organization was made up of business leaders. One of its goals was to "oppose legislation which tended to harass business."[9]

Leicester served as president of the Industrial Aid for the Blind. In 1953, he was named chairman of the Red Cross Fund Campaign.[10] Like his father, Leicester had an interest in the arts. He served on the board of the St. Louis Symphony Society. And he donated several works of art to various institutions. In 1941, Leicester and his sister

Audrey gave the Murillo painting *St. Joseph and the Infant Christ* to Washington University. The painting, once owned by Edward and Anna, was given in their memory. In 1962, Leicester and Mary gave the triptych portraying the Crucifixion, also inherited from his parents, to the City Art Museum.[11]

Leicester and Mary enjoyed Claire and Ann's children. Leicester, especially, doted on his grandkids. Ann brought her daughters to the Farm to lunch with their Booba and Cici every Saturday. Ann's children grew to know and love the Farm. They often stayed overnight, occupying the bedrooms built onto the big house for their mother and aunt. The nighttime wind sometimes blew the curtains of the opened windows into the un-air-conditioned rooms. With her nightgown blowing, Mary closed the windows, sternly admonishing the girls that any fears were unwarranted. When Ann and her husband traveled for a couple of weeks each year, their two daughters stayed with their Cici and Booba. How embarrassing to be picked up at school by their driver! Leicester's granddaughters delighted in Leicester's return from a trip to Florida, when he brought home an alligator and plopped it in the pond on the Farm. Of course, the critter died in the unnatural environment, but Leicester always told the children that the alligator had made its way to the Mississippi.

Ann and her children traveled with their Booba and Cici during the summers of the 1960s. They'd visit zoos, cathedrals, and botanical gardens all over Europe and Scandinavia. Leicester and Mary wished to educate them, and they told Ann, "The girls need to see this."[12]

Leicester was fairly close to his sister, Audrey. Audrey, like

Leicester, had agrarian knowledge that she applied to benefit her family during World War II. Audrey gardened; milked cows; and raised hogs, turkeys, and chickens to supplement her family's war ration. Audrey and Mahlon B. Wallace Jr. also owned a farm in Rolla, Missouri, where they raised Hereford cattle. Naturally, she and Leicester engaged in lively debates regarding the superiority of Angus vs. Herefords.

Audrey's children had a fanciful childhood on the grounds of the St. Louis Country Club, which was still a rural area during the early 1940s. The children climbed trees, ran with their dogs, and rode their pony. The family had a team of workhorses, Star and Blaze, before they purchased their first tractor.

Mahlon Jr. and Audrey went on extensive hunting expeditions and filled their home with taxidermy. When young Lonnie and Tolie grew old enough, they joined their parents on hunting expeditions. Tolie took her first trip when she was 12 and Lonnie was 14. The family took a train to Chicago, then on to Banff and Lake Louise in Canada. Their train took them through Canada and on to Juneau, where they chartered an Alaskan boat. Together, the family hunted polar bears.

The Wallaces went on hunting expeditions every couple of years. They hunted antelope in Wyoming. They went twice again to Alaska, then on an African safari. And they took a ship to Norway, where they again hunted polar bears.[13]

For years, Audrey and Mahlon Jr. ran dog kennels on their property along the St. Louis Country Club. They bred and showed their dogs. Lonnie and Tolie took handling classes and participated in dogs shows as children. The family kenneled wire hair fox terriers, then became active in field trials with Labrador retrievers. In 1954, Mahlon Jr. and Audrey purchased property in the western portion of St. Louis County. There they began Casa Audlon Kennels, which became a great success.[14]

A year after she began her dog kenneling business in western St. Louis County, Audrey was named Director of the Office of Volunteers of the Red Cross's Midwestern 16-state area. Both she and her brother served the Red Cross loyally throughout their adult years.[15]

Audrey continued to golf, more for leisure than competition. In addition, in 1958 she and Mahlon Jr. furthered their love of hunting by purchasing a plantation in Georgia, where they hunted quail.[16]

Donald Sellenriek was the oldest son of Fred and Myrtle Sellenriek, born in 1928. As Leicester's farm manager's son, Donald spent his entire childhood on the Farm. Donald worked alongside his father and took on many responsibilities. He was "being groomed" to replace his father as the head hired man one day. It was okay with his younger brother, Allen. He agreed it was a natural progression, especially as Allen wished to move off of the place after high school.

In the early 1950s, Donald was drafted into the Korean War. He spent two years in Japan, just missing action. He returned home and continued transitioning into the position as the Farm's foreman. One day he went on a picnic with friends along a river. Without a lifejacket, Donald fell out of the boat and drowned.

Donald's death "put out the spark" in Fred. Fred retired from the Farm and died a few years later—of sorrow, some surmised. Leicester's light, too, was dimmed, as he grieved the great loss. This tragedy was a catalyst for Leicester to seriously begin considering the future of the Farm and the legacy of the Faust family name. After Donald's death, he opened a dialogue with St. Louis County.[17]

Donald Sellenriek, raking hay, July 1946.
Courtesy of Allen Sellenriek

Everything was changing. Development was moving farther away from St. Louis and was pushing farther west. The St. Louis County Historic Buildings Commission was formed in 1957 to identify and recommend the preservation of the county's historic buildings before the claws of development overtook them. Leicester served on the commission.[18]

He had always been mindful of historic architecture. In 1941, Leicester oversaw a Historic American Building Survey (HABS) conducted on the Bates house.[19] Leicester knew, though, that the property boasted even more history than the home of the Missouri's second governor. His evidence was in the mason jars filled with Indian arrowheads found around Thornhill.[20]

By the mid-1960s, Leicester had leased most of his farm ground and pastures. Around that time, several factors deemed the Chesterfield Farmers Elevator and Supply Company unnecessary. Farmers began pooling their grain into bigger trucks and hauling it to St. Louis; farmers began raising horses, not grain; and development pushed further west. In the late 1960s, Beckmann Turf & Irrigation Supply, Inc., purchased the grain elevator. Soon after, the Beckmanns closed the elevator and ran just the store.[21]

In 1968, Leicester and Mary Faust donated 98.5 acres of their land to St. Louis County, which included Thornhill.[22] This was the end of the Angus era.

In 1975, Leicester and Mary's daughter Ann died, overtaken by illness. Through their own sorrow, the family ached at Leicester's devastation. He was heartbroken, and was never again the same. Four years later, 81-year-old Leicester Faust passed away. His family held a funeral Mass for him at the St. Louis Priory. On September 3, 1979, Leicester Faust, son of Edward and grandson of Tony, was buried at Bellefontaine cemetery.[23]

Chapter 6
SUNSET ON THE FARM, SUNRISE ON FAUST PARK

After 57 years of marriage, Mary was on her own. She had absolutely no intention of ever leaving the Farm, and she remained there with her Schnauzer, Hans. For the rest of her life, she worked to ensure that the Farm's integrity and beauty would be maintained. She watched as St. Louis County began to transform the 98 acres donated by the Fausts.[1]

It was slow going. The Fausts donated the land in 1968, and in 1971 St. Louis County put together their "Master Site Development Plan" for Thornhill. A year later, in an attempt to "outline the original extent of the buildings on the estate," an archaeological investigation of the house, privy, well, gardens, and walks was completed.[2] Through the duration of the 1970s, the county carefully restored the Bates house at Thornhill as well as its outbuildings. The barn, in particular, was a gem, "put together with mortise and tenon, each beam fitting in with tabs and cross pins."[3] The county hoped to complete the restoration by 1982. Restoration of Thornhill continued, however, through the 1980s. It was completed in 1990.[4]

Mary was pleased with the carousel that was installed at what was now called Faust Park. The carousel, with its colorful horses, had survived a fire that destroyed the Forest Park Highlands amusement park in 1963. The carousel had been built in the 1920s by the Dentzel Company of Philadelphia; the St. Louis County Historic Buildings Commission and Faust Cultural Heritage Foundation raised the money to restore it. In 1987, the carousel was installed in a climate-controlled building in Faust Park.[5]

The Governor Bates home, fully restored to its 1820s grandeur, located in Faust Park.
Courtesy of St. Louis County Parks

In 1986, a bond issue was passed by voters in St. Louis County that allotted $725,000 for improvements for the new Faust Park. Thus came the idea for the Historical Village.[6] Leicester's love of vernacular historic architecture fed into this concept. The plan was to identify buildings that played a role in the history of St. Louis County. Selected buildings were to be moved to Faust Park to create a nineteenth-century village. Virginia Stith, Director of Historic Sites and Preservation for the county, said, "There are a large number of buildings being lost in St. Louis County to development because the land is so valuable. We keep running around trying to collect them before they go. It breaks my heart the buildings we've had to refuse."[7] The Hoch House made such a journey to the park in 1988.

Henry Hoch's parents came from Germany in 1844. Hoch, first a bricklayer, then operator of Rinkel's Market, paid $100 in 1876 for the land where he built his little brick home. The house was donated to the county in 1988 when widening of Olive Street Road "threatened destruction." It needed to be moved one mile along Olive Street Road to reach its destination at Faust Park. Even after the roof and several rows of brick had been removed, Union Electric Company had to raise some power lines to allow the house to proceed down the road. The Hoch House was moved at 3:00 a.m. on a Sunday because, explained Director Stith, "historic preservation does not get priority rights of way on the roads under Missouri law." It was an expensive undertaking. Stith said, "The costs are getting prohibitive. We probably won't be able to prevent demolition by moving them down the road any more."[8] Nevertheless, the Historical Village at Faust Park grew.

In January 1995, a private fund-raising group announced plans to build a butterfly house at Faust Park. The group, the Forest Park Conservancy, had initially approached the City of St. Louis for permission to establish the butterfly house at the Jewel Box in Forest Park. They abandoned that idea in favor of a location at Faust Park. The group conceived of a sunlit building to house butterflies in various stages of development. The group's hope was to establish a butterfly house in St. Louis before any other midwestern city had one. There were only 12 of its kind nationwide. St. Louis County Executive George R. "Buzz" Westfall was enthusiastic. He planned to rename Faust Park "Faust Children's Park." He felt the butterfly house represented his vision of gearing the park toward children.[9]

The plan, however, was to build the butterfly house in the midst of the Historical Village. Battle lines were drawn.

Jack Leonard was the mayor of Chesterfield, the newly incorporated city which had quickly grown around Faust Park. He said, "I'm going down guns blazing on this one." He explained that he did not want to waste the efforts of the people of Chesterfield who put "time and effort to the village project."[10] By then the Historical Village was home to several houses and cabins, smoke houses, a blacksmith shop, and a carriage house. All were under restoration. Director Virginia Stith waffled. The *St. Louis Post-Dispatch* reported, "Stith said that after much soul-searching, she reluctantly came to the conclusion that the county doesn't have the resources to build a village that accurately reflects the life of the mid-1800s."[11] Mary Faust was furious. She resounded, "Most emphatically, the village cannot be touched. I want it completed....I want to make it beautiful."[12] Stith suggested the houses in the village could instead be used for offices, or among other things, a tea room.[13]

Other solutions were offered. County Councilman Mark Brodsky of Creve Coeur, R-3rd District, "urged County Executive George R. "Buzz" Westfall to put the butterfly house in Creve Coeur Park" so as not to "destroy the work of so many people."[14] Then came the next idea: build the butterfly house where the Historical Village sat on the southeast side of the park, and *move* the entire Historical Village to the southwest side of the park.

Chesterfield residents chorused their concern. They acknowledged that the proposed butterfly house might indeed bring visitors and revenue to the park. But, argued a Girl Scout leader, "...about 200 Girl Scouts had devoted many hours on projects." Those included "a clay-bake oven behind the Mertz cabin [and] a brick walkway at the Conway House." Robert J. Hall, director of St. Louis

County Parks Department, assured residents that no buildings would be destroyed. Nevertheless, "regardless of the butterfly house...the village should be moved." The park officials argued that the historic buildings should be nearer Thornhill.[15]

Finally, after several months of debate, plans were drawn to build the butterfly house on the southwest portion of the park. The Historical Village would remain on the southeast portion of the park.[16] In June 1995, the *St. Louis Post-Dispatch* reported,

> A compromise plan to put a butterfly house in Faust Park in Chesterfield without disturbing historic buildings there won final approval Thursday of the St. Louis County Council. The vote was 7-0.[17]

The Butterfly House was built. And in July 1996, 10 years after it was conceptualized, Faust Park celebrated the Grand Opening of the Historical Village.[18]

Late in her life, Mary remained very close with her granddaughters. She also began letting others in, finding friends in a younger generation. Such was the unlikely friendship that blossomed with Chesterfield sculptor Don Wiegand.

Don was in his early 30s in the late 1970s. He often accompanied his girlfriend and her friend to the Missouri Botanical Garden. The women loved to sketch in the lily garden. One day they decided to go for a bike ride instead of going to the Garden to sketch. Don loaded up the girls' bikes in his van and the group drove off into the country. He waved goodbye as his friends set off down a country road. The young women had an accident, and one eventually died of her injuries. The young woman's grieving parents contacted Don. They asked him to create a sculpture of a little girl in a timeless dress, in memory of their lost daughter.

For a model, Don used four-year-old Cora, the daughter of a friend. As she grew tired of modeling during one sitting, the little girl threw her arms over her head in frustration, bent at the elbow. Perfect! That was the pose for the sculpture, *Cora*. Upon completing the work, Don, along with his friends and the young woman's family, made numerous requests to place *Cora* in the Missouri Botanical Garden, to no avail.

Don Wiegand was raised in Chesterfield. His family attended the same church as the Fausts, and he saw Leicester and Mary in the grain elevator and Chesterfield smokehouse market now and then. He knew Leicester to be a kind and good man. Mary, he thought, was not interested in small talk. His mind changed in the 1980s when he made her acquaintance. He became enamored of his elder friend's stern, yet giving, personality.

Don's property was heavily damaged when the Missouri River flooded in 1993. His studio home in Chesterfield filled with water "up to the chandelier." Mary asked Don's friend how she could help. His friend replied, "Get *Cora* into the Missouri Botanical Garden." The Garden responded favorably to their longtime friend and benefactor. The sculpture, officially donated by Mary's granddaughters, was installed in memory of Leicester Busch Faust. *Cora* finally took up residence in the gardens where Don's friends once loved to sketch.[19]

Mary commissioned Don to create a sculpture of her great-grandson, Samuel. She also gave him exotic plants from her greenhouse and boosted his own plant conservatory. Formerly private and uninviting, Mary now called Don frequently. She asked him over to the big house for an afternoon visit, sometimes twice a week. Though Mary was in her 90s and her eyesight was failing, Don marveled at her acute senses and her wit. The unlikely pair sat in a sun-filled nook with their toddies, discussing art, Mary's long past, and the future of Faust Park.[20]

Mary found another friend in Julie Constantino, whom she met when Julie worked at the St. Louis Priory. One day in the late 1980s, Julie gladly accepted an invitation for an afternoon tea at the big house. After that, the two women, each of a different generation, had rum tea often in the nook off of the great room. Mary shared tales of her childhood and her adoration for her father, Samuel Plant. She also told her younger friend stories about the early days of the monks and the Priory, while Julie filled her in on all of the school's happenings.[21]

Mary had a long history with the priory. In the mid-1950s, Catholics in St. Louis wanted a high-caliber secondary school for boys. Fred M. Switzer Jr. and several other St. Louis go-getters persuaded those at Ampleforth Abbey in England to send three Benedictine monks to the heartland of the United States to begin a school. The Abbey in England had been contemplating a new monastery, so a deal was struck. Before approaching those at Ampleforth, Switzer had already purchased an old farm with a 1937 house in St. Louis County.

In 1955, the three Benedictine monks arrived in the wilds of middle America. In the following days, a group of eager St. Louisans, including Leicester and Mary Faust, welcomed the monks. The Fausts became regular worshippers at the new Abbey. Leicester had become a Catholic and, with his devout wife, found a spiritual home there. The Fausts began a deep friendship with the monks.[22]

Abbot Luke Rigby (then Father Luke) was one of the three monks first to arrive. He said, "Mary and Leicester soon came to appreciate Priory's distinctive mission of monastic education. They contributed to that mission from their favored perspective – the educative value of beautiful objects and surroundings." The Fausts shared their love of horticulture. They donated trees and shrubs for planting around the church and the school, all "carefully chosen and placed."[23] They landscaped a lovely winding lane "sweeping up to and around the church."[24] The Fausts donated great amounts of art, including sculptures, paintings, and books. They hoped to contribute in the education of the boys through art.

Both Leicester and Mary devoted a great deal of time to the Priory. Leicester sat on the board and actively participated in meetings and events. Leicester and Mary visited Abbot Luke's parents when they vacationed in England. They grew equally fond of his mother, Ursula, as they had of Abbot Luke. One day in the 1980s, after Mary lunched at the Abbey with Abbot Luke, Mary asked to see the dining hall. She was horrified. Soon Mary made plans to donate the funds to renovate it. She carefully supervised the new dining hall project, built with a state-of-the-art kitchen. Once it was completed, she donated French Cathedral etchings for the walls of the new dining hall. Mary insisted that the kitchen be named for her dear friend's mother. So it was named St. Ursula's kitchen.[25]

Mary's love of historic architecture mirrored Leicester's.

Long after the campus was constructed, Mary dedicated herself to the restoration of the original 1937 house. It had been used by the monks as their primary building for the first few years of the Priory's existence. She gave time, money, and furniture, and she was instrumental in overseeing the restoration of the house to its original Georgian Colonial style. The Switzer House proudly stands as a testament to the monks' hard work.[26]

Mary Faust was celebrated as a Luke Rigby Honoree in 1991. In his tribute, Abbot Luke stated,
> Mary and Leicester, her husband, have very consciously over many years, made possible much of what we can offer to the boys of beauty… Lastly – and this weighs very heavily for us at the Priory School and at the Abbey – Mary, as was Leicester, is a dear, dear friend whose loving encouragement to us is incalculable.

Mary's acceptance speech was read by her granddaughter, Mary. Leicester was as present in her speech as he was in her heart,
> I want you to know that I am accepting it in the name of Leicester as well as myself. He so loved the Priory and his dear friends, the monks…. Our lives have been gratefully enriched through our close association with the monks since their arrival here from Ampleforth. Our deep friendship with men of such intelligence, kindness, wit, devotion and great humor and devotion to their church and school has brought us the greatest happiness…. In accepting it in Leicester's name as well as my own, I feel that I am only continuing the work we began together, and that gives me great happiness. Thank you all very much."[27]

Abbot Luke came to the Farm during those last years of Mary's life. It had become too difficult for Mary to travel to the Abbey, and her dear friend was happy to minister to her at home. A devout Catholic to the end, Mary always knelt at the prie dieu in her bedroom to pray. Mary Plant Faust died May 3, 1996. After a small service, she was buried next to Leicester in the Faust family plot in Bellefontaine Cemetery.[28]

EPILOGUE

In her will, Mary Plant Faust gave 102 acres of the Farm to St. Louis County Parks and Recreation.[1]

The Saint Louis Symphony Community Music School moved into what once was the big house. It was called the Leon R. Strauss Center – West County Branch at Faust Park. It was so named after the civic leader dubbed "Urban Pioneer and Preservationist." Like the Fausts, he was deeply committed to both architectural preservation and the St. Louis Symphony. In September 2001, the Community Music School joined with Webster University.[2]

The sounds are different now. One hears children shouting and the creak of swings from the playground at Faust Park. A strain of calliope music escapes when someone opens the door to the Carousel. On event days, one hears the distant ping! ping! of a hammer on an anvil in the blacksmith shop.

The renowned hiking trails that wind around the park allow one to hear even more: perhaps a piano or violin from an open window in an upstairs studio room in the Community Music School. Or maybe a family opening their picnic basket near the Bates house. Or honking geese in the pond near the Butterfly House.

But if one really listens, not with the ears but with the heart, one can hear the soft, distant low of the Angus cattle. Listen even more, and one can hear the *click, click* of the German maid's footsteps on the shiny floor at 1 Portland Place. Really, really listen, and the sounds of men hauling oysters into Tony's restaurant will mix with the sound of Tony's grandson splashing in his fountain. Oysters to Angus.

NOTES

BOOK ONE

Chapter 1
The Industrious German

[1] John Rodabough, *Frenchtown* (St. Louis: Sunrise Publishing Company, Inc., 1980), 9.

[2] Ibid., 13-18; James Neal Primm, *Lion of the Valley: St. Louis Missouri, 1761-1980*, 3rd ed. (St. Louis: Missouri Historical Society Press, 1998), 7-9, 164.

[3] Audrey L. Olson, "St. Louis Germans, 1850-1920: The Nature of an Immigrant Community and Its Relation to the Assimilation Process" (dissertation, University of Kansas, 1970), 24.

[4] Primm, *Lion of the Valley,* 164-173; Rodabough, *Frenchtown*, 23-24, 53-62.

[5] Primm, *Lion of the Valley,* 234-240; "The Camp Jackson Incident," *The Museum Gazette* (May 1999):www.nps.gov.

[6] *1864-1865 Saint. Louis City Directory* (St. Louis), 230.

[7] Mollie Faust, scrapbook, "A Birthday Gift to Mollie Faust, From Her Mama: May 31, 1878," Missouri History Museum, St. Louis, 12; Mollie Faust, scrapbook, 147-a; "Tony Faust Dies Suddenly Abroad," *St. Louis Republic*, September 29, 1906.

[8] Robert V. Kennedy, *Kennedy's Saint Louis City Directory for the Year 1857* (Saint Louis: R.V. Kennedy, 1857).

[9] "TRRA History," Terminal Railroad Association of St. Louis, accessed February 9, 2010, www.terminalrailroad.com; Frances Hurd Stadler, *St. Louis: From Laclede to Land Clearance* (St. Louis: Radio Station KSD and Kriegshauser Mortuaries, 1962), 72; Ernst D. Kargau, *Mercantile, Industrial and Professional Saint Louis* (St. Louis: Nixon-Jones Ptg. Co., 1902), 86.

[10] "The Southern Hotel of St. Louis," *New York Times,* October 8, 1863.

[11] "Campbell House Museum Family History," Campbell House Museum, accessed September 9, 2009, http://stlouis.missouri.org/501c/chm/campbell.htm.

[12] "Southern Hotel Calamity," *St. Louis Post-Dispatch*, April 11, 1877; "Rebuild the Southern," *St. Louis Post-Dispatch*, April 11, 1877; "The Fire: A Repetition of the Great Brooklyn Holocaust," *St. Louis Post-Dispatch*, April 11, 1877, 1st edition; "Later Horrors: Further Facts From the Burning of the Southern," *St. Louis Post-Dispatch*, April 11, 1877, 2nd edition; "The Worst Yet: Death-Roll Hourly Increasing," *St. Louis Post-Dispatch*, April 11, 1877, 3rd edition; "More Saved: The List of Missing Still Increases." *St. Louis Post-Dispatch*, April 11, 1877, 4th edition; "The Southern Hotel Fire: Number of Missing Unknown," *New York Times*, April 14, 1877; "The Southern Hotel Disaster: An Investigation by the Chief of the Fire Department," *New York Times*, April 15, 1877; "The Southern Hotel Fire: Defending the Fire Department," *New York Times*, April 16, 1877; "The Southern Hotel Fire: The Coroner's Inquest Begun," *New York Times*, April 17, 1877; "The St. Louis Hotel Inquest: Testimony as to the Progress of the Fire When the Alarm Was Heard," *New York Times*, April 18, 1877; "The Southern Hotel Inquest," *New York Times*, April 19, 1877; "General Telegraph News: The Hotel Disaster in St. Louis," *New York Times*, April 20, 1877; "The Southern Hotel Disaster: Further Testimony Taken by the Coroner," *New York Times*, April 21, 1877; "Phelin Toole's Story: His Quaint Description of How He Saved Lives at the St. Louis Hotel Fire," *New York Times*, April 28, 1877; "The Southern Hotel Fire: Close of the Coroner's Inquest," *New York Times*, April 28, 1877; "Editorial," *New York Times*, May 3, 1877.

[13] "Tony Faust," *St. Louis Post-Dispatch*, April 11, 1877.

[14] "A Delightful Resort: What Has Been Provided for Summer Evening Enjoyment," *St. Louis Post-Dispatch*, June 2, 1884; "Tony Faust's Enterprise," *St. Louis Globe-Democrat*, May 16, 1880.

[15] "The Money in Saloons: Exaggerated Statements of the Cost of Drinking Resorts," *St. Louis Post-Dispatch*, July 8, 1888.

[16] Mollie Faust, scrapbook, 18, 119; Adele Heagney and Jean Gosebrink, *Historic Photos of St. Louis* (Nashville, TN: Turner Publishing Co., 2007), 8; "Marley's Ghost Mingles with the After-Theater Crowd," *St. Louis Post-Dispatch*, March 8, 1903.

[17] Thomas Pickering, comp., *Paris Universal Exposition MDCCC LXXVIII: Official Catalogue of the United States Exhibitors* (London: Chiswick Press, 1878), accessed September 15, 2010, Googlebooks.com; St. Louis Electrical Board, *A 'Century Plus' of Electrical Progress*, 7.

[18] Jean Gosebrink, e-mail message to author, July 30, 2009; "The Electric Light: It is Being Tested in the Polytechnic Building," *St. Louis Globe-Democrat*, October 20, 1878; "Answers to Correspondents," *St.*

Louis Post-Dispatch, December 12, 1901; "First Electric Dynamo Shipped to City in 1878," *St. Louis Star-Times,* September 8, 1926, Faust, Anthony Edward (1836-1906) file, St. Louis Historical Society; St. Louis Electrical Board, *A 'Century Plus,'* 7; Mollie Faust, scrapbook, 21.

[19] "Illumination by Electricity," *St. Louis Globe-Democrat,* October 8, 1878.

[20] St. Louis Electrical Board, *A 'Century Plus,'* 6-8, 10, 17, 23, 25, 31.

[21] "City News," *St. Louis Post-Dispatch,* October 12, 1885.

[22] *St. Louis, Queen City of the West* (St. Louis: Mercantile Advancement Company, 1899), 195; Mollie Faust, scrapbook, 107.

[23] Harry M. Hagen, *This is Our St. Louis* (St. Louis: Knight Publishing Company, 1970), 365; *Pen and Sunlight Sketches of St Louis* (Chicago: Phoenix Publishing Company, 1892), 110; Mollie Faust, scrapbook, 10-11, 13, 18, 21.

[24] "Delmonico's History," accessed September 16, 2010, www.delmonicosny.com.

[25] "The Faust Building," description of Tony Faust's Restaurant building, circa 1888, "Restaurants" file, Fine Arts Department, St. Louis Public Library.

[26] "The Money in Saloons: Exaggerated Statements of the Cost of Drinking Resorts," *St. Louis Post-Dispatch,* July 8, 1888; Harry M. Hagen, *This is Our St. Louis,* 365; "Faust's Old Market to Make Way for Parking Lot," *St. Louis Globe-Democrat,* February 19, 1941; "Headwaiters: They Organize to Protect Themselves Against Irresponsible and Disreputable Employes [sic]," *St. Louis Globe-Democrat,* June 24, 1881; Lola L. Schaub to Edward F. Goltra, March 27, 1906. Letter regarding her employment. Edward F. Goltra Papers, Correspondence B2/F9, Missouri History Museum, St. Louis; "Shut Off Their Beer: And Now the Waiters at Faust's Are Going Dry," *St. Louis Post-Dispatch,* June 23, 1895.

[27] "Sidewalk Signs Must Go: Police Will Proceed to Enforce the Ordinance Strictly," *St. Louis Post-Dispatch,* February 10, 1899.

[28] "St. Louis in Splinters," *St. Louis Globe-Democrat,* December 29, 1878.

[29] "Tony Faust's Exhibition," *St. Louis Globe-Democrat,* March 30, 1880.

[30] "Sprague & Butler's Star Oyster Opener, James Mangan," *St. Louis Post-Dispatch,* February 1, 1878; Mollie Faust, scrapbook, 9.

[31] Mollie Faust, scrapbook, 22.

[32] Mollie Faust, scrapbook, 128-129.

[33] Ibid.

[34] "A Cab-Stand Decision: Which Will Entirely Do Away With Private Stands Now Occupied," *St. Louis Post-Dispatch,* June 3, 1887.
[35] "A Brewer's Suggestion: He Thinks the Government's Stamp Idea Might Apply to the Beer Traffic," *St. Louis Post-Dispatch,* February 2, 1883.
[36] "Think $4,000 Too Much: Saloon-Keepers Discuss the License to be Fixed by the Legislature," *St. Louis Post-Dispatch,* February 7, 1889.
[37] "The Bell Punch: St. Louis Threatened with the Moffett Register," *St. Louis Post-Dispatch,* April 2, 1878; "The Other Side: What the Saloon-Keepers Have to Say About the Bell-Punch," *St. Louis Post-Dispatch,* April 24, 1879.
[38] "At The Mercy of the Meat Trust," *St. Louis Post-Dispatch,* April 17, 1895; "Hunting a Beef Trust: Federal Grand Jurors Looking for Evidence," *New York Times,* December 5, 1896; "Big Meat Packers Indicted in Jersey," *New York Times,* February 26, 1910; "Meat Trust Sued: Government Seeks to Dissolve the National Packing Company as Illegal Combination," *New York Times,* March 22, 1910; *Meat-Packer Legislation Hearings Before the Committee on Agriculture, House of Representatives, Sixty-Sixth Congress, Second Session, on Meat Packer Legislation* (Washington, DC: Washington Government Printing Office, 1920), 1863, 1870. Accessed September 21, 2010, www.googlebooks.com; "National Packing Company," accessed September 21, 2010, www.encyclopedia.chicagohistory.org; "Meatpacking," accessed September 21, 2010, www.encyclopedia.chicagohistory.org; Mark Wahlgren Summers, *The Gilded Age: or, The Hazard of New Functions* (Upper Saddle River, NJ: Prentice Hall, 1997), 91; Howard Zinn, *A People's History of the United States: 1492-Present* (New York: Harper Perennial, 1995), 251; James A. Henretta, David Brody, and Lynn Dumenil, *America: A Concise History* (Boston: Bedford / St. Martin's, 1999), 480.
[39] "Oysters For All: Some of the Leading St. Louis Dealers in the Luscious Bivalve," *St. Louis Globe-Democrat,* September 3, 1876.
[40] "Faust's Fulton Market," *St. Louis Globe-Democrat,* February 5, 1879.
[41] Ibid; Mollie Faust, scrapbook, 12.
[42] "Multiple News Items," *St. Louis Globe-Democrat,* October 24, 1878.
[43] "Anti-Dust: The Post-Dispatch Subscription Still Increasing," *St. Louis Post-Dispatch,* April 16, 1880.
[44] "War on the Dust: How the Sprinkling Fund Stands Now," *St. Louis Post-Dispatch,* April 30, 1880.
[45] "Vehicle Licenses: A Determined Effort Being Made to Have them Reduced," *St. Louis Post-Dispatch,* November 19, 1891.

[46] "Faust's Fulton Market: An Enterprise That is a Credit to St. Louis," *St. Louis Post-Dispatch,* October 16, 1880.
[47] Ibid.
[48] "About Town," *St. Louis Post-Dispatch,* May 6, 1884; "A Delightful Resort: What Has Been Provided for Summer Evening Enjoyment," *St. Louis Post-Dispatch,* June 2, 1884; "Tony Faust," *St. Louis Globe-Democrat,* November 21, 1885.
[49] "Ye Connoisseurs in Good Grub," *St. Louis Post-Dispatch,* December 22, 1886; "The Fulton Markets: Where Those Who Want Delicacies for Christmas Ought to Go," *St. Louis Post-Dispatch,* December 20, 1888; "A Suitable Menu: For Your Xmas Dinner," *St. Louis Post-Dispatch,* December 20, 1893.
[50] "Our Tony," *St. Louis Post-Dispatch,* June 4, 1884; "Christening of the 'Tony Faust'," *Sea World and Packers' Journal* (June 12, 1884). Faust, Anthony Edward file, Missouri History Museum, St. Louis.
[51] Robert W. Cherny, *American Politics in the Gilded Age: 1868-1900* (Wheeling, IL: Harlan Davidson, Inc., 1997), 78-81; Howard Zinn, *A People's History,* 214-215, 240-246; Richard Hofstadter, *The Age of Reform* (New York: Vintage Books, 1995), 233; Henretta, Brody and Dumenil, *America,* 474.
[52] "Spanish-American Club: The New Quarters – Opening of the Rooms This Evening," *St. Louis Post-Dispatch,* September 26, 1883.
[53] Mollie Faust, scrapbook, 14; *St. Louis Up To Date: The Great Industrial Hive of the Mississippi Valley* (St. Louis: Consolidated Illustrating Company, 1895), 88-89.
[54] "Faust's Fulton Market Prices," *St. Louis Post-Dispatch,* December 2, 1897; "Faust's Fulton Market," *St. Louis Post-Dispatch,* April 8, 1903; Mollie Faust, scrapbook, 106.
[55] "Almost an Oyster Famine in the West," *St. Louis Globe-Democrat,* September 17, 1878.
[56] "The Household: The Market – What is There, What is Not, and What is Paid," *St. Louis Globe-Democrat,* March 6, 1881.
[57] "Business and Pleasure," *St. Louis Post-Dispatch,* April 20, 1883; "Local Personals," *St. Louis Globe-Democrat,* July 21, 1882; "Direct Imports: A Striking Feature of St. Louis Commerce," *St. Louis Globe-Democrat,* November 30, 1884; "Direct Importations," *St. Louis Globe-Democrat,* October 16, 1886; February 12, 1887; April 23, 1887; September 24, 1887; October 15, 1887; December 10, 1887.

Chapter 2
The Perils of Beer

[1] "City News," *St. Louis Post-Dispatch,* May 18, 1882.
[2] "Hit in the Head," *St. Louis Post-Dispatch,* February 17, 1883.
[3] "Had a Free Fight: Lively Scrimmage Resulting From an Objection to a Bill at Faust's," *St. Louis Post-Dispatch,* June 5, 1893.
[4] "Col. Abe Slupsky Comes to Grief," *St. Louis Post-Dispatch,* July 19, 1896.
[5] "Stabbed by a Tout," *St. Louis Post-Dispatch,* November 14, 1895.
[6] "Wand Cut M'Gee: The Livery Man Uses His Knife in a Fight at Faust's Saloon," *St. Louis Post-Dispatch,* October 18, 1896.
[7] "Inharmonious Histrionics: Two Theatrical Stars Indulge in a Furious Fight at Faust's," *St. Louis Post-Dispatch,* March 4, 1889.
[8] "A Couple of Bloods: And the Way Their Companions Behaved," *St. Louis Post-Dispatch,* June 21, 1882.
[9] "Diddlebock and Garrett: The Browns' Manager Goes to Headquarters with his Grievances," *St. Louis Post-Dispatch,* March 6, 1896.
[10] "Back at his Trade: Jack M'auliffe, Once Champion Lightweight, Retires from the Ring," *St. Louis Post-Dispatch,* September 6, 1897.
[11] "A Bad Man: Dr. Englebert Voerster in Another Saloon Fight," *St. Louis Post-Dispatch,* September 10, 1886; "Broke Loose Again: Dr. Voerster Beats Two Men in the Early Morning Hours," *St. Louis Post-Dispatch,* January 27, 1887.
[12] "The Courts: At the Justices'," *St. Louis Globe-Democrat,* September 5, 1879.
[13] Carol Berkin, Christopher L. Miller, Robert W. Cherny, and James L. Gormly, *Making America: A History of the United States,* 3rd ed. (Boston: Houghton Mifflin Company, 2003), 342-343, 394-395; Mark Wahlgren Summers, *The Gilded Age: or, The Hazard of New Functions* (Upper Saddle River, NJ: Prentice Hall, 1997), 10-11; James A. Henretta, David Brody, and Lynn Dumenil, *America: A Concise History* (Boston: Bedford / St. Martin's, 1999), 512-514.
[14] Richard Hofstadter, *The Age of Reform* (New York: Vintage Books, 1955), 9, 182.
[15] Mark Wahlgren Summers, *The Gilded Age,* 206; Berkin, Miller, Cherny, and Gormly, *Making America,* 516; Robert W. Cherny, *American Politics in the Gilded Age: 1868-1900* (Wheeling, IL: Harlan Davidson, Inc., 1997), 24-25.
[16] "Give Generously: The Request of the Citizens' Entertainment

Committee," *St. Louis Post-Dispatch*, March 19, 1888; "Silver Convention Finances: Sub-Committees Appointed to Raise the Fund Required," *St. Louis Post-Dispatch,* October 8, 1889.

[17] "German Democrats: An Enthusiastic Meeting Last Night at Union Capitol Hall," *St. $_{Louis}$ Post-Dispatch,* November 4, 1888.

[18] "He Pulled a Knife: Sensational Scene at Tony Faust's Very Early This Morning," *St. Louis Post-Dispatch,* October 26, 1888.

[19] "Hit Him Hard: The Knock-Down Argument Between Frank O'Neill and Judge Noonan," *St. Louis Post-Dispatch,* December 19, 1887.

[20] "The Brewers: They Are Leaving the Republican Party on Account of Prohibition," *St. Louis Post-Dispatch,* July 17, 1882.

[21] "The Sunday Problem: The Police Board Will Consult the City Counsellor [sic]," *St. Louis Post-Dispatch,* July 9, 1883.

[22] "Sunday in St. Louis: One Hundred Thousand People in the Parks, Beer Gardens and Other Resorts," *St. Louis Post-Dispatch,* July 16, 1883.

[23] "Blue Sunday: The General Law to be Enforced the Next Sabbath, *St. Louis Post-Dispatch,* July 25, 1883; "To-Morrow: List of Avocations That Are Allowed," *St. Louis Post-Dispatch,* July 28, 1883.

[24] "Travelers' Grievances: Inconveniences Occasioned by the Closing of Ticket Offices on Sunday," *St. Louis Post-Dispatch,* June 4, 1884.

[25] "St. Louis Saloon-Keepers Win: Judge Noonan Decides a Test Case Under the Downing Law," *New York Times,* August 28, 1883.

[26] "Anti-Saloonists Win: St. Louis Must Close Her Saloons on Sunday," *New York Times,* May 8, 1888.

[27] "Rest and Water: The Privileges to be Bestowed Upon St. Louisans To-Morrow," *St. Louis Post-Dispatch,* June 25, 1887.

[28] "Sunday Acquittals: What They Will Probably Result in Very Soon," *St. Louis Post-Dispatch,* June 13, 1888; "The Liquor Men's Convention," *St. Louis Post-Dispatch,* February 17, 1889; Article citing name change from the Saloon-Keepers' Protective Association to the Liberal Brotherhood of America, *St. Louis County Watchman,* December 20, 1883.

[29] "Warrants for Sunday Violators," *St. Louis Post-Dispatch,* March 18, 1895; "Sunday and the Saloons," *St. Louis Post-Dispatch,* March 19, 1895; "Will Close Up the Town: State Sunday Law to be Enforced to the Limit," *St. Louis Post-Dispatch,* March 19, 1895; "Carl Unger Out of Town: Therefore Sabbath-Breakers May Rest in Peace," *St. Louis Post-Dispatch,* March 20, 1895.

[30] "Sunday and the Saloons," *St. Louis Post-Dispatch,* March 19, 1895; "Will Close Up the Town: State Sunday Law to be Enforced to the Limit," *St. Louis Post-Dispatch,* March 19, 1895.

[31] "Carl Unger Out of Town: Therefore Sabbath-Breakers May Rest in Peace," *St. Louis Post-Dispatch,* March 20, 1895.
[32] "Open on Sundays," *St. Louis Post-Dispatch,* September 3, 1905.
[33] Henretta, Brody, Dumenil, *America,* 281, 513, 566; John M. Murrin et al., *Liberty, Equality, Power: A History of the American People,* vol. 2 (Orlando: Harcourt, Brace & Company, 1999), 700; Robert W. Cherny, *American Politics,* 36, 134; Mark Wahlgren Summers, *The Gilded Age,* 11.
[34] "Kansas City's Dry Day: The Sunday Law Effective for the First Time," *New York Times,* July 22, 1889.
[35] Doris Weatherford, *Foreign and Female: Immigrant Women in America, 1840-1930* (New York: Facts on File, Inc., 1995), 198; Robert W. Cherny, *American Politics,* 36.
[36] Murrin et al., *Liberty, Equality, Power,* 695

Chapter 3
Enterprising and Active

[1] Isaac H. Sturgeon and J. Stanley Brown correspondence, September 12, 1881. Isaac H. Sturgeon Papers, Missouri History Museum, St. Louis.
[2] "The Quail Match: Mr. Henry Dahmer Undertakes to Eat 35 Quail in 35 Days," *St. Louis Post-Dispatch,* January 27, 1883; "The Quail Eaters," *St. Louis Post-Dispatch,* January 29, 1883; "The Gastronomes: Dahmer's Daily Dose of Quail – A Cracker Match Proposed," *St. Louis Post-Dispatch,* January 31, 1881.
[3] "To Be Prosecuted: Game Wardens After Those Who Have Game Out of Season," *St. Louis Post-Dispatch,* February 5, 1897; "Caterers Will Feel the Law: Too Free in Serving 'Young Owls' and 'Snow Birds'," *St. Louis Post-Dispatch,* February 6, 1887.
[4] Michael Everman, Archivist, Missouri State Archives, email messages to author, October 13, 15, 18, 2010.
[5] "The West Greets the East: Game for Christmas Presents," *St. Louis Post-Dispatch,* December 17, 1897.
[6] "Multiple News Items," *St. Louis Globe-Democrat,* September 17, 1878.
[7] "Taking a Hand: Merchants Resolve to Push the Work of the Immigration Society," *St. Louis Globe-Democrat,* December 20, 1880; "$5,527.95: This is the Sum Contributed to the 'Post-Dispatch' Flood

Fund," *St. Louis Post-Dispatch,* May 22, 1892; Mollie Faust, "A Birthday Gift to Mollie Faust, From Her Mama, May 31, 1878." Scrapbook filled with newspaper articles, passenger lists, memorabilia, etc. Missouri History Museum, St. Louis, 114.

[8] Mark Wahlgren Summers, *The Gilded Age: or, The Hazard of New Functions* (Upper Saddle River, NJ: Prentice Hall, 1997), 168; Summers, *The Gilded Age,* 167-170.

[9] Howard Zinn, *A People's History of the United States: 1492-Present* (New York: Harper Perennial, 1995), 254-257; Carol Berkin, Christopher L. Miller, Robert W. Cherny, and James L. Gormly, *Making America: A History of the United States* 3rd ed. (Boston: Houghton Mifflin Co., 2003), 506-509.

[10] Howard Zinn, *A People's History of the United States: 1492-Present* (New York: Harper Perennial, 1995), 255.

[11] "Rex M'Donald's View of the Show," *St. Louis Post-Dispatch,* November 3, 1898.

[12] "The Citizens' Committee: A Large and Enthusiastic Meeting – Four Thousand More Presents," *St. Louis Post-Dispatch,* December 21, 1888; "Post-Dispatch Committeemen," *St. Louis Post-Dispatch,* December 25, 1900; "Lend a Helping Hand and Make Poor Children Happy on Christmas Day," *St. Louis Post-Dispatch,* December 11, 1904.

[13] "The First Meal," *St. Louis Globe-Democrat,* March 30, 1881.

[14] "A Silver Celebration: The Twenty-Fifth Anniversary of the Marriage of Mr. and Mrs. Adolph Busch," *St. Louis Post-Dispatch,* April 8, 1886.

[15] "Gardens Are About Ready: Forest Park Highlands Will Open Sunday and Delmar Garden Two Weeks Later," *St. Louis Post-Dispatch,* May 6, 1900; Faust, Mollie, "A Birthday Gift to Mollie Faust, From Her Mama: May 31, 1878." Scrapbook filled with newspaper articles, passenger lists, memorabilia, etc. Missouri History Museum, St. Louis, 134.

[16] *St. Louis Up To Date: The Great Industrial Hive of the Mississippi Valley* (St. Louis: Consolidated Illustrating Company, 1895), 89.

[17] "The First Ten Days: Show a Decided Increase in Receipts Over Former Years," *St. Louis Globe-Democrat,* September 18, 1887; "The Crowds Increase: Every Night Witnesses a Crush at the Great Exposition," *St. Louis Post-Dispatch,* September 20, 1890; "The Exposition Call: Payments on Stock Coming in Rapidly," *St. Louis Globe-Democrat,* March 8, 1883; James Neal Primm, *Lion of the Valley: St. Louis Missouri, 1761-1980,* 3rd ed. (St. Louis: Missouri Historical Society Press, 1998), 372.

[18] "St. Louisans Investing in Arkansas," *St. Louis Globe-Democrat,* February 10, 1887; Jane Wilkerson, Historian, Arkansas History Commission, telephone discussion with author, January 19, 2010.

[19] "Forewarned: St. Louis Brewers in Texas Arranging for Protection of their Interests," *St. Louis Post-Dispatch*, December 8, 1889; "Texas Breweries," accessed August 9, 2009, www.texasbreweries.com.

[20] "Grand Pyrotechnic Display: Tony Faust's Southern Terrace Ablaze With Glory," *St. Louis Post-Dispatch*, October 5, 1881.

[21] "The Boulevard Lights: Committees Appointed to Solicit Funds for the Fair Week Display," *St. Louis Globe-Democrat*, August 24, 1883; "The Fall Illuminations," *St. Louis Globe-Democrat*, June 9, 1887.

[22] "Aquariums at the Ex: Inauguration of the Missouri Fish Commission's Exhibit To-Day," *St. Louis Post-Dispatch*, September 13, 1889.

[23] "The Centennial: Definite Measures to Secure a Proper Representation of Missouri," *St. Louis Globe-Democrat*, August 12, 1875; "The Knights of St. Patrick," *St. Louis Globe-Democrat*, March 7, 1886; "The Capture of Camp Jackson," *St. Louis Globe-Democrat*, April 12, 1886; *List of Members*, Missouri History Museum Bulletin I, no. 11 (June 1, 1894): 30.

[24] "Jolly Germans: Who Are Members of One of the Largest Clubs in the City," *St. Louis Post-Dispatch*, April 24, 1886; St. Louis Turner Veterans Will Soon Celebrate Their Semi-Centennial," *St. Louis Post-Dispatch*, May 8, 1898.

[25] "Plundering the Pilgrims: How the St. Louis Singers are Being Held Up in Chicago," *St. Louis Post-Dispatch*, July 2, 1881.

[26] "The Faust Prize Cup: To Be Rowed for To-morrow by the Barge Crews of This City," *St. Louis Post-Dispatch*, October 12, 1878.

[27] Ibid.; "Aquatic Athletes: Who Our City's Representative Amateur Oarmen Are," *St. Louis Post-Dispatch*, August 14, 1885.

[28] "Scholarly Scullers: The Most Brilliant of the Many University Races," *St. Louis Globe-Democrat*, March 23, 1880; "Local Sporting Notes: Interesting Events in Aquatic, Athletic and Base Ball Circles," *St. Louis Post-Dispatch*, August 21, 1880; "The Modocs: Annual Meeting and the Election of Officers – The List of Membership," *St. Louis Globe-Democrat*, March 15, 1881; "Modoc's New Boat," *St. Louis Post-Dispatch*, April 26, 1881.

[29] "The Modocs: Annual Meeting and the Election of Officers – The List of Membership," *St. Louis Globe-Democrat*, March 15, 1881; "The Trickett-Plaisted Match," *St. Louis Post-Dispatch*, October 7, 1881.

[30] "Aquatic Athletes: Who Our City's Representative Amateur Oarmen Are," *St. Louis Post-Dispatch*, August 14, 1885; "The Modocs: Trophies Won By Their Blades on Lake and River," *St. Louis Post-Dispatch*, May 1, 1886; "A Pleasant Affair," *St. Louis Post-Dispatch*, October 12, 1886.

[31] Certificate of acceptance into the Masonic Lodge. April 9, 1875, Faust, Anthony E. file, Missouri History Museum, St. Louis.
[32] "History of Freemasonry," Mason Service Association, accessed September 28, 2010, www.msana.com.
[33] "The Charity Ball: Three Important Committees Appointed and the Date Fixed," *St. Louis Globe-Democrat,* November 27, 1878.
[34] "A Masonic Muddle: The Order in Missouri Torn Up on the Liquor Question," *St. Louis Post-Dispatch,* September 13, 1887.
[35] Ibid.
[36] Ibid.
[37] "Tony Faust Not Liable," *St. Louis Post-Dispatch,* February 12, 1893; "Tony Faust's Case Appealed," *St. Louis Post-Dispatch,* February 15, 1893; "Decided in Faust's Favor," *St. Louis Post-Dispatch,* May 8, 1893.

Chapter 4
The 1904 World's Fair

[1] James Neal Primm, *Lion of the Valley: St. Louis, Missouri, 1761-1980,* 3rd ed. (St. Louis: Missouri Historical Society Press, 1998), 373-374.
[2] Ibid., 374-375.
[3] Ibid., 303, 360-369.
[4] Ibid., 362-363, 377.
[5] Ibid., 377-381.
[6] Ibid., 382-383.
[7] Ibid., 376.
[8] Adolphus Busch to Wm. H. Thompson and D. R. Francis. Letters in Executive Committee meeting minutes, 1902. Louisiana Purchase Exposition Company collection, Missouri History Museum, St. Louis.
[9] Primm, *Lion of the Valley,* 382-385.
[10] Ibid., 385-386.
[11] "Europe Has the Fair Fever: Letter From St. Louis Visitor in Italy Tells of Interest," *St. Louis Post-Dispatch,* May 13, 1904.
[12] Primm, *Lion of the Valley,* 386-391; Martha R. Clevenger, ed., *Indescribably Grand: Diaries and Letters From the 1904 World's Fair* (St. Louis: Missouri Historical Society Press, 1996), 16, 29.
[13] Primm, *Lion of the Valley,* 390-391; Clevenger, ed., *"Indescribably Grand,"* 79; Margaret Johanson Witherspoon, *Remembering the St. Louis World's Fair* (St. Louis: Margaret Johanson Witherspoon, 1973),

44-45; "Tyrolean Alps," Display ad, *St. Louis Post-Dispatch,* May 22, 1904; "Killed Himself in Central Park," article about Fair in St. Louis within this piece, *St. Louis Post-Dispatch,* June 13, 1904.

[14] "Lüchow's Restaurant," The New York Preservation Archive Project, accessed September 3, 2009, http://www.nypap.org; "Lüchow's," Tips on Tables, accessed September 3, 2009, http://www.tipsontables.com/Lüchows.html; New York, "Soundex Index to Petitions for Naturalizations Filed in Federal, State and Local Courts," *Footnote,* accessed August 13, 2009,www.footnote.com/image/79563707,:, entry for August Lüchow of Germany, 1880; citing New York County Superior Court; *City Directories for New York, New York* (New York: The Trow City Directory Company, 1884), 1023; *City Directories for New York, New York* (New York: The Trow City Directory Company, 1885), 1061; *City Directories for New York, New York* (New York: The Trow City Directory Company, 1888), 1196; *City Directories for New York, New York* (New York: Trow Directory Printing and Bookbinding Company, 1902), 1135; *City Directories for New York, New York* (New York: Trow Directory Printing and Bookbinding Company, 1902), 116; *City Directories for New York, New York* (New York: Trow Directory Printing and Bookbinding Company, 1903), 1467; *City Directories for New York, New York* (New York: Trow Directory Printing and Bookbinding Company, 1903), 1195; *City Directories for New York, New York* (New York: Trow Directory Printing and Bookbinding Company, 1905), 154; *City Directories for New York, New York* (New York: Trow Directory Printing and Bookbinding Company, 1906), 936.

[15] "Biggest Kitchen in the World," *St. Louis Post-Dispatch,* August 21, 1904.

[16] Ibid.

[17] Luchow-Faust World's Fair Restaurant Co. menus, May 24, May 25, July 9, August 17, October 14, 1904, St. Louis: 1904 World's Fair, menu numbers 1-5, Missouri History Museum; Luchow-Faust World's Fair Restaurant Co. menu, November 1904, St. Louis: St. Louis Fairs & Expositions, Box #2, St. Louis Mercantile Library.

[18] "Biggest Kitchen in the World," *St. Louis Post-Dispatch,* August 21, 1904; Primm, *Lion of the Valley,* 391.

Chapter 5
Tony's Family

[1] St. Louis, Missouri, "Naturalization Records," *St. Louis Genealogical Society*, : accessed September 12, 2007, http://www.stlgs.org/NatDetail.aspx?naturalid=21987, entry for Anton Faust of Prussia, 1865; citing St. Louis Circuit Court; "IGI Individual Record database, *FamilySearch International Genealogical Index*, accessed January 19, 2010, http://www.familysearch.org :, entry for Anton Faust – Elis. Bischof, May 12, 1864; citing Saint Louis city, Missouri. Batch no. M515697, dates 1865-1869, source call no. 0528178, film.

[2] 1870 United States Federal Census, St. Louis Ward 2, St. Louis, Missouri, www.ancestry.com; 1880 United States Federal Census (June and November), St. Louis, Missouri, www.ancestry.com; Missouri. St. Louis City. Registry of Births (September 4, 1871), Faust, Anthony R., Missouri State Archives, Jefferson City.

[3] Smith Academy Catalogs, 1856-1917. Washington University Archives, St. Louis.

[4] Ibid.

[5] Benson J. Lossing, *History of New York City, Embracing an Outline Sketch of Events From 1609 to 1830, and a Full Account of its Development from 1830 to 1884* (New York: The Perine Engraving and Publishing Co., 1884), 684.

[6] Ibid., 684-686; "Opening of a Business College," *New York Times*, June 10, 1870; "A College Coming of Age," *New York Times*, December 18, 1879; "Packard's Business College," *Scientific American*, 43, no. 25 (December 18, 1880): 388-389; "Packard's College Fall Opening," *New York Times*, August 13, 1886; "Business Colleges: Packard Commercial School," *New York Daily Tribune*, September 7, 1907.

[7] Kate Cordes, Milstein Division of United States History, Local History & Genealogy, The New York Public Library, e-mail message to author regarding Tode Brothers' locations listed in New York City Directories, February 24, 2009; "Leases Recorded," *New York Times*, January 31, 1882; "Troubles of Business Men," *New York Tribune*, March 2, 1891; "Failures in Business," *New York Times*, March 26, 1891; "Failures in Business," *New York Times*, April 8, 1891; "Failures in Business," *New York Times*, April 21, 1891; "Petitions in Bankruptcy," *New York Times*, September 27, 1899; "In the District Court of the Unites States for the Southern District of New York: In Bankruptcy," *New York Times*,

October 9, 1899; "Discharges in Bankruptcy," *New York Times,* November 16, 1899.

[8] Ernst D. Kargau, *Mercantile, Industrial and Professional Saint Louis* (St. Louis: Nixon-Jones Printing Company, 1902), 552; *St. Louis: Queen City of the West* (St. Louis: Mercantile Advancement Co., 1899), 195; Mollie Faust, "A Birthday Gift to Mollie Faust, From Her Mama, May 31, 1878." Scrapbook filled with newspaper articles, passenger lists, memorabilia, etc. Missouri History Museum, St. Louis, 17.

[9] "Admitted His Guilt: An Employe [sic] at Faust's Confesses to Swindling His Employer, *St. Louis Post-Dispatch,* April 1, 1894.

[10] "Robbed Tony Faust: Waiters Had a Scheme That Was Better Than Tips," *St. Louis Post-Dispatch,* September 3, 1895.

[11] "Tony Faust's Home Looted: Systematic Robbery Extending Over One Year," *St. Louis Post-Dispatch,* October 11, 1900; "Tony Faust Robbed by Headwaiter: Joseph Weaver Confessed When Arrested," *St. Louis Post-Dispatch,* October 28, 1900; "Had Rich Tastes in His Thefts: Louis Weber Confronted By His Costly Stealings," *St. Louis Post-Dispatch,* October 29, 1900; "Bunch of Convicts: St. Louis Sends Up 22 Distinguished Prisoners," *St. Louis Post-Dispatch,* December 27, 1900.

[12] "Shut Off Their Beer: And Now the Waiters at Faust's Are Going Dry," *St. Louis Post-Dispatch,* June 23, 1895.

[13] "Wife is Hoping Against Hope For Faust's Recovery," *St. Louis Post-Dispatch,* November 9, 1911; "Beau Brummell," accessed April 27, 2010, www.wikipedia.com.

[14] "An Affair of Honor – and Oysters," *St. Louis Post-Dispatch,* September 25, 1897; "Oyster War Now Personal: The House of Gallais Now Arrayed Against the House of Faust," *St. Louis Post-Dispatch,* September 24, 1897.

[15] "The Delmar Jockey Club," display ad, *St. Louis Post-Dispatch,* June 30, 1901.

[16] "At The Liederkranz: A Series of Brilliant Tableaux Given Last Night," *St. Louis Post-Dispatch,* December 1, 1889; "The French Ball: Two Liederkranz Members Object to Insinuations of Disloyal Conduct," *St. Louis Post-Dispatch,* February 2, 1894.

[17] Edward A. Faust, "Last Bachelor Dinner of Ernest Holm," March 13, 1897. Souvenir book, #A2309 Faust, E.A. file, Missouri History Museum, St. Louis.

[18] Mollie Faust, scrapbook, 91-93.

[19] Ibid., 98-104; "Will Be Married To-Night: Nuptials of Miss Anna Louise Busch and Mr. Edward Faust," *St. Louis Post-Dispatch,* March 20, 1897.

[20] Mollie Faust, scrapbook, 103; Missouri. St. Louis City, birth record

reel C628 (December 1897), Faust, Leicester Busch; Missouri State Archives, Jefferson City.

[21] 1910 United States Federal Census, St. Louis Ward 10, St. Louis, Missouri, www.ancestry.com; Esley Hamilton, "The Faust Estate: A History," 3, Faust Park Records, Chesterfield, Missouri.

[22] 1900 United States Federal Census, St. Louis Wards 5 and 21, St. Louis, Missouri, www.ancestry.com; "Pretty Voice Won Mr. Faust's Heart," *St. Louis Post-Dispatch,* August 17, 1904; Mollie Faust, scrapbook, 109.

[23] "Tony Faust, Son of Café Founder, Dies in Sanitarium," *St. Louis Post-Dispatch,* May 4, 1914; "New Marquette Hotel Leased," *St. Louis Post-Dispatch,* October 13, 1906; "Webster Groves, Missouri: Area History," accessed October 18, 2010, http://www.webstergroves.org.

[24] Mollie Faust scrapbook, 66, 130; "Revel Still Reigns: Lent Does Not Prevent the Success of the Liederkranz Masquerade Ball," *St. Louis Globe-Democrat,* February 26, 1882; Mollie Faust report card, Lindenwood College, 1881. Faust, Anthony E. file, Missouri History Museum, St. Louis; "Mary Institute and St. Louis Country Day School (MICDS): A Brief History of Our School," accessed October 19, 2010, www.micds.org/aboutus.

[25] Mollie Faust, scrapbook, 27, 39, 43-45, 94.

[26] Ibid., 27.

[27] 1860 United States Federal Census, New York Ward 14 District 2, New York, New York, www.ancestry.com; "City Personals," *St. Louis Post-Dispatch,* February 17, 1886; "Society Gossip," *St. Louis Post-Dispatch,* February 27, 1886; "Wedded To-Day: Nuptials of Miss Mollie Faust and Mr. A.D. Giannini," *St. Louis Post-Dispatch,* February 24, 1886; "Wedding Bells: Celebration of Giannini-Faust Wedding Nuptials Last Evening," *St. Louis Globe-Democrat,* February 25, 1886; Mollie Faust, scrapbook, 43; Early U.S. French Catholic Church Records (Drouin Collection), 1695-1954," database *Ancestry.com,* accessed November 2, 2010, http://www.ancestry.com :, entry for Arthur David Ginannini – Mollie Faust, February 24, 1886; citing St. Louis city Catholique marriages. Original data: Gabriel Drouin, comp. *Drouin Collection.* Montreal, Quebec, Canada: Institut Genealogique Drouin.

[28] "Society News," *St. Louis Globe-Democrat,* October 30, 1887; "Society Gossip," *St. Louis Post-Dispatch,* December 11, 1888; Mollie Faust, scrapbook, 29, 32; *City Directories for New York, New York* (New York: The Trow City Directory Company, 1892), accessed September 12, 2009, www.footnote.com.

[29] Mollie Faust, scrapbook, 114; "Will Live in St. Louis," *St. Louis Post-Dispatch,* March 27, 1896.

[30] Mollie Faust, scrapbook, 105, 132.

[31] Ibid., 128, 153.

[32] Ibid., 123; 1900 United States Federal Census, St. Louis Ward 5, St. Louis, Missouri, www.ancestry.com; Postcard from Vera Giannini to her father, A.D. Giannini, August 8, 1911. St. Louis: Photographic collection, Missouri History Museum.

[33] "Local Personals," *St. Louis Globe-Democrat,* August 23, 1875.

[34] "St. Louisans in the Surf: How Western People Enjoy Themselves When They Go to the Seashore," *St. Louis Globe-Democrat,* July 2, 1879; "Leaving For a Rest," *St. Louis Globe-Democrat,* June 25, 1881; "Local Personals," *St. Louis Globe-Democrat,* July 20, 1882; "Washington: News and Notes From the Capital," *St. Louis Globe-Democrat,* March 29, 1882; "Society News," *St. Louis Globe-Democrat,* July 21, 1887; "Society News," *St. Louis Globe-Democrat,* August 7, 1887; "Society News," *St. Louis Globe-Democrat,* August 10, 1887; "New York Passenger Lists, 1820-1957," *Ancestry.com,* accessed April 14, 2010, http://www.search.ancestrylibrary.com , entry for Mr. and Mrs. A.E. Faust, Eddie and Tony Faust, arrived New York, New York 1887 aboard the *Norddeutscher.*

[35] Mollie Faust, scrapbook, 29; "Society News," *St. Louis Globe-Democrat,* April 3, 1887; "Society News," *St. Louis Globe-Democrat,* July 15, 1887; "In Society," *St. Louis Post-Dispatch,* June 20, 1888; "Departures," *St. Louis Post-Dispatch,* April 23, 1891; "Back From Europe: Tony Faust Returns to St. Louis After a Three Months' Visit," *St. Louis Post-Dispatch,* September 28, 1895; "All Aboard for Europe," *St. Louis Post-Dispatch,* May 16, 1897; "Society Events of Mid-Week," *St Louis Post-Dispatch,* May 16, 1897; "Society Gossip," *St. Louis Post-Dispatch,* May 28, 1899; "Mid-Week Society," *St. Louis Post-Dispatch,* June 22, 1899; "Society: St. Louisans Go To Europe," *St. Louis Post-Dispatch,* June 9, 1901.

[36] "Returns," *St. Louis Post-Dispatch,* April 17, 1892; "Society in Mid-Week: Gossip," *St. Louis Post-Dispatch,* March 16, 1899; "Society: St. Louisans in Hot Springs," *St. Louis Post-Dispatch,* March 19, 1899.

[37] "Faust," *The Spectator* 4, no. 128 (September 22, 1883): 26.

[38] "Sudhoff Was a Mark," *St. Louis Post-Dispatch,* September 3, 1901.

[39] "Tony Faust Injured Abroad," *St. Louis Post-Dispatch,* December 8, 1902.

[40] "New York Passenger Lists, 1820-1957," *Ancestry.com,* accessed April 14, 2010, http://www.search.ancestrylibrary.com , entry for Mr. and Mrs. A.E. Faust, Mrs. Mollie Faust and Miss Vera Giannini,

arrived New York, New York April 12, 1904 aboard the *Bluecher*; Anton Faust, March 24, 1905, passport application for himself, Elizabeth Faust, Mollie and Vera Giannini, City of St. Louis, State of Missouri. Record taken from Anthony E. Faust probate file 33329, Probate Court office; Civil Courts Building, St. Louis; "Tony Faust, Famed as Caterer, Dead," *St. Louis Post-Dispatch,* September 29, 1906.

[41] Mollie Faust, scrapbook, 153; "Tony Faust is Injured," *St. Louis Post-Dispatch,* August 3, 1906; "Tony Faust Dies Suddenly Abroad," *St. Louis Republic,* September 29, 1906.

[42] Mollie Faust, scrapbook, 139, 156, 158; "Myriad of Roses on Faust's Coffin," *St. Louis Post-Dispatch,* October 28, 1906.

BOOK TWO

Chapter 1
Life and Death

[1] "Faust Leaves $260,000: Widow Will Lose Her Share if She Weds Again," *St. Louis Post-Dispatch,* November 3, 1906; St. Louis City, Missouri. St. Louis: Anthony E. Faust probate file 33329.

[2] Edward F. Goltra, List of members of the Entertainment & House Committee of the Aero Club of St. Louis, September 29, 1909. (St. Louis: Edward F. Goltra Papers, Missouri History Museum); "This is Open Season for Aeroplanes: Aero Club Members Flighty," *St. Louis Post-Dispatch,* October 11, 1908; "Dozier Elected Aero Club Head Despite Protest," *St. Louis Post-Dispatch,* February 3, 1910.

[3] "Society," *St. Louis Post-Dispatch,* April 22, 1908; "Carnival Crowd Breaking Records; So Are Receipts," *St. Louis Post-Dispatch,* May 16, 1908; "German Village Girls At Picnic for Altenheim: Waitresses at Charity Carnival Will Serve Once More," *St. Louis Post-Dispatch,* May 31, 1908; "Society Women Aid Festival for Altenheim: Managers of German Village Have Charge of Next Sunday's Event," *St. Louis Post-Dispatch,* June 4, 1908; "Thousands in Joyous Crowd at Altenheim: Annual Spring Festival Included Singing and Exhibition by Turners," *St. Louis Post-Dispatch,* June 8, 1908.

[4] "Society," *St. Louis Post-Dispatch,* November 20, 1904.

[5] "Summer Work to Save the Babies Now Well Begun," *St. Louis Post-Dispatch,* May 24, 1911.
[6] "Mrs. Busch gives $8000, Mrs. Faust $5000 to Y.W.C.A.: $35,163.66 is Added to the Building Fund by Workers Monday," *St. Louis Post-Dispatch,* May 9, 1910; "Three Days Left to Get $45,729 for the Y.W.C.A," *St. Louis Post-Dispatch,* May 15, 1910.
[7] "Society Girls Aiding Y.W.C.A. to Snub Stingy Men: Beaux Who Do Not Contribute Liberally Will Be Blacklisted," *St. Louis Post-Dispatch,* May 10, 1910.
[8] "New Year's Day: List of Ladies Who Will Receive Callers," *St. Louis Post-Dispatch,* December 31, 1885; "Year's Calls," *St. Louis Globe-Democrat,* January 1, 1886.
[9] "Euchre," last modified December 26, 2011, accessed July 19, 2010, http://en.wikipedia.org/wiki/Euchre.
[10] "Society Gossip," *St. Louis Post-Dispatch,* January 23, 1889; "Active in Society," *St. Louis Post-Dispatch,* January 26, 1893; "The Week in Society," *St. Louis Post-Dispatch,* February 16, 1896; "Society," *St. Louis Post-Dispatch,* February 21, 1897; "Midweek in Society," *St. Louis Post-Dispatch,* May 3, 1900.
[11] "The Week in St. Louis Society," *St. Louis Post-Dispatch,* March 20, 1898; "In and Of Society," *St. Louis Post-Dispatch,* March 13, 1898; "All About Society," *St. Louis Post-Dispatch,* March 27, 1898.
[12] Mollie Faust, "A Birthday Gift to Mollie Faust, From Her Mama, May 31, 1878." Scrapbook filled with newspaper articles, passenger lists, memorabilia, etc. Missouri History Museum, St. Louis, 39; "News of St. Louis Society," *St. Louis Post-Dispatch,* January 25, 1910; "Society," *St. Louis Post-Dispatch,* February 7, 1897; "The Passing Show," *St. Louis Post-Dispatch,* March 15, 1896; "Society," *St. Louis Post-Dispatch,* February 12, 1908.
[13] "Tony Faust Suffers Breakdown in East," *St. Louis Post-Dispatch,* May 13, 1911; "Faust Not Seriously Ill," *St. Louis Post-Dispatch,* May 26, 1911; "Tony Faust's Sanity Questioned in Suit," *St. Louis Post-Dispatch,* November 8, 1911; "Wife is Hoping Against Hope For Faust's Recovery," *St. Louis Post-Dispatch,* November 9, 1911; "Tony Faust is Found Insane in Three Minutes: Whole Proceedings of the Case Last Less Than Quarter of an Hour," *St. Louis Post-Dispatch,* November 21, 1911.
[14] "Doings in Society," *St. Louis Post-Dispatch,* February 2, 1908; "Society," *St. Louis Post-Dispatch,* July 26, 1908; "Society," *St. Louis Post-Dispatch,* August 28, 1908; "Society," *St. Louis Post-Dispatch,* December 16, 1908; "Society," *St. Louis Post-Dispatch,* March 12, 1909; "Society," *St. Louis Post-Dispatch,* December 14, 1909;

"Holidays Bring Younger Set From School to Society Whirl: Many St. Louisans Return From Far Places to Dance, Dine, and Go to the Play While Others Spend Their Yuletide at Distant Firesides," *St. Louis Post-Dispatch,* December 26, 1909.

[15] Mollie Faust, scrapbook, 162-170.

[16] Carol Ferring Shepley, *Movers & Shakers, Scalawags & Suffragettes: Tales From Bellefontaine Cemetery* (St. Louis: Missouri History Museum, 2008), 47; Mollie Faust, scrapbook, 180; "Florists Taxed to Supply Busch Funeral Emblems: Pieces Larger and More Numerous Than Any Ever Seen Here Before," *St. Louis Post-Dispatch,* October 24, 1913.

[17] St. Louis City, Missouri. St. Louis: Elizabeth Bischoff Faust probate file 42888.

[18] Ibid.; "Tony Faust, Son of Café Founder, Dies in Sanitarium," *St. Louis Post-Dispatch,* May 4, 1914; "Obituaries," *St. Louis Post-Dispatch,* May 5, 1914; "Burial Permits," *St. Louis Post-Dispatch,* May 6, 1914; Mollie Faust, scrapbook, 46.

[19] B. John Melloni, June L. Melloni, Ida G. Dox, and Gilbert M. Eisner, eds., *Melloni's Illustrated Medical Dictionary* 4th ed. (Nashville: Parthenon Publishing Group, 2002), 486.

Chapter 2
A Member of the Posse

[1] "St. Louis News," *The Builder* 10, no. 32 (August 17, 1903): 4; Charles C. Savage, *Architecture of the Private Streets of St. Louis: The Architects and The Houses They Designed* (Columbia: University of Missouri Press, 1987), xi, 182-183; Julius K. Hunter, *Westmoreland and Portland Places: The History of America's Premier Private Streets, 1888-1988,* with a Foreword by James Neal Primm and Essay on the Architecture by Esley Hamilton, (Columbia: University of Missouri Press, 1988), 191, 206; Smith Academy Catalogues, 1909-1913, Washington University Archives, St. Louis.

[2] James A. Henretta, David Brody, and Lynn Dumenil, *America: A Concise History* (Boston: Bedford / St. Martin's, 1999), 548-549.

[3] Savage, *Architecture of the Private Streets,* 42-44, 62, 66-67; Elizabeth McNulty, *St. Louis Then & Now* (San Diego: Thunder Bay Press, 2000), 142.

[4] Savage, *Architecture of the Private Streets,* 67.

[5] Hunter, *Westmoreland and Portland Places*, 191.
[6] "New Homes in St. Louis: Residence of Mr. and Mrs. E.A. Faust, No. 1 Portland Place," *St. Louis Post-Dispatch*, April 5, 1914.
[7] Ibid.
[8] Mark McCloskey, 1 Portland Place (tour, 1 Portland Place, St. Louis, Missouri, January 24, 2010).
[9] "Faust to Open Mansion to Public for Charity: New Marble Palace to be Scene of Big Tea Party, Orphans' Home Will Receive Proceeds," *St. Louis Post-Dispatch*, June 4, 1914.
[10] "Baronial Castle is to be Erected by Gussie Busch: Grant Farm on Gravois Road Will Be Transformed into Fairyland," *St. Louis Post-Dispatch*, June 12, 1910; Roland Krebs and Percy J. Orthwein, *Making Friends is Our Business: 100 Years of Anheuser-Busch* (St. Louis: Anheuser-Busch, 1953), 67; Hunter, *Westmoreland and Portland Places*, 47; Peter Hernon and Terry Ganey, *Under the Influence: The Unauthorized Story of the Anheuser-Busch Dynasty* (New York: Avon Books, 1991), 78-79.
[11] Hernon and Ganey, *Under the Influence*, 79; Mary Bartley, *St. Louis Lost* (St. Louis: Virginia Publishing, 1994), 89; Krebs and Orthwein, *Making Friends is Our Business*, 67-68; "Gifts Worth Half Million at Busch Golden Wedding Include Kaiser's Tribute," *St. Louis Post-Dispatch*, March 7, 1911; "Brewery Closed, Salute is Fired: Employes [sic] Will Gather in Coliseum, With Fausts as Acting Hosts," *St. Louis Post-Dispatch*, March 7, 1911.
[12] Edward Faust to David R. Francis. Response to Adolphus Busch's invitation to World's Fair Directors' meeting, April 24, 1913. St. Louis: Louisiana Purchase Exposition Company Collection, Missouri History Museum.
[13] *Men of Affairs in St. Louis* (St. Louis: Press Club, 1915), 51; "Property of Mrs. Busch, Taken by U.S. Custodian, is Valued at $15,000,000," *St. Louis Republic*, June 18, 1918; "$50,000 Private Car Elaborately Furnished Given to Adolphus Busch," *St. Louis Post-Dispatch*, November 3, 1901; "'Hi-Lee, Hi-Lo' in Busch's Honor: Generous Donor to San Francisco Relief Serenaded by Liederkranz," *St. Louis Post-Dispatch*, May 3, 1906; Krebs and Orthwein, *Making Friends is Our Business*, 440.
[14] Hunter, *Westmoreland and Portland Places*, 36, 51; Henretta, Brody and Dumenil, *America*, 547-548; "The Fourth National Bank" ad, *St. Louis Post-Dispatch*, May 5, 1902; "The Fourth National Bank" ad, *St. Louis Post-Dispatch*, January 7, 1903.
[15] Jim Healey (expert on the history of St. Louis golf), interview with author, October 22, 2009; Jim Healey, e-mail message to author,

February 6, 2010; "Society," *St. Louis Post-Dispatch,* July 6, 1902; Hunter, *Westmoreland and Portland Places,* 42; "Sunset Country Club," accessed November 18, 2010, www.sunsetcountryclub.org; "Glen Echo Country Club History," accessed November 19, 2010, www.gecc.org.
[16] "Sunset Country Club," accessed November 18, 2010, www.sunsetcountryclub.org.
[17] Lawrence O. Christensen, William E. Foley, Gary R. Kremer and Kenneth H. Winn, *Dictionary of Missouri Biography* (Columbia, MO: University of Missouri Press, 1999), 137.
[18] Mollie Faust, "A Birthday Gift to Mollie Faust, From Her Mama, May 31, 1878." Scrapbook filled with newspaper articles, passenger lists, memorabilia, etc. Missouri History Museum, St. Louis, 97.
[19] "The News in Society," *St. Louis Post-Dispatch,* April 29, 1900.
[20] "Some Things Concerning the 'Somebodies' in St. Louis: Edward A. Faust, Prince of the Royal House, or Another Big Man From the Little American Cabin," *St. Louis Post-Dispatch,* June 21, 1903.
[21] Hunter, *Westmoreland and Portland Places,* with Foreword by Primm, 9, 24, 42-43; Henretta, Brody and Dumenil, *America,* 547-549; Alexander Scot McConachie, "The 'Big Cinch': A Business Elite in the Life of a City, Saint Louis, 1895-1915." PhD diss., Washington University, St. Louis, 1976, 24-27.
[22] Krebs and Orthwein, *Making Friends is Our Business,* 259; *Book of St. Louisans: A Biographical Dictionary of Leading Living Men of the City of St. Louis and Vicinity* (St. Louis: St. Louis Republic, 1912), 191; Ronald Jan Plavchan, *A History of Anheuser-Busch, 1852-1933* (North Stratford, NH: Ayer, 1969), 79-81.
[23] McConachie, "The 'Big Cinch,'" 57-58.
[24] Ibid., 60.
[25] Ibid., 61; *Men of Affairs in Saint Louis* (St. Louis: Press Club, 1915), 51.
[26] McConachie, "The 'Big Cinch,'" 67, 70-71, 79; "The Fourth National Bank" ad, *St. Louis Post-Dispatch,* May 5, 1902; "The Fourth National Bank" ad, *St. Louis Post-Dispatch,* January 7, 1903; Hunter, *Westmoreland and Portland Places,* 51; James Cox, *Old and New St. Louis: A Concise History of the Metropolis of the West and Southwest, With a Review of its Present Greatness and Immediate Prospects* (St. Louis: Central Biographical Publishing Co., 1891), 212.
[27] McConachie, "The 'Big Cinch,'" 141, 158-159; James Neal Primm: *Lion of the Valley: St. Louis, Missouri, 1761-1980* 3rd ed., (St. Louis: Missouri Historical Society Press, 1998), 353-354.
[28] Ibid., 354-355.

[29] "St. Louis in Year After Fair as an Eastern Writer Sees It," *St. Louis Post-Dispatch,* May 14, 1905.
[30] Lana Stein, *St. Louis Politics: The Triumph of Tradition* (St. Louis: Missouri Historical Society Press, 2002), 18.
[31] McConachie, "The 'Big Cinch,'" 158.
[32] Ibid., 141, 164-166, 169; Primm, *Lion of the Valley,* 353-354.
[33] Ibid., 358-359.
[34] "Several Lines Open This Afternoon: Police Say All Cars Can Run if There Are Men – Transit Co. Asks Strikers to Return," *St. Louis Post-Dispatch,* May 11, 1900.
[35] "Incidents of the Strike: Brief Items About Minor Happenings in the Present Street Railway Situation," *St. Louis Post-Dispatch,* May 21, 1900.
[36] "Some Untold Tales of the Street Car Strike," *St. Louis Post-Dispatch,* May 20, 1900.
[37] Truman A. Post to Col. John H. Cavender. Letter discussing the general type of men volunteering for the posse comitatus, June 13, 1900. Cavender, John H. – St. Louis Streetcar Strike Papers. St. Louis: Missouri History Museum.
[38] McConachie, "The 'Big Cinch,'" 213-214; Primm, *Lion of the Valley,* 359.
[39] George S. Stoodman to Wallace D. Simmons. Letter offering assistance in Streetcar Strike, June 8, 1900. Cavender, John H. – St. Louis Streetcar Strike Papers, Missouri History Museum, St. Louis.
[40] "Account of Sheriff's Posse Supplies as Delivered to Wagons of Commissioner of Supplies," June 28, June 29, July 6, 1900. St. Louis: Cavender, John H. - St. Louis Streetcar Strike Papers, Missouri History Museum.
[41] John H. Cavender to Sheriff's Posse commanders of detachments. Letter of instruction, June 4, 1900. Cavender, John H. – St. Louis Streetcar Strike Papers. Missouri History Museum, St. Louis.
[42] Captain McEntire and Captain Clarkson to citizens of St. Louis. Letter warning citizens to disperse assemblies and keep peace, June 10, 1900. Cavender, John H. – St. Louis Streetcar Strike Papers, Missouri History Museum, St. Louis.
[43] *New York World* to Col. John H. Cavender. Telegram regarding St. Louis Streetcar Strike, 1900; Cavender, John H. – St. Louis Streetcar Strike Papers, Missouri History Museum, St. Louis.
[44] "The St. Louis Strike," *Collier's Weekly,* June 30, 1900. Cavender, John H. – St. Louis Streetcar Strike Papers, Missouri History Museum, St. Louis.
[45] "The St. Louis Strike," *Harper's Weekly,* June 23, 1900. Cavender,

John H. – St. Louis Streetcar Strike Papers, Missouri History Museum, St. Louis.
[46] Primm, *Lion of the Valley,* 362.

Chapter 3
The American German-American

[1] Gerhard K. Friesen and Walter Schatzberg, eds., *The German Contribution to the Building of the Americas* (Hanover, NH: Clark University Press, 1977), 292-293; Audrey L. Olson, "St. Louis Germans, 1850-1920: The Nature of an Immigrant Community and Its Relation to the Assimilation Process" (dissertation, University of Kansas, 1980), 4-6.
[2] Frances Hurd Stadler, *St. Louis: From Laclede to Land Clearance* (St. Louis: Radio Station KSD and Kriegshauser Mortuaries, 1962), 26; Friesen and Schatzberg, eds., *The German Contribution,* 296-299.
[3] Wm. L. Montague, *The Saint Louis Business Directory for 1853-4* (Saint Louis: E.A. Lewis, 1853).
[4] Ernst D. Kargau, *Mercantile, Industrial and Professional Saint Louis* (St. Louis: Nixon-Jones Printing Co., 1902), 39-40.
[5] Ibid., 40.
[6] Don Heinrich Tolzmann, ed. and William G. Bek, trans., *The German Element in St. Louis. A translation from German of Ernst D. Kargau's St. Louis in Former Years: A Commemorative History of the German Element* (Baltimore: Clearfield Company, Inc., 2000), 138.
[7] Wm. S. Bryan and Robert Rose, *A History of the Pioneer Families of Missouri* (St. Louis: Bryan, Bran and Co., 1876), 450.
[8] Olson, "St. Louis Germans," 95.
[9] Smith Academy Catalogues, 1856-1917. Washington University Archives, St. Louis.
[10] Olson, "St. Louis Germans," 91-101; Friesen and Schatzberg, eds., *The German Contribution,* 303.
[11] Olson, "St. Louis Germans," 134.
[12] Ibid.
[13] Ibid., 133-141; "Liederkranz Masquerade," *St. Louis Post-Dispatch,* January 26, 1896.
[14] Olson, "St. Louis Germans," 114; Friesen and Schatzberg, eds., *The German Contribution,* 300.
[15] "German-American Veterans," *St. Louis Post-Dispatch,* June 3, 1885.

[16] Olson, "St. Louis Germans," 176-177.
[17] Ibid., 178-179.
[18] Ibid., 186.
[19] Ibid., 186-187.
[20] Ibid., 188.
[21] Ibid., 191.
[22] Ibid., 192-194.
[23] "Reserves Throng to Answer Calls: Marching Germans Cheer the Kaiser and Sing 'Watch on the Rhine,'" *New York Times,* August 4, 1914.
[24] Olson, "St. Louis Germans," 203-205.
[25] Michael Warner, "The Kaiser Sows Destruction: Protecting the Homeland the First Time Around," *Center for the Study of Intelligence Journal* 46, no. 1 (April 2007): 1, www.cia.gov/library.
[26] Ibid., 2-5.
[27] Olson, "St. Louis Germans," 205-207.
[28] Robert Lansing, *War Memoirs of Robert Lansing, Secretary of State* (Westport, Conn: Greenwood Press, 1970), 84.
[29] Olson, "St. Louis Germans," 208; "Gets Five Years for Espionage," *St. Louis Post-Dispatch,* October 23, 1918.
[30] Olson, "St. Louis Germans," 208-209; Peter Hernon and Terry Ganey, *Under the Influence: The Unauthorized Story of the Anheuser-Busch Dynasty* (New York: Avon Books, 1991), 90-91; "Planning Return of Mrs. Lilly Busch to United States," *St. Louis Post-Dispatch,* November 15, 1917; Ronald Jan Plavchan, *A History of Anheuser-Busch, 1852-1933* (North Stratford, NH: Ayer Company Publishers, Inc., 1969), 140-141.
[31] Ibid.
[32] "Property of Mrs. Busch, Taken by U.S. Custodian, is Valued at $15,000,000," *St. Louis Republic,* June 18, 1918.
[33] Ibid; "Relatives Greet Mrs. Lilly Busch at Union Station," *St. Louis Post-Dispatch,* June 22, 1918; Hernon and Ganey, *Under the Influence,* 103.
[34] Olson, "St. Louis Germans," 209.
[35] "Mrs. A.W. Lambert Chairman of Buy-in-St. Louis League," *St. Louis Post-Dispatch,* May 12, 1915; "Woman to Lecture Here on Her Experiences in War Zone," *St. Louis Post-Dispatch,* January 4, 1917; "Red Cross Here Gets Pledges for 15,000 Members," *St. Louis Post-Dispatch,* February 24, 1917; "Entertainment for Hospital in France: Will Be Given Three Evenings at Odeon by Children of America Loyalty League," *St. Louis Post-Dispatch,* October 2, 1918; "Patronesses Named for the Victory Ball: Include Some of the Best

Known Women in the St. Louis Social World," *St. Louis Post-Dispatch*, February 6, 1919; "Saving on Dinner Tuesday Urged to Aid Hoover Fund: All St. Louisans Are Asked to Eat Meager Meal and Give Difference in Cost to Relief in Europe," *St. Louis Post-Dispatch*, February 6, 1921.

[36] "Liberty Bond Rally Day" ad, *St. Louis Post-Dispatch*, October 23, 1917; "Social Items," *St. Louis Post-Dispatch*, June 13, 1918; "Events in the Social World: Society People are Eagerly Looking Forward to Automobile Fashion Parade in Connection With Patriotic Meet for America Fund for French Wounded at Maxwelton Park, Oct. 5 and 6," *St. Louis Post-Dispatch*, September 22, 1918; "Subscriptions to War Fund Not Yet Totaled: Uncertain Whether They Will Reach City's Minimum Quota of $2,250,000," *St. Louis Post-Dispatch*, November 28, 1918; "Events in the Social World," *St. Louis Post-Dispatch*, February 23, 1919.

[37] "How Deaf Hear With Eyes To Be Shown: Demonstrations Will Be Given at Reception for Institute Pupils at Faust Home Today," *St. Louis Post-Dispatch*, December 11, 1921.

Chapter 4
The Art of Making Money

[1] "Events in the Social World," *St. Louis Post-Dispatch*, December 30, 1917; "Society," *St. Louis Post-Dispatch*, May 15, 1916; "Social Items," *St. Louis Post-Dispatch*, October 29, 1919.

[2] "Events in the Social World," *St. Louis Post-Dispatch*, August 14, 1921; "Social Items," *St. Louis Post-Dispatch*, September 27, 1921.

[3] "Elaborate Springtime Setting for Ball at Faust Home," *St. Louis Post-Dispatch*, November 20, 1921.

[4] "Colorful East Indian Ball Friday: Affair at Faust Home Will Be Outstanding Among Events of the Pre-Holiday Period," *St. Louis Post-Dispatch*, December 3, 1922.

[5] Ibid.; "Oriental Splendor Marks East Indian Ball at Faust Home: Princesses, Rajahs, Hindoo Dancers and Snake Charmers Among Guests at Brilliant Affair," *St. Louis Post-Dispatch*, December 10, 1922; "Sketched by Marguerite Martyn at the East Indian Durbar Ball Given by Mr. and Mrs. Edward A. Faust," *St. Louis Post-Dispatch*, December 17, 1922; "Durbar," *A Dictionary of World History*, 2000. www.encyclopedia.com.

[6] "Social Items," *St. Louis Post-Dispatch,* May 22, 1922; "Social Items," *St. Louis Post-Dispatch,* May 25, 1922; "Social Items: Debutantes and Escorts at the Papa Club Fete Yesterday," *St. Louis Post-Dispatch,* May 26, 1922.

[7] "Society," *St. Louis Post-Dispatch,* December 6, 1917; "Social Items," *St. Louis Post-Dispatch,* May 6, 1918; "Patriotic Luncheon for Eastern Visitor," *St. Louis Post-Dispatch,* May 8, 1918; "Society to Entertain Junior League Visitors: Many Affairs Planned for Those Who Will Attend Four-Day Conference Next Week," *St. Louis Post-Dispatch,* April 29, 1920; "Junior League Convention: Delegates to be Entertained at Several Affairs Here Today," *St. Louis Post-Dispatch,* May 7, 1920; "Events in the Social World," *St. Louis Post-Dispatch,* October 17, 1920; "Social Items," *St. Louis Post-Dispatch,* April 10, 1922; "Needlework Guild to Convene May 4: St. Louis Organization Last Year Distributed 12,000 Garments to Charitable Institutions," *St. Louis Post-Dispatch,* April 18, 1922.

[8] "Events in the Social World," *St. Louis Post-Dispatch,* November 24, 1918; "'Dollar Dance' at Coliseum Tonight: Grand March and Community Sing on Program of Benefit for Children's Hospital," *St. Louis Post-Dispatch,* May 23, 1919; "Events in the Social World," *St. Louis Post-Dispatch,* June 11, 1922; "Events in the Social World: Society Matrons and Maids, in Midst of What Promises to Be a Brilliant Season, Turn Attention to $300,000 Campaign for Additions to Buildings at Children's Hospital," *St. Louis Post-Dispatch,* September 24, 1922; "Society and the Veiled Prophet," *St. Louis Post-Dispatch,* October 1, 1922; "$156,247 Pledged to Children's Hospital," *St. Louis Post-Dispatch,* October 13, 1922; "Benefit Performance for Orphan Asylum," *St. Louis Post-Dispatch,* November 21, 1920; "Ball for Benefit of Orphans' Home," *St. Louis Post-Dispatch,* December 6, 1920; "Children to See Stone in Tip-Top Tomorrow," *St. Louis Post-Dispatch,* December 26, 1922.

[9] "New Directors are Elected by Missouri Welfare League," *St. Louis Post-Dispatch,* June 18, 1922.

[10] "Campaign for Washington U. Fund Starts With $100,000," *St. Louis Post-Dispatch,* January 6, 1920; "Hospital Collection Committees Names," *St. Louis Post-Dispatch,* November 13, 1921; "'Proctor for Senator' Club Organized in St. Louis," *St. Louis Post-Dispatch,* July 1, 1922; "Municipal Theater Officers Elected," *St. Louis Post-Dispatch,* October 21, 1921; "10 Weeks of Municipal Opera for Next Year," *St. Louis Post-Dispatch,* October 6, 1922; James A. Henretta, David Brody, and Lynn Dumenil, *America: A Concise History* (Boston: Bedford / St. Martin's, 1999), 546-547.

[11] "When St. Louis Society Dances Downtown After the Theater," *St. Louis Post-Dispatch*, December 19, 1920.

[12] "B.M.L. to Raise Endowment Fund to Aid Symphony: Campaign Launched to Provide $45,000 Annually for Next Four Years," *St. Louis Post-Dispatch*, March 3, 1914.

[13] "Symphony Seeks $11,000 to Meet Deficit: Effort Being Made to Collect Funds to Prevent Closing of Season in Debt," *St. Louis Post-Dispatch*, March 12, 1917.

[14] "Symphony Society to Campaign for $12,000: Committee to Open Drive Tomorrow to Complete Guarantee Fund," *St. Louis Post-Dispatch*, September 30, 1917.

[15] "$30,000 Needed to Keep Symphony Orchestra Intact: Heavy Expense of Organization This Year Attributed to Competition of Moving Picture Houses," *St. Louis Post-Dispatch*, December 16, 1920.

[16] "Three Officers of Symphony Re-Elected to Make Donations," *St. Louis Post-Dispatch*, January 7, 1919.

[17] "Symphony Needs $15,000 More to Meet Deficit: All But This Amount of $105,000 Loss for Year Has Been Raised – Public Asked to Contribute," *St. Louis Post-Dispatch*, March 29, 1922; "Successful Season of Symphony Orchestra: $5,000 Contributed at Annual Meeting on $17,901 Deficit of Previous Years," *St. Louis Post-Dispatch*, May 20, 1922.

[18] "American Opera," *St. Louis Post-Dispatch*, January 5, 1911.

[19] Ibid.; "Site is Acquired for New Home for Grand Opera: Syndicate Buys the Old Hunter-Fraley Mansion at 3650 Lindell Boulevard," *St. Louis Post-Dispatch*, January 28, 1917.

[20] "St. Louis Season of Grand Opera is Now Outlined," *St. Louis Post-Dispatch*, January 4, 1914; "Boxes for Opera Season Rapidly Are Being Taken," *St. Louis Post-Dispatch*, October 4, 1914.

[21] "Site is Acquired for New Home for Grand Opera: Syndicate Buys the Old Hunter-Fraley Mansion at 3650 Lindell Boulevard," *St. Louis Post-Dispatch*, January 28, 1917.

[22] Ibid.

[23] Ibid.

[24] Ibid.; "The Opera House Project," *St. Louis Post-Dispatch*, January 30, 1917.

[25] St. Louis, Missouri, "Deed Records," City Block 1960, Deed Books 488:5, 467:67, 526:101, Edward A. Faust and the Thirty-Six Fifty Lindell Corporation, 1917-1920; St. Louis City Hall.

[26] "Society," *St. Louis Post-Dispatch*, July 13, 1916; "Events in the Social World," *St. Louis Post-Dispatch*, July 8, 1917; "Many St. Louisans at Biddeford Pool: Another Large Colony Has Gone to Rye

Beach, N.H. for Summer," *St. Louis Post-Dispatch,* July 7, 1920; "What St. Louisans Away for Summer Months Are Doing," *St. Louis Post-Dispatch,* July 18, 1920; "Social Items," *St. Louis Post-Dispatch,* July 18, 1921; "Events in the Social World: Many St. Louisans at Resorts on the New England Coast," *St. Louis Post-Dispatch,* July 24, 1921; "Events in the Social World: Informal Attractions of Smaller Resorts Draw Many From St. Louis to the Ozarks and Other Missouri Summering Points," *St. Louis Post-Dispatch,* July 31, 1921; "Social Items," *St. Louis Post-Dispatch,* September 2, 1921; "Social Items," *St. Louis Post-Dispatch,* September 8, 1921; "Social Items," *St. Louis Post-Dispatch,* January 27, 1922; "Events in the Social World: Migration of St. Louisans to Winter Resorts Will be on in Full Blast," *St. Louis Post-Dispatch,* January 29, 1922; "Social Items," *St. Louis Post-Dispatch,* February 6, 1922; "Society News," *St. Louis Post-Dispatch,* March 27, 1922; "Social Items," *St. Louis Post-Dispatch,* June 13, 1922; "Will Sail for Europe Soon," *St. Louis Post-Dispatch,* December 31, 1922.

[27] Edward Faust to Edward F. Goltra. Letter regarding Rochester, New York, telephone deal, June 11, 1907. St. Louis: Edward F. Goltra Papers, Missouri History Museum; "Local Money in $6,000,000 Phone Offer," *St. Louis Post-Dispatch,* June 11, 1907; "Big 'Phone Co. is Formed by St. Louis Men," *St. Louis Post-Dispatch,* June 14, 1907; "Legal Notices," *St. Louis Post-Dispatch,* January 20, 1908; "Rochester Telephone Corporation," *Funding Universe,* accessed February 14, 2011, www.fundinguniverse.com/company-histories/; "Legal Notices," *St. Louis Post-Dispatch,* January 27, 1908; "Local Investors Lose Fortune in Telephone Deal," *St. Louis Post-Dispatch,* February 14, 1908; "Phone Concern Fails; St. Louis Men Interested: Stock and Bonds of United States independent Co. Held Here," *St. Louis Post-Dispatch,* April 5, 1908; Edward Faust to Edward F. Goltra. Letter regarding Rochester, New York telephone deal, May 15, 1908. St. Louis: Edward F. Goltra Papers, Missouri History Museum; "Wall Street in Plot to Change Jersey Courts: Three Recent Decisions Have Hit Corporation Methods Severe Blows," *St. Louis Post-Dispatch,* March 22, 1909; "Jones Got His Money Back in Phone Failure," *St. Louis Post-Dispatch,* May 24, 1909; "Breckinridge Jones Asserts He Got No Money For Losses: Worthless Bonds Given for His Telephone Stock, Says Former Promoter," *St. Louis Post-Dispatch,* May 25, 1909; "Independents in Telephone Fight Raise $150,000," *St. Louis Post-Dispatch,* January 8, 1910; "Telephone Suit a Fight for Life Against Trust: Charge of Conspiracy to Destroy Independents Back of St. Louis Hearing," *St. Louis Post-Dispatch,* January 9, 1910; "Missouri Takes Hand in War on Tel-Tel Merger," *St. Louis Post-Dispatch,* February 9, 1910; "Priest Led

Jones to Buy Telephone Stock, Is Evidence," *St. Louis Post-Dispatch*, September 8, 1910; "Jones Denies He Dodged Inquiry on Telephone Stock," *St. Louis Post-Dispatch*, September 9, 1910; "Morgan Deal On For Kansas City Phone Co.'s Stock," *St. Louis Post-Dispatch*, February 8, 1911; "Phone Company Voting Trustees Held To Be Liable," *St. Louis Post-Dispatch*, June 20, 1912; "Busch Sued For $750,000; Gotham Realty Attached: Six Actions Filed in Rochester to Recover Money Invested in Telephone Company," *St. Louis Post-Dispatch*, February 6, 1913; "C.M. Forster's Widow Sued by Phone Concern," *St. Louis Post-Dispatch*, February 14, 1913; "Four St. Louisans Sued in Bond Deal for $105,000," *St. Louis Post-Dispatch*, August 26, 1913; "Busch's Body is on Ship, on Way to United States," *St. Louis Post-Dispatch*, October 14, 1913; "Morgan Loses Control of Ohio Phone Lines," *St. Louis Post-Dispatch*, May 21, 1914; "Busch Executors Fight Claim of $20,000 Against Estate: Suit Brought to Prevent Eastern Company From Collecting the Amount," *St. Louis Post-Dispatch*, December 15, 1915; "St. Louis Investors Lose U.S. Telephone Recovery Suits," *St. Louis Post-Dispatch*, January 17, 1917; *Men of Affairs in Saint Louis* (St. Louis: Press Club, 1915), 51; "The Northeastern Reporter: Comprising All the Decisions of the Supreme Courts," *National Reporter System – State Series* 116, permanent ed. (June 5 – September 25, 1917): 24-28. www.googlebooks.com.

[28] "St. Louisans to Urge U.S. Use of River on M'Adoo," *St. Louis Post-Dispatch*, May 19, 1918.

[29] "Mississippi Put Into Use as a Carrier," *St. Louis Post-Dispatch*, July 12, 1918.

[30] "Plans for River Traffic Are To Be Hurried Here," *St. Louis Post-Dispatch*, July 14, 1918.

[31] "Plans Federal Barge Line in 2 Months," *St. Louis Post-Dispatch*, July 17, 1918.

[32] "Government Barge Service Starts Today," *St. Louis Post-Dispatch*, September 28, 1918.

[33] "$6,170,000 Barge Line Contract Let by U.S." *St. Louis Post-Dispatch*, October 23, 1918.

[34] "St. Louisans to Urge U.S. Use of River on M'Adoo," *St. Louis Post-Dispatch*, May 19, 1918; "M'Adoo Aid Wants River Used at Once," *St. Louis Post-Dispatch*, July 10, 1918; "Mississippi Put Into Use As a Carrier," *St. Louis Post-Dispatch*, July 12, 1918; "Plans for River Traffic Are To Be Hurried Here," *St. Louis Post-Dispatch*, July 14, 1918; "Plans Federal Barge Line in 2 Months," *St. Louis Post-Dispatch*, July 17, 1918; "Maj. Fordyce to Build River Terminals Here," *St. Louis Post-Dispatch*, August 31, 1918; "Barge Service Will Start Late in

Month," *St. Louis Post-Dispatch,* September 8, 1918; "Government Barge Service Starts Today," *St. Louis Post-Dispatch,* September 28, 1918; "$6,170,000 Barge Line Contract Let by U.S." *St. Louis Post-Dispatch,* October 23, 1918.

[35] "$1,000,000 Contract for River Barges Won by St. Louisans: Edward A. Faust Home From Washington, Says Company May Also Get Towboats Award," *St. Louis Post-Dispatch,* February 2, 1919.

[36] "Officers Here Today to Let Towboat Order," *St. Louis Post-Dispatch,* June 16, 1919.

[37] "4 River Barges Will Be Built in Local Plant: Company Represented by E.A. Faust is Lowest Bidder on Several More Craft and May Get Contract," *St. Louis Post-Dispatch,* February 1, 1919; "Government Engineer Places Contract for Four Towboats," *St. Louis Post-Dispatch,* June 17, 1919; "Men From Valley to Urge Passage of Newton Bill," *St. Louis Post-Dispatch,* January 16, 1921; "Valley Association Committee to Meet Here," *St. Louis Post-Dispatch,* May 20, 1921; "Champagne Shower Christens 'Mobile,'" *St. Louis Post-Dispatch,* April 20, 1921; "James E. Smith Heads Valley Association: Convention Urges Completion of River Development and Furthering of Great Lakes Project," *St. Louis Post-Dispatch,* April 27, 1922.

[38] "What 317,000 Wanted to See and What Only 317 Saw on New Year's Eve," *St. Louis Post-Dispatch,* January 3, 1909.

[39] "Promoters Plan to Move 'Faust's' to 15-Story Hotel," *St. Louis Post-Dispatch,* May 24, 1912; "Southern Hotel to Close Aug. 1: For 31 Years a City Landmark," *St. Louis Post-Dispatch,* July 21, 1912; "What of Faust's?" *St. Louis Post-Dispatch,* February 11, 1915; "Fond Farewell," *St. Louis Globe-Democrat,* June 24, 1916; "Faust's Café But a Memory in Few Days: Famous Restaurant, for 45 Years a 'Show Place' of St. Louis, to Close for All Time on June 30 or July 3," *St. Louis Globe-Democrat,* June 25, 1916; "St. James Hotel and Faust's Café Close Their Doors," *St. Louis Republic,* July 1, 1916; "Faust's Café Will Probably Close Tonight," *St. Louis Post-Dispatch,* June 30, 1916; Description of closing of Tony Faust's Restaurant, July 2, 1916, "Restaurants" file, Fine Arts Department, St. Louis Public Library; "$5 Champagne $1.05 a Quart at Fausts' Auction," *St. Louis Post-Dispatch,* July 26, 1916; "Faust Furnishings, Valued at $30,000, Sold for $4,000," *St. Louis Post-Dispatch,* July 27, 1916; "Faust's, Famous for 45 Years, Closes its Doors," *St. Louis Post-Dispatch,* July 1, 1916; "Stories of Faust's; How Adolphus Busch Made a 'Tight Wad' Pay for Wine," *St. Louis Post-Dispatch,* July 2, 1916.

BOOK THREE

Chapter 1
The Joys of Youth

[1] Mary Plant Faust, audiocassette interview with unknown person, July 2, 1986.
[2] Smith Academy Catalogues, 1909-1913, Washington University Archives, St. Louis; "Knocked Down by Gus Busch," *St. Louis Post-Dispatch,* November 8, 1895; Peter Hernon and Terry Ganey, *Under the Influence: The Unauthorized Story of the Anheuser-Busch Dynasty* (New York: Avon Books, 1991), 55-56.
[3] Smith Academy Catalogues, 1909-1913, Washington University Archives, St. Louis; Ernest Kirschten, *Catfish and Crystal* (Garden City, NY: Doubleday & Co., 1960), 347.
[4] Mary Plant Faust, audiocassette interview with unknown person, July 2, 1986; Smith Academy Catalogues, 1856-1917, Washington University Archives, St. Louis; *The Lake Placid School with Winters in Florida, 1915-1916,* Northwood School, Lake Placid, New York; *Lists and Directory of Officers and Students, 1918-1919,* Yale University Archives, New Haven, Connecticut. Nancy F. Lyon, e-mail message to author, November 26, 2007.
[5] "$20,000 Chicken Farm is Bought for L. Busch Faust: Father Edward A. Faust, Purchases 80-Acre Tract on Missouri River Heights, 14 Miles West of Clayton," *St. Louis Post-Dispatch,* July 2, 1917; Clayton, Missouri, "Deed Records," Deed Book 412:174, July 5, 1917, and Deed Book 565: 607, December 21, 1918; St. Louis County Government Building. Faust Park Records, Chesterfield, Missouri.
[6] *Lists and Directory of Officers and Students, 1918-1919,* Yale University Archives, New Haven, Connecticut. Nancy F. Lyon, e-mail message to author, November 26, 2007; Faust, Leicester B., WWI Service Card and Registration Record, "Soldiers' Records: War of 1812-World War I," Missouri Digital Heritage, Missouri State Archives, www.sos.gov.
[7] *Lists and Directory of Officers and Students, 1918-1919,* Yale University Archives, New Haven, Connecticut. Nancy F. Lyon, e-mail message to author, November 26, 2007; Washington University Catalogs, 1918-1921, Washington University Archives, St. Louis; *The*

Hatchet, Washington University yearbook, 1921. Washington University Archives, St. Louis; Mary Plant Faust, audiocassette interview with unknown person, July 2, 1986.

[8] Clayton, Missouri, "Deed Records," Deed Book 412:174, July 5, 1917 and Deed Book 565: 607, December 21, 1918; St. Louis County Government Building. Faust Park Records, Chesterfield, Missouri; Missouri Office of Historic Preservation, Historic Inventory of Leicester B. Faust Estate dated circa 1980s, Faust Park records, St. Louis County Parks, 2; Dan A. Rothwell, *A Guide to Chesterfield's Architectural Treasures,* with a Foreword by Esley Hamilton (Chesterfield, MO: City of Chesterfield, 1998), 57-58.

[9] Missouri Office of Historic Preservation, Historic Inventory of Leicester B. Faust Estate dated circa 1980s, Faust Park records, St. Louis County Parks, 2.

[10] Missouri Office of Historic Preservation, Historic Inventory of Leicester B. Faust Estate dated circa 1980s, Faust Park records, St. Louis County Parks, 2; Rothwell, *A Guide,* 57-58.

[11] 1920 United States Federal Census, St. Louis Ward 28, St. Louis, Missouri, www.ancestry.com; Allen Sellenriek, interviews with author, March 25 and April 8, 2010.

[12] "The History of St. Louis County: L Busch Faust" *St. Louis Watchman Advocate,* 1919; 1920 St. Louis County Directory (St. Louis), 99.

[13] "Society," *St. Louis Post-Dispatch,* November 18, 1915; "Weekly Calendar of Social Events," *St. Louis Post-Dispatch,* December 24, 1916; "Social Items," *St. Louis Post-Dispatch,* December 11, 1917; "Social Items," *St. Louis Post-Dispatch,* December 17, 1918; "Social Items," *St. Louis Post-Dispatch,* December 26, 1918; "80 Young Men Form Dancing Club," *St. Louis Post-Dispatch,* March 18, 1920; "'Le Minuet' Dance at Woman's Club Tonight," *St. Louis Post-Dispatch,* November 19, 1920.

[14] "Social Items," *St. Louis Post-Dispatch,* March 23, 1921.

[15] "Social Items," *St. Louis Post-Dispatch,* January 16, 1922.

[16] "Missouri Death Certificates, 1910-1958," database, *Missouri Digital Heritage,* accessed March 11, 2010, http://www.sos.mo.gov/archives/resources/deathcertificates/), entry for Mollie Faust Giannini, March 29, 1918; citing St. Louis City, Certificate 11558; "Frau Mollie Faust Giannini Gestorben: Tochter des Vestorbenen Restaurateurs 'Tony' Faust Erliegt Einem Krebsleiden," *St. Louis Westliche Post,* March 30, 1918; "Mrs. Giannini, Daughter of Anthony E. (Tony) Faust, Dies," *St. Louis Post-Dispatch,* March 29, 1918.

[17] Mary Plant Faust, audiocassette interview with unknown person, July 2, 1986.

[18] Esley Hamilton, "The Creation of Faust Park," Faust Park records, Chesterfield, Missouri; Esley Hamilton, "The Faust Estate: A History," Faust Park records, Chesterfield, Missouri; "Samuel Plant, Retired Miller, Dies at 81," *St. Louis Globe-Democrat,* December 30, 1953; United States Department of the Interior, National Park Service, National Register of Historic Places Nomination Form of Samuel Plant House dated September 1983, Faust Park records, St. Louis County Parks, 3.

[19] Hamilton, "The Creation of Faust Park"; Hamilton, "The Faust Estate".

[20] Mary Plant Faust, audiocassette interview with unknown person, July 2, 1986.

[21] Ibid.

[22] Ibid.; United States Department of the Interior, National Park Service, National Register of Historic Places Nomination Form of Samuel Plant House dated September 1983, Faust Park records, St. Louis County Parks, 2.

[23] "Events in the Social World," *St. Louis Post-Dispatch,* June 19, 1921.

[24] Mary Plant Faust, audiocassette interview with unknown person, July 2, 1986; Bryn Mawr Alumnae Directory, 1916. Lorett Treese, Archivist, Bryn Mawr College, e-mail message to author, May 17, 2010. Gerald Francis, President, Lower Merion Historical Society, e-mail message to author, May 19, 2010; "Society," *St. Louis Post-Dispatch,* December 20, 1916; "Society," *St. Louis Post-Dispatch,* May 24, 1916; "Society," *St. Louis Post-Dispatch,* May 26, 1916.

[25] "Saturday Afternoon at Sunset Hill Country Club," *St. Louis Post-Dispatch,* July 13, 1919; Mary Plant Faust, audiocassette interview with unknown person, July 2, 1986.

[26] "Events in the Social World," *St. Louis Post-Dispatch,* October 26, 1919; "Miss Mary Plant to Make Bow Tonight: Parents Have Invited 400 Guests to Ball at St. Louis Country Club," *St. Louis Post-Dispatch,* November 26, 1919.

[27] Mary Plant Faust, audiocassette interview with unknown person, July 2, 1986.

[28] "Mrs. David O'Neil to be 'Liberty' in Women's Tableau: Will Pose in Role of the Goddess on Steps of Old Art Museum," *St. Louis Post-Dispatch,* June 10, 1916.

[29] "Junior League Officers Comment on Elinor Glyn's Charges: Activities of Young Women in This Organization Refute Many of Criticism of English Writer Directed at American Girls," *St. Louis Post-*

Dispatch, December 5, 1921.

30 "Events in the Social World: Wedding of Miss Mary Plant and Leicester Faust and Imperial Club Ball Next Big Events on Social Calendar," *St. Louis Post-Dispatch,* January 8, 1922.

31 "Events in the Social World," *St. Louis Post-Dispatch,* January 1, 1922; "Social Items," *St. Louis Post-Dispatch,* January 9, 1922.

32 "Events in the Social World: Brilliant Wedding of Miss Mary Plant and Leicester Faust Yesterday, One of Most Important of the Year – Ceremony Performed at 'Easton Farms' by the Rev. Francis J. O'Connor," *St. Louis Post-Dispatch,* January 15, 1922; "Events in the Social World," *St. Louis Post-Dispatch,* January 22, 1922.

Chapter 2
Golf, Tulips, Angus, and Finally, Beer

[1] Jim Healey (expert on the history of St. Louis golf), interview with author, October 22, 2009.
[2] Dorothy Campbell Hurd, "Women's Golf at Home and Abroad," *Golf Illustrated* (August 1924): www.1a84foundation.org/SportsLibrary/GolfIllustrated/1924/gi25s.pdf, accessed October 22, 2009.
[3] Grantland Rice, "Will Miss Collett Make It Two in a Row?" *The American Golfer* (September 1923): 7.
[4] Jim Healey, *Golfing Before the Arch* (St. Louis: James F. Healey, 1997), 145.
[5] "Miss Collett Wins Medal With an 81," *New York Times,* September 26, 1922; Healey, *Golfing Before the Arch,* 145-146.
[6] Jim Healey (expert on the history of St. Louis golf), interview with author, October 22, 2009.
[7] Jim Healey, "Ladies on the Links: Audrey Faust Wallace and Virginia Pepp," 1998. www.stlgolfhistory.com, accessed October 22, 2009; Healey, *Golfing Before the Arch,* 146.
[8] Esley Hamilton, "The Faust Estate: A History," Faust Park Records, Chesterfield, Missouri; Audrey "Tolie" Wallace Otto, interview with author, September 29, 2009.
[9] *The Book of St. Louisans: A Biographical Dictionary of Leading Living Men of the City of St. Louis and Vicinity* (St. Louis: The St. Louis Republic, 1912), 618-619; "Brookings Institution History," Brookings

Institute, www.brookings.edu/about/History.aspx, accessed January 11, 2012.

[10] McCune Gill, *The St. Louis Story: Library of American Lives* (Hopkinsville, KY: Historical Record Association, 1952), 1126-1128; *Polk's St. Louis County (Missouri) Directory, 1928* (St. Louis: R.L. Polk & Co., 1928), 786, 1373; "They've Made Their Mark With Pencils," *St. Louis Post-Dispatch,* June 18, 1965.

[11] Audrey "Tolie" Wallace Otto, interview with author, September 29, 2009; Mahlon "Lonnie" Wallace, III, interview with author, June 15, 2009.

[12] "Son Pays Tribute to Eugene H. Angert in Memorial Volume," *St. Louis Globe-Democrat,* December 19, 1930.

[13] "E.G. Angert Gardens Open to Public," *St. Louis Globe-Democrat,* April 27, 1930; "Angert Gardens Open as Usual: Public Invited to View Gardens Despite Death of Owner Last Year," *St. Louis Globe-Democrat,* April 23, 1930.

[14] "Eugene H. Angert Dies in Hospital of Septic Poisoning," *St. Louis Globe-Democrat,* May 3, 1929.

[15] "Son Pays Tribute to Eugene H. Angert in Memorial Volume," *St. Louis Globe-Democrat,* December 19, 1930.

[16] "Missouri Marriage Records, 1805-2002," database, *Ancestry.com* (http://search.ancestrylibrary.com : accessed April 12, 2010), entry for Borden S. Veeder – Vera G. Angert, September 15, 1930; citing St. Louis County [Missouri Marriage Records]; "Mrs. Eugene Angert Becomes Bride of Dr. Borden S. Veeder," Harry Sprague clipping scrapbook, 191, Missouri History Museum, St. Louis.

[17] Mary Plant Faust, audiocassette interview with unknown person, July 2, 1986; Allen Sellenriek, interviews with author, March 25 and April 8, 2010.

[18] Mary Plant Faust, audiocassette interview with unknown person, July 2, 1986; Allen Sellenriek, interviews with author, March 25 and April 8, 2010; Lily Claire Keeler and Claire Beck, interviews with author, April 9, 2009.

[19] "L. Busch Faust, Beginning 10 Years Ago, Now at 31, Owns a Unique and Beautiful Farm Development," *St. Louis Watchman-Advocate,* November 2, 1928.

[20] Ibid.; Allen Sellenriek, interviews with author, March 25 and April 8, 2010.

[21] Allen Sellenriek, interviews with author, March 25 and April 8, 2010.

[22] Esley Hamilton, "The Lamella Barn at Faust Park, Chesterfield, Missouri," Faust Park Records, Chesterfield, Missouri.

[23] "The Flying Lamella and How it Turned Into a Dinosaur," *St. Louis Post-Dispatch,* August 14, 1983.
[24] Ibid.; Esley Hamilton, "The Lamella Barn at Faust Park, Chesterfield, Missouri," Faust Park Records, Chesterfield, Missouri; C.D. Stelzer, "Bringing the Roof Down," *Riverfront Times,* February 10-16, 1999.
[25] Ibid.
[26] Allen Sellenriek, interviews with author, March 25 and April 8, 2010.
[27] *Gould's St. Louis (Missouri) City Directory, 1933* (St. Louis: Polk-Gould Directory Co., 1933), 368; *St. Louis City Directory, 1935* (St. Louis: Polk-Gould Directory Co., 1935), 391, 904; *Gould's St. Louis (Missouri) City Directory, 1936* (St. Louis: Polk-Gould Directory Co., 1936), 390, 900.
[28] Robbi Courtaway, *Wetter Than the Mississippi: Prohibition in St. Louis and Beyond* (St. Louis: Reedy Press, 2008), 29.
 52; Jeff Hill, *Defining Moments in Prohibition* (Detroit: Omnigraphics, 2004), 47.
[29] Courtaway, *Wetter Than,* 52.
[30] "Beer or No Beer: Prominent Brewers Discuss the Proposed Prohibition Bill," *St. Louis Globe-Democrat,* February 8, 1881.
[31] Daniel Okrent, "The Man Who Turned Off The Taps," *Smithsonian* (May 2010): 30-37; "Constitutional Amendments," *United States Government Printing Office,* www.gpoaccess.gov/constitution/html : accessed March 15, 2011.
[32] Okrent, "The Man," 35.
[33] Courtaway, *Wetter Than,* 29; "Social Items," *St. Louis Post-Dispatch,* January 9, 1922.
[34] Henry Herbst, Don Roussin and Kevin Kious, *St. Louis Brews: 200 Years of Brewing in St. Louis, 1809-2009* (St. Louis: Reedy Press, 2009), 19.
[35] Mary Bartley, *St. Louis Lost* (St. Louis: Virginia Publishing, 1994), 89; Ernst Kirschten, *Catfish and Crystal* (Garden City, NY: Doubleday & Co., 1960), 348.
[36] Mary Plant Faust, audiocassette interview with unknown person, July 2, 1986; Kirschten, *Catfish and Crystal,* 356; Annemarie Offer, Anheuser-Busch Manager of Communications, representing Anheuser-Busch Archives, interview, July 25, 2008.

Chapter 3
The Great Depression

[1] *Gould's St. Louis City Red-Blue Book, 1921* (St. Louis: Polk-Gould Directory, 1921), 186; *Gould's St. Louis (Missouri) City Directory, 1932* (St. Louis: Polk-Gould Directory Co., 1932), 372; *Gould's St. Louis (Missouri) City Directory, 1933* (Polk-Gould Directory Co., 1933), 368; *Who's Who in North St. Louis* (St. Louis: North St. Louis Businessmen's Association, 1925), 339; "Tony Faust's Sons Chartered," *St. Louis Post-Dispatch*, August 10, 1933.

[2] "Faust's Old Market to Make Way for Parking Lot," *St. Louis Globe-Democrat*, February 19, 1941; "Faust's Market Files Debtor's Plea: Concern in Operation Over 50 Years Seeks to Reorganize," *St. Louis Globe-Democrat*, January 10, 1935; *Gould's St. Louis (Missouri) City Directory, 1935* (Polk-Gould Directory Co., 1935), 391.

[3] Mary Plant Faust, audiocassette interview with unknown person, July 2, 1986; James Neal Primm: *Lion of the Valley: St. Louis, Missouri, 1761-1980* 3rd ed., (St. Louis: Missouri Historical Society Press, 1998), 439-440; "E. A. Faust Collection of Art is Loaned to City's Museum: Exhibit to Remain in Galleries for Several Months," *St. Louis Globe-Democrat*, November 8, 1931.

[4] Allen Sellenriek, interviews with author, March 25 and April 8, 2010.

[5] Mary Plant Faust, audiocassette interview with unknown person, July 2, 1986; Roland Krebs and Percy J. Orthwein, *Making Friends is Our Business: 100 Years of Anheuser-Busch* (St. Louis: Anheuser-Busch, 1953), 267; *Gould's St. Louis (Missouri) City Directory, 1933* (St. Louis: Polk-Gould Directory Co., 1933), 368; *Gould's St. Louis (Missouri) City Directory, 1935* (St. Louis: Polk-Gould Directory Co., 1935), 391, 904.

[6] Allen Sellenriek, interviews with author, March 25 and April 8, 2010.

[7] Mary Plant Faust, audiocassette interview with unknown person, July 2, 1986; Mary Dangremond, interview with author, October 20, 2008; Jane Keough, interview with author, April 28 and May 1, 2009; Esley Hamilton, "The Faust Estate: A History," Faust Park Records, Chesterfield, Missouri.

[8] Allen Sellenriek, interviews with author, March 25 and April 8, 2010.

[9] "Missouri Death Certificates, 1910-1958," database, *Missouri Digital Heritage* (http://www.sos.mo.gov/archives/resources/deathcertificates/ : accessed March 11, 2010), entry for Anna Busch Faust, April 16, 1936; citing St. Louis City, Certificate 17414;"Missouri Death Certificates,

1910-1958," database, *Missouri Digital Heritage* (http://www.sos.mo.gov/archives/resources/deathcertificates/ : accessed March 11, 2010), entry for Edward Anthony Faust, July 5, 1936; citing St. Louis City, Certificate 28066.

[10] "E. A. Faust Buried in Bellefontaine: Funeral Services Attended by Several Hundred St. Louisans," *St. Louis Globe-Democrat,* July 8, 1936.

[11] Bellefontaine Cemetery map of Faust burial plots, Bellefontaine Cemetery records, Bellefontaine Cemetery, St. Louis, Missouri.

[12] "Allows $102,125 Faust Estate Claim," *St. Louis Globe-Democrat,* October 30, 1936;"$82, 906 Claims Against Faust Estate Allows," *St. Louis Globe-Democrat,* September 17, 1936;"$1,908,139 Value Placed on Estate of Mrs. E. A. Faust: Bulk of Vast Wealth is in Stocks, Inventory Shows," *St. Louis Globe-Democrat,* July 9, 1936; "Edward A. Faust Estate Valued at Total of $296, 982: $163,465 Assets Are Pledge for Loans of $190,000," *St. Louis Globe-Democrat,* November 10, 1936.

[13] St. Louis City, Missouri, Edward A. Faust probate file 82976, Probate Court office; Civil Courts Building, St. Louis; "$82, 906 Claims Against Faust Estate Allows," *St. Louis Globe-Democrat,* September 17, 1936; "$1,908,139 Value Placed on Estate of Mrs. E. A. Faust: Bulk of Vast Wealth is in Stocks, Inventory Shows," *St. Louis Globe-Democrat,* July 9, 1936; "Edward A. Faust Estate Valued at Total of $296, 982: $163,465 Assets Are Pledge for Loans of $190,000," *St. Louis Globe-Democrat,* November 10, 1936.

[14] St. Louis City, Missouri, Anna Busch Faust probate file 82591, Probate Court office; Civil Courts Building, St. Louis.

[15] Mahlon "Lonnie" Wallace, III, interview with author, June 15, 2009.

[16] St. Louis City, Missouri, Anna Busch Faust probate file 82591, Probate Court office; Civil Courts Building, St. Louis; "Mrs. Faust Leaves Bulk of Fortune in Trust Estates: Husband and Two Children Chief Beneficiaries of Will," *St. Louis Post-Dispatch,* April 29, 1936.

[17] "E. A. Faust Adds $75,000 Murillo to Art Collection: 'St. Joseph and the Infant Christ' Formerly Owned by King Louis Phillippe," *St. Louis Post-Dispatch,* April 8, 1917; "Notable Paintings in the Homes of St. Louisans," *St. Louis Post-Dispatch,* June 19, 1921.

[18] "News of the St. Louis Art World," *St. Louis Star,* July 31, 1921, *Art in St. Louis* scrapbook II, Missouri History Museum, St. Louis.

[19] "E. A. Faust Acquired 1475 Italian Painting: Panel by Fungai Was Originally Side of Wedding Chest," *St. Louis Globe-Democrat,* February 22, 1929.

[20] "Italian Villa Inspired Art Collection of Mr. and Mrs. Edward A. Faust: Triptych by Fifteenth Century Seer is Most Important Single Piece in Famous Group of Paintings," *St. Louis Star-Times,* July 7, 1936.

[21] "E. A. Faust Collection of Art is Loaned to City's Museum: Exhibit to Remain in Galleries for Several Months," *St. Louis Globe-Democrat,* November 8, 1931.

[22] "Art League Announces Award for Playlets," *St. Louis Post-Dispatch,* November 27, 1918; "Second Industrial Art Show Planned: Backers of Exposition Will Meet Tomorrow to Discuss Details," *St. Louis Post-Dispatch,* March 21, 1920; "Edward Faust is Made President of City Art Commission," *St. Louis Globe-Democrat,* February 12, 1930; "Edward A. Faust Elected Head of Art Commission," *St. Louis Post-Dispatch,* February 12, 1930; "E. A. Faust, Director of Bank and Business Leader, Dies at 67: Son-in-Law of Late Adolphus Busch Was Art Connoisseur and Chairman of Muny Art Commission Since 1930," *St. Louis Globe-Democrat,* July 6, 1936.

[23] "Edward A. Faust Estate Valued at Total of $296, 982: $163,465 Assets Are Pledge for Loans of $190,000," *St. Louis Globe-Democrat,* November 10, 1936.

[24] Mary Plant Faust, audiocassette interview with unknown person, July 2, 1986.

[25] Julius K. Hunter, *Westmoreland and Portland Places: The History of America's Premier Private Streets, 1888-1988,* with a Foreword by James Neal Primm and Essay on the Architecture by Esley Hamilton, (Columbia: University of Missouri Press, 1988), 84; "Museum Declines Use of Faust Home," *St. Louis Globe-Democrat,* August 13, 1937.

[26] Hunter, *Westmoreland and Portland Places,* 84; "150,000 Mansion Offered as Gift to City, But No One Wants It," *St. Louis Post-Dispatch,* January 7, 1943; "150,000 Faust Home May Be Torn Down: Heirs Say, It Is Still at Disposal of City, However, For Public Use," *St. Louis Globe Democrat,* January 8, 1943; "Installation of $11,000 Pipe Organ at Ferris Home Made: Only Few of Instruments Are in Private Homes of St. Louis Citizens, It Is Said," *St. Louis Post-Dispatch,* July 16, 1922.

[27] "Science Academy Asks Faust Home: Use as Memorial Depends on Consent of Portland Pl. Residents," *St. Louis Globe-Democrat,* January 23, 1943.

[28] "$150,000 Mansion of Faust Family in Portland Pl. Sold," *St. Louis Globe-Democrat,* December 7, 1945.

[29] Clayton, Missouri, "Deed Records," Deed Book 1094:118, August 1, 1930, and Deed Book 1623:331, December 27, 1939; St. Louis County Government Building. Faust Park Records, Chesterfield, Missouri.

[30] United States Department of the Interior, National Park Service, National Register of Historic Places Inventory Nomination Form of "Thornhill," dated March 23, 1973, Faust Park records, St. Louis County Parks; Historic Buildings Commission and W. Philip Cotton, Jr.,

ed., *Interim Survey Report 1970: 100 Historic Buildings in St. Louis County* (Clayton, MO: St. Louis County Department of Parks and Recreation, 1970), 8; David L. Browman, "Thornhill: The Governor Frederick Bates Estate," *Missouri Historical Society Bulletin* 30 (October 1973 – July 1974): 89-100; Gloria Dalton, ed., *Heritage of the Creve Coeur Area* (Creve Coeur, MO: City of Creve Coeur, 1976), 11-12, 20-21.
[31] Allen Sellenriek, interviews with author, March 25 and April 8, 2010.

Chapter 4
Life on the Farm

[1] Dan Rothwell, *A Guide to Chesterfield's Architectural Treasures*, with a Foreword by Esley Hamilton (Chesterfield, MO: City of Chesterfield, 1998), 66; Mary Plant Faust, audiocassette interview with unknown person, July 2, 1986; Allen Sellenriek, interviews with author, March 25 and April 8, 2010.
[2] Allen Sellenriek, interviews with author, March 25 and April 8, 2010.
[3] Rothwell, *A Guide*, 67; Allen Sellenriek, interviews with author, March 25 and April 8, 2010.
[4] Ibid.
[5] Jack Rinkel, interview with author, July 21, 2009.
[6] Gloria Dalton, ed., *Heritage of the Creve Coeur Area* (Creve Coeur, MO: City of Creve Coeur, 1976), 57.
[7] Gloria Autenrieth Ruck, interview with author, February 13, 2010.
[8] Ibid.; Jim Gerst and Bob Gerst, interviews with author, January 21, 2009; "Herbert L. Autenrieth: One of Area's Oldest Residents," *St. Louis Post-Dispatch*, February 14, 2001; David Fiedler, *The Enemy Among Us: POWs in Missouri During World War II* (St. Louis: Missouri Historical Society Press, 2003), 40, 281, 290-310.
[9] Ibid., 306-310.
[10] Mary Plant Faust, audiocassette interview with unknown person, July 2, 1986.
[11] Lawrence O. Christensen, William E. Foley, Gary R. Kremer and Kenneth H. Winn, eds., *Dictionary of Missouri Biography* (Columbia, MO: University of Missouri Press, 1999), 137-138.
[12] Ibid.
[13] Ibid.; Jean Rose Buchanan and Bob Buchanan, *The King's Reign: The History of the Brewery in St. Louis* (St. Louis: Post-Dispatch Books,

2008), 26-32; Ronald Jan Plavchan, *A History of Anheuser-Busch, 1852-1933* (North Stratford, NH: Ayer Company Publishers, Inc., 1969), 232; Donna S. Baker, *Vintage Anheuser-Busch: An Unofficial Collector's Guide* (Atglen, PA: Schiffer Publishing, LTD., 1999), 13.

[14] Peter Hernon and Terry Ganey, *Under the Influence: The Unauthorized Story of the Anheuser-Busch Dynasty* (New York: Avon Books, 1991), 167-168.

[15] Ibid.; 128; Roland Krebs and Percy J. Orthwein, *Making Friends is Our Business: 100 Years of Anheuser-Busch* (St. Louis: Anheuser-Busch, 1953), 269.

[16] Ibid.; Hernon and Ganey, *Under the Influence,* 87, 124, 126, 198; Christensen, Foley, Kremer and Winn, eds., *Dictionary,* 137-138.

[17] "L. Busch Faust to Sell His Stock in Brewery," *St. Louis Globe-Democrat,* October 1, 1952; "Seeks SEC Permit to Sell Anheuser-Busch Stock," *St. Louis Post-Dispatch,* October 15, 1952; "7,847,000 Busch Stock Will Be Offered Today," *St. Louis Globe-Democrat,* October 29, 1952.

Chapter 5
Times are Changin'

[1] Allen Sellenriek, interviews with author, March 25 and April 8, 2010; Jim Gerst and Bob Gerst, interviews with author, January 21, 2009.

[2] Jane Keough, interviews with author, April 28 and May 1, 2009.

[3] Ibid.; Lily Claire Keeler and Claire Beck, interviews with author, April 9, 2009.

[4] Jane Keough, interviews with author, April 28 and May 1, 2009; Allen Sellenriek, interviews with author, March 25 and April 8, 2010.

[5] Jane Keough, interviews with author, April 28 and May 1, 2009; Dan A. Rothwell, *A Guide to Chesterfield's Architectural Treasures* with a Foreword by Esley Hamilton (Chesterfield, MO: City of Chesterfield, 1998), 66; "Honolulu, Hawaii, Passenger Lists, 1900-1953," *Ancesry.com* (http://search.ancestrylibrary.com : accessed April 14, 2010), entry for Leicester and Mary Faust, arrived Honolulu, Hawaii August 30, 1948 aboard the *Lurline*; "Honolulu, Hawaii, Passenger Lists, 1900-1953," *Ancesry.com* (http://search.ancestrylibrary.com : accessed April 14, 2010), entry for Leicester and Mary Faust, arrived Honolulu, Hawaii July 29, 1950 aboard the *Lurline*.

[6] "Garden Club Prepares Exhibit," *St. Louis Globe-Democrat,*

November 21, 1954; "Christmas Around the World'," *St. Louis Post-Dispatch,* November 21, 1954; "Recent Visitors to the Garden," *Missouri Botanical Garden Bulletin* 48, no. 8 (October 1960): 144; "Annual Report of the Director," *Missouri Botanical Garden Bulletin* 54, no. 1 (January 1966): 3.

[7] "Leicester Faust Becomes Honorary Trustee," *Missouri Botanical Garden Bulletin* 62, no. 2 (March 1973): 5-6.

[8] "Notes and Comments: New Board Members," *Missouri Historical Society Bulletin* 4, no. 2 (January 1948): 57; "News and Comment: Membership Drive," *Missouri Historical Society Bulletin* 5, no. 3 (April 1949): 227; "News and Comment: The Women's Association," *Missouri Historical Society Bulletin* 10 (October 1953-July 1954): 524.

[9] "Group to Sponsor Passage of Sane Laws is Organized: L. B. Faust Heads Association Pledge to Legislation to Benefit All," *St. Louis Globe-Democrat,* September 8, 1934.

[10] "Leicester B. Faust Funeral; Was Anheuser-Busch Official," *St. Louis Post-Dispatch,* September 2, 1979; "L. B. Faust Named Chairman of 1954 Red Cross Campaign," *St. Louis Globe-Democrat,* November 26, 1953; "The Red Cross Fund Drive Goes Over The Top," *St. Louis Globe-Democrat,* May 26, 1954.

[11] "Washington U. Given Murillo Painting," *St. Louis Globe-Democrat,* January 11, 1941; "Unique Work Given to Art Museum," *St. Louis Globe-Democrat,* November 28, 1962.

[12] Jane Keough, interviews with author, April 28 and May 1, 2009; Mary Dangremond, interview with author, October 20, 2008; "UK Incoming Passenger Lists, 18781960," *Ancestry.com* (http://search.ancestrylibrary.com : accessed April 14, 2010), entry for Leicester and Mary Faust, arrived Southampton, England, November 25, 1960 aboard the *Polish Ocean Liners.*

[13] Audrey "Tolie" Wallace Otto, interview with author, September 29, 2009.

[14] Ibid.

[15] "Mrs. Mahlon B. Wallace, Jr." *St. Louis Globe-Democrat,* March 3, 1955.

[16] Jane Keough, interviews with author, April 28 and May 1, 2009; Audrey "Tolie" Wallace Otto, interview with author, September 29, 2009; Mahlon "Lonnie" Wallace, III, interview with author, June 15, 2009.

[17] Allen Sellenriek, interviews with author, March 25 and April 8, 2010.

[18] "St. Louis County Historic Buildings Commission," St. Louis County Parks, www.co.st-louis.mo.us/parks/hbc.html, accessed May 29, 2009; "Organization of the St. Louis County Historic Buildings Commission,

in June, 1957," 3873 van Ravenswaay Papers, f. 363, Correspondence, St. Louis County Department of Parks & Recreation; Western Historical Manuscript Collection, Columbia, Missouri.

[19] United States Department of the Interior, National Park Service, National Register of Historic Places Inventory Nomination Form of "Thornhill," dated March 23, 1973, Faust Park records, St. Louis County Parks, 1.

[20] Allen Sellenriek, interviews with author, March 25 and April 8, 2010.

[21] Jane Keough, interviews with author, April 28 and May 1, 2009; Jim Gerst and Bob Gerst, interviews with author, January 21, 2009.

[22] Esley Hamilton, "The Creation of Faust Park," Faust Park records, Chesterfield, Missouri; Esley Hamilton, "The Faust Estate: A History," Faust Park records, Chesterfield, Missouri.

[23] "Leicester B. Faust Funeral Today," *St. Louis Globe-Democrat,* September 3, 1979; "Leicester B. Faust Funeral; Was Anheuser-Busch Official," *St. Louis Post-Dispatch,* September 2, 1979.

Chapter 6
Sunset on the Farm, Sunrise on Faust Park

[1] Jane Keough, interviews with author, April 28 and May 1, 2009.

[2] United States Department of the Interior, National Park Service, National Register of Historic Places Inventory Nomination Form of "Thornhill," dated March 23, 1973, Faust Park records, St. Louis County Parks, 2, 7; David L. Browman, "Thornhill: The Governor Frederick Bates Estate," *Missouri Historical Society Bulletin* 30 (October 1973 – July 1974): 89.

[3] Gloria Dalton, ed. *Heritage of the Creve Coeur Area* (Creve Coeur, MO: City of Creve Coeur, 1976), 20; "The Saint Louis County Department of Parks and Recreation presents A Restoration in Progress at Thornhill Historic Site: Governor Bates' Estate (St. Louis: vertical file, Faust Park File, Missouri History Museum).

[4] Faust Park: Park History, Faust Park Records, Chesterfield, Missouri.

[5] "St. Louis Carousel at Faust Park," www.stlouisco.com/ParksandRecreation/ChildrensFun/StLouisCarouselatFaustPark, accessed May 26, 2011.

[6] Faust Park: Park History, Faust Park Records, Chesterfield, Missouri.

[7] "Plans are Under Way to Set Up in Faust Park a Historical Oasis of Vintage Buildings Rescued From the Rapid Development of West St. Louis County," *St. Louis Post-Dispatch*, May 15, 1988.

[8] "Faust Park Takes on Frontier Flavor: Historic Homes Turning Park into Museum," *St. Louis Post-Dispatch*, July 18, 1988; "German Heritage Uprooted: More History Moved to Faust Park," *Clayton Citizen Journal*, July 22, 1988.

[9] "Taking Wing: Forest Park is Loser as County Gets Site for 'Butterfly House'," *St. Louis Post-Dispatch*, January 26, 1995.

[10] "Butterflies Threaten Restored Village: Insect House Plan Upsets Backers of Faust Park Project," *St. Louis Post-Dispatch*, February 15, 1995.

[11] Ibid.

[12] Ibid.

[13] Ibid.

[14] "Briefs: Public Meeting to Discuss Plans for Butterfly House," *St. Louis Post-Dispatch*, March 9, 1995.

[15] "Residents are Getting 'Butterflies': Project Sparks Concern for Faust Historic Village," *St. Louis Post-Dispatch*, March 13, 1995; "Ex-Parks Director Puts History Before Butterflies," *St. Louis Post-Dispatch*, May 8, 1995; "Briefs / Region: Council Approval Sought for Park Butterfly House," *St. Louis Post-Dispatch*, May 12, 1995; "Butterflies are Free to Fly: But Eyebrows Raised Over Plan to Put Them in Faust Park – And Move Historic Buildings," *St. Louis Post-Dispatch*, May 15, 1995.

[16] "Briefs: New Location Picked for Butterfly House, *St. Louis Post-Dispatch*, May 19, 1995; "A Case of Butterflies," *St. Louis Post-Dispatch*, May 21, 1995; "Historic Village Decision Pleases Critics of Plan for Butterfly House," *St. Louis Post-Dispatch*, May 22, 1995; "County Council Advances Plan for Butterfly House," *St. Louis Post-Dispatch*, May 26, 1995.

[17] "Briefs: Butterfly Plan Wins Unanimous Approval," *St. Louis Post-Dispatch*, June 2, 1995.

[18] "The Grand Opening of Faust Historical Village," July 13-14, 1996. St. Louis: Faust Historical Village vertical file, Missouri HIstory Museum.

[19] Don Wiegand, interview with author, October 10, 2010.

[20] Ibid.

[21] Julie Constantino, interview with author, October 28, 2008.

[22] "Profiles of the Laymen and the Monks Who Formed the Earliest Nucleus of the Monastery and School," St. Louis Abbey, www.stlouisabbey.org, accessed May 23, 2011; "History: St. Louis Abbey," St. Louis Abbey, www.stlouisabbey.org, accessed May 23,

2011; Abbot Luke Rigby, interview with author, April 1, 2009.
[23] "Luke Rigby Honoree: Mary Plant Faust," *From the Monastery* (February 1991): 8.
[24] Program for Luke Rigby Honoree celebration of Mary Plant Faust, January 26, 1991. St. Louis: files of St. Louis Priory.
[25] "Luke Rigby Honoree: Mary Plant Faust," *From the Monastery* (February 1991): 8; Abbott Luke Rigby, interview with author, April 1, 2009; Julie Constantino, interview with author, October 28, 2008.
[26] Ibid.
[27] "Luke Rigby Honoree: Mary Plant Faust," *From the Monastery* (February 1991): 8.
[28] "Obituaries: Mary Plant Faust, 95; Civic Leader and Philanthropist," *St. Louis Post-Dispatch,* May 5, 1996.

Epilogue

[1] St. Louis County, Missouri, Mary Plant Faust estate number 121894, Probate Division; St. Louis County Government, Clayton; Esley Hamilton, "The Creation of Faust Park," Faust Park records, Chesterfield, Missouri; Esley Hamilton, "The Faust Estate: A History," Faust Park records, Chesterfield, Missouri; "Jewel in the Park: St. Louis County Has Big Plans for the Former Faust Estate," *St. Louis Post-Dispatch,* May 5, 1997.
[2] "Faust House Could Be Home to Music School," *St. Louis Post-Dispatch,* June 11, 1997; "Music School Shows Off New Branch," *St. Louis Post-Dispatch,* May 2, 1999; "Leon R. Strauss," St. Louis Public Art Consortium, www.stlpack.org/FeaturedArt/strauss.html, accessed May 26, 2011; "History of the CMS," Webster University, www.webster.edu/cms/history.shtml, accessed January 17, 2012.